ABUSES OF THE EROTIC

ABUSES OF

Expanding Frontiers Interdisciplinary Approaches
to Studies of Women, Gender, and Sexuality

SERIES EDITORS / Karen J. Leong / Andrea Smith

THE EROTIC

Militarizing Sexuality in the Post–Cold War United States

JOSH CERRETTI

University of Nebraska Press / Lincoln

An earlier version of chapter 1 appeared as "Rape as a Weapon of War(riors): The Militarisation of Sexual Violence in the United States, 1990–2000" in *Gender and History* 28, no. 3 (November 2016): 794–812. © 2016 by John Wiley and Sons Ltd. Used with permission.

An earlier version of chapter 2 appeared as "Confronting an Enemy Abroad, Transforming a Nation at Home: Domestic Militarism in the US, 1990–1996" in *Radical History Review* 126 (October 2016): 50–70. Used with permission of Duke University Press.

Library of Congress Cataloging-in-Publication Data
Names: Cerretti, Josh, author.
Title: Abuses of the erotic: militarizing sexuality in the post–Cold War United States / Josh Cerretti.
Description: Lincoln: University of Nebraska Press, [2019] | Series: Expanding frontiers: interdisciplinary approaches to studies of women, gender, and sexuality | Includes bibliographical references and index.
Identifiers: LCCN 2018043071
ISBN 9781496205568 (cloth: alk. paper)
ISBN 9781496215857 (epub)
ISBN 9781496215864 (mobi)
ISBN 9781496215871 (pdf)
Subjects: LCSH: Women and war—United States. | Women and the military—United States. | Gay military personnel—United States. | Militarism—United States. | Sex—United States. | United States—Military policy.
Classification: LCC JZ6405.W66 C47 2019 |
DDC 306.70973—dc23
LC record available at
https://lccn.loc.gov/2018043071

Set in Chaparral Pro by Mikala R. Kolander.

CONTENTS

ABUSES OF THE EROTIC

Introduction

ABUSES OF THE EROTIC

In the wake of the September 11, 2001, hijackings, amid a storm of anxieties about everything from new airport security procedures to envelopes of anthrax powder, people in the United States from across the political spectrum also appeared profoundly anxious about sexuality.

Seeking to condemn those who lifted the "veil of protection" that he believed "allowed no one to attack America on our soil since 1812," conservative Christian pastor Jerry Falwell used the September 13 episode of the television show *The 700 Club* to levy an accusation. Falwell said "you helped this happen" to "the abortionists, and the feminists, and the gays and the lesbians who are actively trying to make that an alternative lifestyle."[1] Falwell's specification of reproductive technology, feminist ideology, and sexual orientation as the forces imperiling his country made clear that he was worried about the power of sexuality. His perspective on geopolitics suggested that national security depended, in large measure, on the proper practice of national sexuality.

Falwell's words were quickly condemned as hyperbolic and divisive, even by close allies like then president George W. Bush. At the same time, Bush's reactions connected the events of September 11 to sexuality too. He began his September 20 address to Congress and the nation by singling out Lisa Beamer, the visibly pregnant widow of a victim from one of the hijacked planes, for a special welcome. In doing so, Bush made clear that not only were "the terrorists" capable of striking at U.S. interests abroad, but also they had now demonstrated their ability to incapacitate heterosexual nuclear families within the United States. Then, in response to this terrifying threat, he simply asked citizens to "live your lives and hug your children."[2] Beyond just appealing to threatened sexuality to mobilize heterosexuals for war, Bush directed civilians to concern themselves with the pursuit of conventional heterosexual life goals, leaving the struggles around geopolitical problems to military professionals.

Those on the U.S. right were not alone in expressing their anxieties about sexuality in their responses to September 11. Liberal New York senator Chuck Schumer referred to the attacks as a figurative sexual assault, saying, "There's a sense that we've been violated, that some horrible person has taken something away from all of us," in a September 15 radio address.[3] Some ostensibly progressive advocates for women's and LGBTQ rights joined Falwell and Bush in seeking to capitalize on the disruptions triggered by the four hijackings and thousands of subsequent deaths. Bucking assertions in the September 10, 2001, *New York Times* claiming that "feminism is not on the radar screen for most young women right now" and that older feminists were "struggling to define feminism," the Feminist Majority Foundation (FMF) spoke unselfconsciously for women, young and old, within both the U.S. and Afghanistan.[4] In a September 18 statement, FMF president Eleanor Smeal decried "gender apartheid" in Afghanistan, claimed the treatment of women under the Taliban government "poses a real threat to global security and our national security" and insisted that the United States had "a unique obligation to end the Taliban's atrocities toward women."[5] Consciously or not, Smeal tapped into a racialized heterosexual script in which heroic white men rescue helpless women from the threatening and improper sexuality of men of color.

Meanwhile, the Servicemembers Legal Defense Network (SLDN) was at work preparing its eighth annual report on the U.S. military's Don't Ask, Don't Tell policy barring openly gay, lesbian, or bisexual individuals from serving in the military. In the report, SLDN's executives wrote, "It has never been more obvious than in the weeks and months following September 11th that [Don't Ask, Don't Tell] weakens our military, deteriorates our readiness and undermines the morale and cohesion of our troops." Furthermore, they asserted, "The time has come to align our priorities and pursue terrorists, not the patriotic Americans who risk their lives for our freedom while denied their own."[6] Investing optimism in an institution that actively punished gay and lesbian people with varying degrees of intensity since its inception, opponents of the military's "gay ban" also minimized the decades of lesbian and gay activism in opposition to the state and its violences, representing gay and lesbian people as "normal," nationalist U.S. citizens first and sexual dissidents last.

Certain themes can be distilled from these statements and events: the connection between national security and national sexuality, the use of critiques of violence against women as camouflage for other violences, the increased willingness in the dominant culture to incorporate those modalities of nonnormative sexuality most amenable to dominant power, and the insistent centering of reproductive heterosexuality coupled with callous disregard for certain lives and bodies. Taken together, these points marked some vertices of the formations of both sexuality and militarism specific to the United States in the early twenty-first century. In *Abuses of the Erotic*, I argue that the connections between sexuality and militarism apparent in the wake of September 11, 2001, are best understood in reference to the decade that immediately preceded that day. The first decade following the Cold War became the last decade before the War on Terror in large measure through changes in the relationship between sexuality and militarism. That is, I argue that a project of *militarizing sexuality* succeeded in the 1990s United States, and, furthermore, the mass mobilizations of state violence collectively known as the "War on Terror" could not have happened without sexualities having been militarized.

Black feminist scholar Audre Lorde, certainly one of the most significant thinkers of the late twentieth century, wrote that "the erotic is a resource within each of us" and "in order to perpetuate itself, every oppression must corrupt or distort those various sources of power."[7] She went on to explain that although "the erotic offers a well of replenishing and provocative force" for social justice, it is susceptible to being "misnamed" and transformed into a tool of oppression. Drawing analyses from Lorde and the many women, LGBTQ, and of color thinkers and activists she has inspired, I ask how the erotic has been corrupted and distorted in order to perpetuate state violence in the years since her death in 1992. Throughout her work, Audre Lorde demonstrated the uses of the erotic. Here, I demonstrate some of the recent *abuses* of the erotic. Doing so requires first explaining my methodological approach to sexuality and to militarization, as well as my archive, before providing a general outline of the chapters to come.

SEXUALITY IN AN INTERSECTIONAL, HISTORICAL PERSPECTIVE

Since at least the end of the nineteenth century, scholars from every discipline have studied how sexuality—the constellation of desires, practices, and identities that constitute the erotic lives of humans—appears in diverse and unpredictable modalities structured by the linguistic, material, and anatomical possibilities envisaged by individuals.[8] Historical and cross-cultural work on sexuality in the second half of the twentieth century convincingly revealed that no aspect of sexuality is either universal to the species or purely individual; rather, sexual acts, thoughts, and communities all arise from a complex mediation of knowledge and power that is at once personal and social. As linguistic anthropologists Deborah Cameron and Don Kulick wrote: "The linguistic construction of identity is not simply about 'authentic' self-expression. . . . The link between a way of speaking and the social meanings it conveys is not created by the individual speaker; individuals can choose whether and how to deploy particular meanings, but the meanings themselves preexist that choice."[9]

What is intelligible as sexuality—what acts "count" as sex, what acts are "desirable" or "normal," what combinations of desires and acts coalesce into a recognizable identity—is always predicated on the social construction of sexuality in that context. In addition, the construction of identities is a perpetual project without a master plan, meaning that social identities are never fixed and always in the process of becoming, as opposed to being.[10] In this work, I propose that the processes through which U.S. sexualities were (re)constructed during the 1990s made these identities particularly reliant on the military and state violence for intelligibility, which has proven particularly useful for the projects of militarization, intervention, and securitization played out in the War on Terror.

For the purposes of this study, sexuality provides a useful matrix through which I maintain an intersectional approach that attends not only to power as distributed through sexuality but also to axes of oppression and privilege based on race, gender, class, and nationality. Intersectional approaches arise out of the feminisms developed by women of color and have a long, complex history but are succinctly summarized by some of their earliest innovators, members of the Combahee River Collective, who wrote: "The most general statement of our politics at the present time would be that we are actively committed to struggling against racial, sexual, heterosexual, and class oppression, and see as our particular task the development of integrated analysis and practice based upon the fact that the major systems of oppression are interlocking. The synthesis of these oppressions creates the conditions of our lives."[11]

Sexuality proves useful for developing such integrated analysis because of the special relationship it has with both gender and race. In contemporary Western thought, the reduction of sexuality to one of its constituent elements (sexual orientation) ties it tightly to the gender binary. The dominant schema requires interpreting each individual as deeply, constitutionally heterosexual or homosexual based on the unstated assumptions that gender is dichotomous, stable, obvious, and the most significant aspect of one's desires.[12] Both those who trouble binaries (bi- and pansexual, gender nonconforming, and genderqueer people) and sexual behaviors that do not eroticize gender (sadomasochism, partialisms) mark boundaries beyond which gender cannot accurately map the world of human sexuality. Still, heterosexuality and homosexuality remain defining organizational poles for sexuality in the contemporary United States, thus orienting sexuality in structural relationships to particular masculinities and femininities. Dichotomous, hierarchal gender roles are both produced by and productive of compulsory heterosexuality. At the same time, conventional lesbian and gay identities also affirm and are affirmed by the gender binary, even as they exceed the dictates of heterosexuality.

While the relationship between gender and sexuality has been well articulated in a great deal of feminist and queer scholarship, fewer thinkers have been willing to grapple with how sexuality is also always constituted in terms of race.[13] Sexual behavior, though far exceeding the strictures of reproduction, is the primary mechanism for reproduction, and reproduction is the instrument through which the fiction of race is propagated and enforced. This is to say that the social process of racialization is obscured by the "fact" of reproduction, which is used to reinforce a belief in the biological bases of social inequity. Taboos about sexual relations across racial borders enable the desire to seek pleasure in the violation of sexual prohibitions while reifying the power inequalities through which racial borders are drawn. As bell hooks writes, "From the standpoint of white supremacist capitalist patriarchy, the hope is that desires for the 'primitive' or fantasies about the Other can be continually exploited, and that such exploitation will occur in a manner that reinscribes and maintains the *status quo*."[14]

At the same time, sex resulting in reproduction can threaten the construction of racial groups as distinct and pure, meaning regulation of reproductive practices has often focused on limiting the potential for intimacy between the racial communities constructed by these regulations. As regulation never achieves total success, children who are born of unions that cross supposedly impermeable boundaries regular undermine the coherence of these regulations.[15] Additionally, hierarchies of sexual behavior that divide practices into categories of normal and acceptable or abnormal and deviant were constructed upon notions of the racialized Others' sexual practices, examples of what "we" are not.[16] So, though the linguistic categories of race may not appear as overtly as those of gender in existing scholarship on sexuality, one must remain aware that, when focused on sexuality, one observes a system historically constituted through and only intelligible in terms of other cross-cutting systems of power and meaning.

Patricia Hill Collins suggests three distinct paths for researching sexuality within an intersectional framework, none of which need be mutually exclusive: First, sexuality "can be analyzed as a freestanding system of oppression similar to oppressions of race, class, and gender. . . . A second approach examines how sexualities become manipulated *within* class, race, nation, and gender as distinctive systems of oppression and draw upon heterosexist assumptions to do so. . . . Yet another approach views sexuality as a specific site of intersectionality where intersecting oppressions meet."[17] Therefore, in this work, I examine sexuality as a distinctive axis of oppression and privilege, an instrument through which other axes of oppression and privilege are expressed, *and* a nexus where the boundaries between oppressed and privileged are both established and crossed.

My interdisciplinary feminist and queer methods echo certain resonances of the thinker whose work has had perhaps the greatest impact on other scholars of the history of sexuality, Michel Foucault. In the first volume of his groundbreaking *History of Sexuality*, Foucault writes: "Sexuality must not be described as a stubborn drive, by nature alien and of necessity disobedient to a power which exhausts itself trying to subdue it and often fails to control it entirely. It appears rather as an *especially dense transfer point for relations of power*. . . . Sexuality is not the most intractable element in power relations, but rather one of those endowed with the greatest instrumentality: useful for the greatest number of maneuvers and capable of serving as a *point of support*, as a linchpin, for the most varied strategies."[18]

Hence, sexuality can be analyzed as a place where struggles over the construction and meaning of other identity categories take place and as a sort of ideological technology that can be used to bulwark or tear down claims made about gender, race, the family, violence, and the economy. Lest we invest too much faith in Foucault's ingenuity, it is worth noting that before the promulgation of his work, similar claims about the instrumentality of sexuality for propagating oppression based on gender and race were made in the work of women of color feminists, such as Claudia Jones's 1940s writings on "manifestations of white chauvinism" and Angela Davis's work on Black women's roles during slavery, as well as that of radical feminists, especially

Adrienne Rich's identification of "compulsory heterosexuality" and Catharine MacKinnon's work on sexual harassment.[19] *Abuses of the Erotic* emerges from a genealogy rooted firmly in the soil of North American feminisms and eschews extensive engagement with any European theorists, despite respect for their contributions. Together, these foundational feminisms and their intellectual descendants attest to the strategic nature of sexuality and allow us to examine it as a matrix through which power relations are defined, justified, expressed, enforced, and, importantly, resisted.

MILITARIZATION IN THE MODERN UNITED STATES

In this work, I focus on sexuality as a point of support for *militarization*, what antimilitarist feminist Cynthia Enloe defines as the process through which "a person or a thing gradually comes to be controlled by the military *or* comes to depend for its well-being on militaristic ideas."[20] Such a definition demands we look beyond the enlisted personnel, policies, weapons, and activities of militaries toward the more indirect but enormously significant connections between military ideology and the culture of civilian life. At the same time, questions about the formal and institutional relationships between the military and the polity that produces it remain highly relevant. My approach to these questions is broadly interdisciplinary, drawing upon traditional disciplines such as history, political science, and sociology, as well as a number of interdisciplinary fields including feminist theory, American studies, media studies, and peace and conflict studies.

Militarization is the historical process through which militarism moves from theory into practice. Militarism is an ideology that advocates for the military's primacy over civilian governance; the close relationship between contemporary nation-states and their militaries over the course of the past century has made that ideology especially significant.[21] Militarism first became a topic of scholarly and political interest soon after the institutionalization of professional militaries across much of Europe in the early nineteenth century, but the study of militarism remained a relatively small and marginal field until after World War I. Whether conducted within Marxist, liberal, or nationalist paradigms, the central concern has remained a military's unique potential for asserting its own internal interests against and over those of the nation-states that raise and nominally administer them. Most early scholars of militarism focused on Germany, and much of the post–World War II work attempted to explain military dictatorships in Latin America and the decolonizing world, but alarm about militarism in the United States rang loudly and mostly unheeded from the early 1960s onward.[22]

In his 1961 farewell address, U.S. president Dwight D. Eisenhower, who had been a military officer his whole adult life and led the U.S. effort in Europe during World War II, cemented the term *military-industrial complex* in the national memory. Eisenhower had a highly optimistic and demonstrably false view of the United States as a historically peaceful country and held that the military was a "vital element in keeping the peace." Still, he insisted that those who followed him "guard against the acquisition of unwarranted influence, whether sought or unsought, by the military-industrial complex" because "potential for the disastrous rise of misplaced power exists and will persist." Eisenhower called for "an alert and knowledgeable citizenry [to] compel the proper meshing of the huge industrial and military machinery of defense with our peaceful methods and goals, so that security and liberty may prosper together," but he presciently cautioned that "domination of the nation's scholars by Federal employment, project allocations, and the power of money" threatened efforts to educate citizens about militarism.[23] Although the study of militarism remains marginal in U.S. institutions, over time, activist scholars embraced Eisenhower's analysis of the confluences of systems structured in opposition to social justice, naming the prison-industrial complex, the nonprofit-industrial complex, and many others.[24]

At the same time, militarization advanced both in many national contexts and globally throughout the second half of the twentieth century. In 1985 peace and conflict researchers Peter Wallensteen, John Galtung, and Carlos Portales claimed, "In the long history of human society, military attitudes, military behavior, and military structures have never been as widely represented as they are today," but "at the same time, ours is an age of questioning militarization."[25]

While the Soviet Union and United States poured immense resources into developing even more weapon systems that would become obsolete before ever being used, advocates for peace and civilian rule increasingly connected with each other and articulated counterpoints to militarism in media, academia, governments, and international forums such as the United Nations.

During the 1980s, United States culture contained an unstable mix of Cold War anxieties about the spread of communism that encouraged militarization and profound doubt about the efficacy of military interventions produced by the disastrous U.S. involvement in Vietnam from 1955 to 1975. In spite of the successes of pro-peace movements, direct U.S. military interventions in Lebanon, Grenada, and Libya coupled with underwriting for armed conflicts in Nicaragua, Afghanistan, and the Persian Gulf demonstrated the persistence of the recourse to militarized violence by the state during the 1980s. Heterosexual white male resentment at the incremental steps taken toward social equity in the mid-twentieth century drove growing interest in paramilitarism, the adoption of military tool and tropes by civilians. This phenomenon both arose from and produced anxieties about the military's ability and interest in defending (certain) citizens. James Gibson wrote that the 1980s "saw the emergence of a highly energized culture of war and the warrior" in which "American men . . . began to dream, to fantasize about the powers and features of another kind of man who could retake and reorder the world."[26] These fantasies, and the deeply erotic investments many people held in them, have persisted through significant changes in circumstance.

After the 1989 Malta Summit between U.S. president George H. W. Bush and Soviet leader Mikhail Gorbachev, considered by many to be the armistice of the Cold War, Bush proudly declared, "We stand at the threshold of a brand new era."[27] The end of decades of global militarization by the two competing superpowers was supposed to open the door for the 1990s to be the first decade of a peaceful epoch, but this did not come to pass. As political scientist Patrick Regan wrote in 1994, "The Cold War is over. . . . Nuclear weapons and large numbers of troops are being removed from the European theater. And rumors of military budget cuts abound. . . . But this putative demise of the military as the central actor in world politics may be too sanguine an interpretation."[28] Instead, as journalist William Greider wrote in 1998, "When the Cold War ended, America did not demobilize. . . . It remains configured and equipped to confront a war of maximum scale, prompted by some large and unknowable threat that no one can yet name."[29]

Clearly, the United States did launch a "war of maximum scale" in 2001, prompted by the "large and unknowable threat" of terrorism manifest on September 11, but many works struggle to place that day in its most useful frame of reference. The intense focus on September 11 and its aftermath, evidenced by the transdisciplinary outpouring of recent scholarly works beginning with reference to that day, blurs our understanding of the crucial years preceding it.[30] At the same time, other works have attempted to explain the post–September 11 War on Terror solely in terms of prior conflicts ranging from the colonization of the Americas to the Cold War, ignoring the distinctive features of post–Cold War militarisms.[31] The 1990s remain an undertheorized point of arrival or departure, shadowed by the penumbras of light shed on the surrounding eras and slipped between the cracks of two solidly studied periods.

A focus on the 1990s also heeds the insight of feminist work on militarism and war that demands we look beyond the formal opening and cessation of hostilities to understand the multiple causes and effects of armed conflict. As Cynthia Enloe wrote in 1993, "A postwar era lasts as long as people affected by a conflict employ that painful or exhilarating experience to assess their own current relationships and aspirations." This work uses the term *post–Cold War* as a frame that recognizes both the official end to the conflict and the continuation of Cold War practices and ideologies through justifications other than anticommunism or Soviet aggression. Following Enloe, I recognize that the Cold War had "a multitude of endings": the fall of the Berlin Wall, the Malta Summit, the dissolution of the Soviet Union, and a plethora of other moments between the late 1980s and early 1990s. Consequently, each of the four body chapters of *Abuses of the Erotic* embarks from a different moment in the closing years of the Cold War and proceeds toward distinct moments in the late

1990s and early 2000s. Recognizing the gendered nature of both war and peace, as Enloe calls us to, I also highlight how the "fresh answers to the old questions" devised in response to the Cold War's multiple endings did "not have the same meanings for women as they [did] for men."[32]

The end of the Cold War also did not have the same meanings for those on the political right and left in the United States. I do not engage in a partisan analysis in this work, finding a great deal to critique in both Republican and the Democratic politicians who administered the country during the time covered by this study, but I cannot disregard the significance of long-term historical forces in both of these parties to the era. Whereas the global left appeared conflicted and directionless following the collapse of the Soviet Union, the Democratic Party in the United States emerged from decades of extremely limited success to control the presidency for two terms with a freshly neoliberal approach that deemphasized traditional class politics in favor of more inclusive cultural politics and austerity measures packaged as work opportunity. Although they did not hold executive office for much of the decade, Republicans also experienced some electoral success during this period and further developed the neoconservative alliance between those advocating hawkish foreign policy and evangelical Christians advocating regressive social policies, returning executive power to Republicans less than a year before the September 11 attacks.[33]

Scholars on the right immediately showed great interest in the possibilities of the 1990s. Francis Fukuyama predicted the decade would be the beginning of an eternal capitalist paradise in *The End of History*, whereas Samuel Huntington envisioned a more dangerous, but still fundamentally changed, world in his *Clash of Civilizations*.[34] This decade has received less attention from scholars critical of the institutions and ideologies to which Fukuyama and Huntington are committed, however. For example, Joseph Masco's *The Theatre of Operations* provides a cogent critique of the continuities between the Cold War and War on Terror but speaks of the "suturing the end of the Cold War to the start of the War on Terror" without any analysis of the decade between them.[35] Consequently, this work addresses both the aftermath of the Cold War and the prelude to the War on Terror, filling a gap between scholarship on militarism in the Cold War and militarism in the War on Terror.[36] I demonstrate throughout that, far from being a decade in which U.S. politics and culture stayed static or turned toward peace, the 1990s were a time of intense militarization. Critics of the U.S. military and intervention abroad have missed many elements of this militarization because much of it happened outside of the formal structures of the military and within the borders claimed by the United States. Furthermore, the advance of militarism during this period cannot be explained simply in terms of the continuities that exist between these conflicts and past bouts of militarization related to wars against indigenous people, the nineteenth-century expansion of the United States, or interventions across the globe in the world wars and Cold War era.

From 1990 to 1999, the U.S. military conducted operations in Panama, Liberia, Saudi Arabia, Kuwait, Iraq, Zaire (DRC), Sierra Leone, Bosnia-Herzegovina, Somalia, Macedonia, Haiti, Central African Republic, Albania, Congo, Gabon, Cambodia, Guinea-Bissau, Kenya, Tanzania, Afghanistan, Sudan, East Timor, Serbia, and Kosovo.[37] Across the world, U.S. troops were deployed to more than 150 countries, and the military maintained bases in more than fifty foreign countries, including a heavy concentration in non-self-governing U.S. territories such as the Marshall Islands, Guam, Puerto Rico, American Samoa, and Johnson Atoll. During this same period, U.S. military units deployed domestically during the 1992 Los Angeles Uprising, National Guard units participated in lethal armed conflicts with civilians in Idaho and Texas, paramilitary Immigration and Naturalization Service troops were concentrated on the U.S.-Mexican border as part of Operation Gatekeeper, and law enforcement agencies fighting the "War on Drugs" increasingly adopted military-style tactics and equipment.[38] Even political scientist Andrew Bacevich, an avowedly conservative Catholic veteran, noted the success of militarization during this decade, writing, "Events of the 1990s made it even more difficult to preserve a clear distinction between the world of the warrior and the world of the politician. . . . As a result, over the course of the 1990s, inhibitions about actually using force eased."[39]

That the United States used military force often and widely during the 1990s is well established, but the means by which militarization succeeded is less settled. Here, I diverge sharply from most scholars of militarism in demonstrating that a great deal of militarization's success depends on the successful manipulation of people's ideas about sexuality.

BRINGING SEXUALITY AND MILITARISM INTO ONE FRAME

Scholars of militarism bound to disciplines historically dominated by men, as Bacevich is, may speak of "how Americans are seduced by war" or "the marriage of a militaristic cast of mind with utopian ends" but are generally uninterested in the sexual politics of militarism.[40] Several interdisciplinary works on Cold War sexualities have been published in the past decade, and a growing number of new works attend to the importance of sexuality to the War on Terror, but few scholars have sought to address sexuality during this inter-war period.[41] Therefore, in addition to marking the significance of a decade obscured by its location between two well-studied eras, this work fills a gap in a growing field demonstrating the undertheorized significance of sexual politics to geopolitical struggles.

In *Abuses of the Erotic*, I operate from the assumption that sexuality and militarism exist in a dialogic relationship in which neither force drives the other. I do not attempt to demonstrate the existence of conscious strategy by defense contractors to use sexuality as a promotional strategy, nor do I suggest that the politics of militarism can be reduced to the frustrated (hetero)sexualities of aging soldiers and politicians. Instead, the process through which sexualities have been militarized is much more diffuse and contested. Both militarism and sexuality are sets of ideological and linguistic resources that different users in different venues have deployed in unpredictable ways with even more unpredictable effects. I demonstrate here that, with the benefit of hindsight, one can see how arguments favoring militarism evidenced with reference to sexuality became increasingly common and successful over the course of 1990s. As a result, a particular "common sense" about the relationships between sexuality and militarism developed by the end of the decade. These cultural norms about sexuality and militarism were especially fertile ground for planting the seeds of the War on Terror that blossomed in the 2000s.

Sexuality can become militarized in several ways.[42] First, sexuality becomes militarized when people accept the argument that people of a particular sexuality should support military action because of their sexuality. Historically, this has often meant accusing men who do not support militarism of being insufficiently virile. More commonly today this takes this form of suggesting that good heterosexuals protect their children and that protecting children requires war, but increasingly some have suggested that people who identify with nonnormative sexualities should support wars against countries with unfriendly legal systems for LGBTQ people. Second, sexuality becomes militarized when people prioritize the military's interests and value system on sexuality over civilian law and consensus. This can take the form of excusing homophobic discrimination in the military as part of the military's internal culture, deferring to military courts' biases against survivors in cases of sexual assault, or prioritizing the military's ability to test weapons of mass destruction over the reproductive health of people living near test sites, among other possibilities. The third modality through which sexuality is militarized relies on defining who is and is not deserving of state violence by way of their sexual practices. Accusations of an imagined enemy's deviant sexuality become justification for state violence, and the self-presentation of one's sexuality as "normal" becomes proof for the righteousness of one's own violence. Each of these three forms appeared throughout the 1990s and increasingly gained the status of cultural truth, advancing militaristic projects at multiple levels.

In addressing the connections between the construction of sexuality and the conduct of war, I walk in the footsteps of many feminists without whom my work would not exist. This is an interdisciplinary work in the tradition established by women of color feminists of the 1970s, a set of interventions that have facilitated the development of transnational feminism (discussed in chapter 1), queer of color critique (utilized extensively in chapters 2 and 3), and indigenous feminisms (the approach most influencing chapter 4). While scholars in each of these fields have acknowledged their common roots, it remains uncommon for their branches to be woven together. In addition to Black feminist innovators like Lorde, Collins, Davis, hooks, and the Combahee River Collective, I owe a debt to the essential work on the intersections of identity and state violence produced by Joy James and M. Jacqui Alexander.[43] James established the critical need for placing the United States at the center of our critiques of violence in her 1996 book *Resisting State Violence*, and Alexander cogently demonstrates how nation-states instrumentalize sexuality in her early 2000s essay "Transnationalism, Sexuality, and the State." Women in antiwar movements, from the hundred-year-old Women's International League for Peace and Freedom to the contemporary activists at Code Pink, have also been at the forefront of developing integrated analyses of militarism and sexuality. Finally, Cynthia Enloe has been the leading feminist scholar on militarism at least since the 1983 publication of her book *Does Khaki Become You? The Militarisation of Women's Lives*, and her influence permeates this book alongside other work in the field of feminist international politics.[44]

I enhance these feminist perspectives with scholarship on the history of sexuality and from queer studies. Allan Berube, Margot Canaday, and Aaron Belkin each produced historical works useful for this study that address sexuality in the military.[45] I extend their works both by focusing on more contemporary moments in history and expanding my frame beyond a focus on sexual orientation to include topics like reproduction and sexual violence. I also find indispensable the scholarship in queer theory on state-sponsored sexualities and the incorporation of certain sexual minorities into the dominant culture by Jasbir Puar, Lisa Duggan, and Lauren Berlant.[46] These theorists' focus on denaturalizing the relationship between bodies, desires, and sexual ideologies produces important tools for examining archives and topics that have escaped their interest. The rhetorical collisions of these feminist, historical, and queer intellectual contributions provide an agile and grounded set of methods for analyzing recent history. Taken together, these influences compose the interdisciplinary methodology through which I read the culture of the United States by way of the texts it produced.

Much of the best and worst work on sexuality, race, and gender focuses on exposition of particular marginalized lives, activities, or ideas. By contrast, *Abuses of the Erotic* is more a work of "studying up," using the perspectives developed in the margins of sexuality, race, and gender to better understand how dominant, hegemonic, and centralized systems maintain their power and perpetuate their existence. To do so, I examine an archive with three major nodes: news media, government documents, and cultural production.

The insistent interdisciplinarity of this work is tempered by my fondness for a historical method grounded in understanding a time period primarily through an analysis of artifacts originating in that period. Consequently, news media is at the heart of my archive, and newspapers are among my most commonly cited and analyzed sources. Though total U.S. newspaper circulation peaked in 1990 and had been in slow decline in proportion to the population since the 1950s, newspapers retained an air of authority even as they lost ground to emerging forms of televised and digital news.[47] As journalists Juan Gonzalez and Joseph Torres write, "For more than 200 years, newspapers were the main source of news to the U.S. public. Even as successive waves of technology transformed our media system . . . newspapers remained the primary source of information for the entire nation."[48]

I focus most extensively on the "newspaper of record," the *New York Times*, a paper that one early 2000s study called "a repository of America's historical memories and cultural contexts . . . a diary of how our history had unfolded from day to day."[49] I also regularly refer to the *Washington Post*, another highly respected newspaper with a particular focus on national politics, and somewhat less often to *USA Today*, a well-circulated but less esteemed publication. Occasionally, especially in reference to stories of local or topical interest, I also make use of the *Wall Street Journal*, *Los Angeles Times*, *San Francisco Chronicle*, and other local newspapers from the *Hampton Roads (VA) Daily Press* (an important source for news pertaining to the U.S. Navy) to the *Honolulu Advertiser* (a small paper in the U.S. media market that loomed large in the Pacific).

While I focus on major daily newspapers, I in no way limit myself to them, and I include major news magazines such as *Time* and *Newsweek*, alternative and subcultural publications such as *The Advocate* and *Indian Country Today*, and some English-language foreign press such as *Japan Times* and *Caribbean News Corporation*. Although I do not dwell extensively on the politics of images and representation, I do look toward televised media at times, including televised presidential addresses and live coverage of the Los Angeles Uprising to anti–Gulf War AIDS activists disrupting the CBS *Evening News*. As I focus most intently on the years 1989–96 and on the most widely distributed ideas and images of this era, I make little reference to exclusively digital forms of news media, though I made extensive use of digitized archives in researching this project.

The second node I use to assess how projects of militarizing sexuality proceeded during this period is government documents. The declarations of elected and appointed officials, the laws they passed and the treaties they signed, as well as the policies they enforced and the research reports they authorized all play an equally important role as news media in this study. Speeches by President George H. W. Bush and President Bill Clinton are laced throughout, and chapter 2 even borrows its name from Bush's "Address on the End of the Gulf War." Military policies regulating the sexual practices and identities of soldiers are key elements of the chapters on sexual violence in the military and debates over LGBT access to the military. My analysis of the militarization of reproduction depends on a close reading of the U.S.–Marshall Islands Compact of Free Association treaty, and I develop the term *domestic militarism* in relation to four 1996 laws relating to criminal justice, immigration, marriage, and the social safety net. I construct a wide-ranging critique of the state by taking its declarations seriously and subjecting them to exacting rigor.

Finally, *Abuses of the Erotic* engages an archive of cultural production to understand how militarized values work their way into and find expression in previously nonmilitary elements of the culture. I foreground popular culture to the exclusion of avant-garde or fine art in order to center what was most widely distributed and consumed by the public. I look toward Hollywood film (*Courage Under*

Fire, G.I. Jane), mass market paperbacks (*Just Cause: The Real Story of America's High-Tech Invasion of Panama, American Terrorist: Timothy McVeigh and the Oklahoma City Bombing*), and popular music (Lee Greenwood's "God Bless the U.S.A.," Sublime's "April 29th, 1992") to assess how militarized ideas about sexuality attain the status of common sense. I approach these cultural objects not as frivolous expressions of spontaneous inspiration but as crystallizations of the values implicit in the specific historical and cultural locations from which they emanate.

To prevent this analysis of dominant power from lapsing into a monolithic representation of unidirectional forces, I bring in a carefully curated set of oppositional pieces to contrast the primary portion of the archive and create a more dynamic account of these always contested processes. I attempt to highlight the words of whoever the most relevant target of state violence is in any situation. When the United States goes to war against Iraq, I look toward Iraqis, and whether U.S. troops appear in Haiti, the former Yugoslavia, or a neighborhood in Los Angeles, I look for the voices of the most affected. Often I make use of direct statements, but key contributions are also made in more literary and poetic forms by artists such as Sapphire and Kathy Jetñil-Kijiner. The final chapter especially focuses on the ongoing work of particular individuals and groups engaged in projects of demilitarizing sexuality and foregrounds their self-descriptions and analyses.

LOOKING AHEAD

The overall organization of this work is thematic, with four chapters addressing militarization of sexual violence, heterosexual domesticity, gay and lesbian identities, and reproduction during the 1990s, followed by a single chapter that unites each of these threads in an analysis of the War on Terror in the first decade of the 2000s. I use the term *post–Cold War* to signal a temporal period beginning in the late 1980s and continuing into the late 2010s, given that I argue sexuality played a crucial role in continuing the Cold War behavior of the U.S. state in the wake of that conflict's close. I apply multiple layers of analysis to one time period to account for the complexity

of sexuality and to lacquer together often bifurcated topics like normative and nonnormative sexualities, sexual violence and sexual
identities, as well as geopolitics and the politics of identity. A richly
textured representation of sexuality and militarism emerges as the
cumulative effect of these layers of analysis.

Chapter 1, "No Politician Can Afford to Let Women Come Home
in Body Bags: The Militarization of Sexual Violence," moves between
incidents of sexual violence committed by U.S. service members and
moments in which proponents of intervention offer the U.S. military
as a bulwark against sexual violence. I ask, if women dying at war is
the ultimate political liability, how does their disproportionate vulnerability to sexual violence become acceptable? Here I contrast the
sexual violence that accompanied the U.S. interventions in Panama,
Kuwait, Haiti, and Kosovo with sexual assaults committed by members
of the military at the Tailhook Convention, on the island of Okinawa,
and at the Aberdeen Proving Grounds. I demonstrate the failure of
the U.S. military to properly address sexual violence within its ranks
and argue that solutions to sexual violence cannot rely primarily
upon institutions that perpetuate sexual violence if they hope to be
effective. To do so, I draw upon a transnational feminist framework
that engages not only feminists working within the U.S. military but
also feminists in Haiti, Japan, and the former Yugoslavia working to
confront the double burdens of localized forms of gender oppression
paired with the patriarchal imperialism of the United States.

Chapter 2, "Confronting an Enemy Abroad, Transforming a Nation
at Home: Heterosexuality and Domestic Militarism," interprets how
what is often considered the first post–Cold War U.S. intervention
abroad, the 1990–91 War on Iraq, produced militarization at home.
The analysis in this chapter embraces the dual meaning of *domestic*
as both the space within the borders claimed by the United States
and the space occupied by a heteronormative family to demonstrate
the slippage between ideas about proper (inter)national relations
and proper kinship relations. Beginning with an analysis of the heteronormative assumptions undergirding the war, I connect its justifications to subsequent episodes of domestic state violence in the
Los Angeles Uprising, Waco siege, Oklahoma City bombing, and

ultimately a series of 1996 laws amending policy on immigration, marriage, public assistance, and the death penalty. Through this, I develop the concept of domestic militarism as an ideology that uses circular appeals to family and nation to excuse the state's use of violence within its borders and with the goal of establishing only certain kinds of kinship as legitimate.

Linking the militarization of heterosexuality to the militarization of homosexuality, chapter 3, "A Propensity or Intent to Engage in Homosexual Acts: Militant Queerness and Militarized Homosexuality," highlights conflicts internal to LGBTQ movements over gay and lesbian service members in contrast to the numerous accounts focused on the debate between integrationists and homophobic government institutions. This chapter draws on material from national gay and lesbian mobilizations, local activist groups, and media oriented toward LGBTQ audiences. In doing so, it demonstrates how widely held assumptions that lesbian and gay politics were radical, oppositional, and antinationalist were overtaken by the assumption that gay and lesbian constituencies built power by assimilating into powerful, nationalistic institutions. This chapter explicates the growing investment in the nation-state attached to the "new homonormativity" described by Lisa Duggan in terms of the neoliberal shrinkage of the state while adding texture and specificity to Jasbir Puar's later, related concept of homonationalism. Highlighting the debate over assimilation into the military within the broader contexts of AIDS, gentrification, and the quest for marriage equality, this chapter explores how gay and lesbian citizens can seek political power without reproducing the hierarchal violences of the U.S. nation-state.

Chapter 4, "A Close and Mutually Beneficial Relationship: The United States, Marshall Islands, and Militarization of Reproduction," turns toward the effects of nuclear testing and the 1986 Compact of Free Association on the futures of indigenous people in U.S.-occupied Micronesia. I argue that one must understand the specifically sexual nature of U.S. intervention in the Pacific to understand the impact of this presence and how it remains oriented, as were the federal Indian policies that preceded it, toward genocide. I demonstrate how mistaken assumptions about the biological dimensions of reproduction, the particular cultural groups that populate the Pacific, and the future viability of these lands and waters have enhanced the power and reach of the U.S. military at the cost of Marshallese and other indigenous lives. Rejecting the model of the "disappearing islander" offered by the U.S. military, I turn toward the work of contemporary Pacific Islander artists like Kathy Jetñil-Kijiner to counter expectations of inevitable death with voices that affirm survival and project resistance into the future.

The conclusion, "The Long War," brings together the insights of the previous four chapters to explain how quickly history can repeat itself. Surveying the first fifteen years of the War on Terror, I frame the militarization of homosexuality, heterosexuality, sexual violence, and reproduction during the 1990s as the preconditions through which the War on Terror has been justified and through which its proponents have continued to militarize sexuality. I complete my analysis of the sexualized metaphors deployed to make sense of the events of September 11 by moving between Iraq, Afghanistan, and issues of domestic securitization in order to clarify how the seeds planted in the 1990s bore fruit in the 2000s. I refuse to provide an unidirectional account of this struggle, however, and finish by turning toward the demilitarization of sexuality. Highlighting U.S., foreign, and transnational organizations, I demonstrate the vital ongoing work reversing the trend of militarization before returning to the words of Audre Lorde to point toward the possibility of a demilitarized future.

A few additional notes reflecting the terminology used in this project are necessary. First, I attempt to use the term *state* to refer exclusively to the institutions and organizations that constitute the sovereign federal government of the United States, not its fifty constituent subnational bodies commonly referred to as *states*. Secondly, I regularly use the term *settler colonial* to characterize U.S. culture, government, and history. Settler colonialism is the ongoing process through which colonists target indigenous people not only for exploitation and removal but also for extermination and replacement by settlers. As Kanaka Maoli scholar J. Kēhaulani Kauanui explains, "Settler colonialism is a structure that endures indigeneity, as it holds out against it."[50] Settler colonialism manifests in historical and contemporary attempts by non-Native people to make the "foreign" space of indigenous territory into their "domestic" space, complicating any easy dichotomy between the two. Therefore, no claims made here about the distinctiveness of post–Cold War U.S. culture should be interpreted as suggesting a discontinuity with the historical and continuing process of settler colonialism. I subscribe to Shawnee and Lenape scholar Steven Newcomb's assessment that "the dominating moral system that underlies federal Indian law and policy is the same moral system that underlies U.S. foreign policy; it is predicated on the presumption . . . that the United States has a divine right of empire, not simply in North America, but throughout the world."[51]

Though first-person pronouns appear rarely after this introduction, throughout this work I cannot avoid relating to my analysis and the objects of my analysis through subjective experience. First, the time period of this study roughly coincides with the years I spent in primary and secondary school. I lived through most of these events, albeit as a distant observer, but I do not discuss my personal experiences with witnessing these events because I am much more interested in the overall system of meaning rather than how one individual navigated it. Furthermore, topics like race and gender cannot be approached neutrally. I approach these topics as someone with deep investments in antimilitarist, anti-heteropatriarchal and anti–white supremacist movements. I also approach them as a white man who has systematically benefited from these oppressions and who has spent life occupying stolen indigenous land. As a U.S.-born citizen, my analysis is limited by the parochialism of my national paradigm, a limitation made all the more dangerous by how rarely we acknowledge that parochialism here.

At the same time, being from the United States gives me, in Edward Said's words, "a special duty to address the constituted and authorized powers" of this country, "particularly when those powers are exercised in a manifestly disproportionate and immoral war, or in deliberate program of discrimination, repression and collective cruelty."[52] Therefore, I openly concede my bias in favor of democratic civilian control of politics, the pursuit of peace instead of war, and social justice at large. Rather than seeing my political commitments as distorting my perspective, I find that these commitments provide relevant evaluative tools and ethical grounding that keeps my scholarship accountable to the social movements from which it arises.

As the following chapters demonstrate, the 1990s were a time of "manifestly disproportionate and immoral wars" as well as "discrimination, repression, and collective cruelty." The most authorized voices in U.S. culture responded to these unfolding events in ways that perpetuated injustice and set the stage for the multiplication of these injustices during the War on Terror. Still, we can discern some glimmers of hope in the sea of money, verbiage, and other limited resources spent on enforcing U.S. global military hegemony, civilian consent for a perpetual war economy, and the social inequalities that structure all lives while making some shorter. The effort expended on producing injustice reveals that it is not our inevitable state; if something has been militarized, it can be demilitarized. Confronting injustice requires understanding how it came into being and has changed the world, and the following chapters document just that. Confronting injustice also requires understanding how it has produced deep changes within us that are difficult to separate from our sense of self. Returning to the words of Audre Lorde:

> We have been raised to fear the yes within ourselves, our deepest cravings. But, once recognized, those which do not enhance our future lose their power and can be altered. . . . The fear that we cannot grow beyond whatever distortions we may find within ourselves keeps us docile and loyal and obedient, externally defined. . . . But . . . as we begin to recognize our deepest feelings, we begin to give up, of necessity, being satisfied with suffering, and self-negation, and with the numbness which so often seems like the only alternative in our society. Our acts against oppression become integral with self, motivated and empowered from within.[53]

Abuses of the Erotic documents how over the course of the 1990s militarization distorted sexuality in a way that does not enhance our future. Clear recognition of this process is one step toward taking power away from these distortions and changing the suffering, self-negation, and numbness Lorde so capably challenged during her own life.

1

No Politician Can Afford to Let Women Come Home in Body Bags

THE MILITARIZATION OF SEXUAL VIOLENCE

Although declining Cold War tensions in the late 1980s stirred hopes for a new era of global peace and cooperation, the 1990s dawned with clouds of black smoke and the sound of warplanes overhead in Panama City. On December 20, 1989, the U.S. military, extensively deployed in Panama since 1903, began a campaign against the government of U.S.-trained Líder Máximo de Liberación Nacional Manuel Noriega, resulting in several hundred deaths and Noriega's eventual surrender and imprisonment. Although long-term geopolitical considerations built a foundation, ranging from the United States' Monroe Doctrine tendency toward intervention in Latin America to more Panama-specific concerns about that country's invaluable canal and potential role in drug trafficking, the rhetoric justifying Operation Just Cause hinged on the threat of sexual assault.

Completing a long list of grievances against Noriega in a televised address, U.S. president George H. W. Bush expressed "that was enough" only when he received a report of Panamanian soldiers sexually terrorizing a civilian woman married to a captured U.S. serviceman.[1] Even though women made up a growing proportion of the military forces deployed against Panama in this confrontation, they continued to be represented as helpless victims either shielded by or violated by masculine violence. The post–Cold War military increasingly confronted questions of women's roles within the institution throughout the 1990s, but despite enormous steps toward gender equity in the preceding decades, women's bodies remained rhetorically hallowed in the institution and confined by the presumption expressed in the 1997 film *G.I. Jane*: "No politician can afford to let women come home in body bags."[2]

At the same time, as we will see, politicians in the United States could afford to let women come home from the military as survivors of sexual assault. Many feminists have rightfully celebrated one of the most significant changes in late twentieth-century warfare: the recognition that sexual violence during times of war is a particular manifestation of gender inequality and gendered violence. Simultaneously, nation-states have increasingly integrated a critique of sexual violence into their justifications for initiating and sustaining armed conflicts.[3] This chapter draws out the contrast between the U.S. government's presentation of its military as global protectors against sexual violence and the commission of sexual assault by military personnel against both fellow service members and civilians. The concept of the *militarization of sexual violence* emerges from my use of a transnational feminist lens to read the intertwined history of militarism and sexual violence during the 1990s.

Transnational feminism begins from the recognition that the unequal and violent relations between nation-states preclude an easy path to solidarity across the borders claimed by those nation-states. As Inderpal Grewal and Caren Kaplan assert in their formative text on transnational feminism, "Without an analysis of transnational scattered hegemonies that reveal themselves in gender relations, feminist movements will remain isolated and prone to reproducing the universalizing gestures of dominant Western culture."[4] Instead of assuming that a nation-state adopting antirape rhetoric is an uncomplicated feminist victory, transnational feminism demands that we examine how such rhetoric has different benefits, limitations, and consequences for women placed differently in terms of race, ethnicity, and nationality. Furthermore, U.S.-based feminists of color like Beth Richie and Sarah Deer have demonstrated the insufficiency of the state to positively intervene in the lives of Black and indigenous women when that state is for them, historically and currently, incarcerator and occupier.[5]

Sexual violence undergoes militarization in two ways. First, and most straightforwardly, promoting military intervention as a viable solution to sexual violence militarizes sexual violence by encouraging the armed response of the state over effective, survivor-centric responses designed by feminists. Second, ignoring, denying, rationalizing, or defending sexual violence as an inevitable part of a military's internal culture, immune to civilian regulation, militarizes sexual violence. In both cases, the interests of the military and its leadership prevail over those of accountability and survivors, making civilian cultural understandings of sexual violence complicit with militarized projects. As we will see, the first modality of militarizing sexual violence was relevant to the U.S. military's actions in Panama, Iraq, Haiti, and Kosovo during the 1990s. The second modality appeared most prominently in reference to sexual assaults committed by members of the military at the Tailhook Convention in Las Vegas, on the Japanese island of Okinawa, and at the Aberdeen Proving Grounds in Maryland.

Although sexual violence has been an element of war throughout history and men in patriarchal societies have been going to war in defense of "their" women since antiquity, wars justified in terms of ethical stance against the mistreatment of women are a relatively recent phenomenon. The U.S. state has long used violence against indigenous and Black men in supposed defense of white women, but assaults against foreign women had never been a prominent or proximate justification for U.S. wars abroad. For example, neither propaganda surrounding Evangelina Cosio y Cisneros and Clemencia Arango before the Spanish-American War nor that articulating the Rape of Belgium in the first year of World War I convinced the U.S. government to declare war or featured prominently in their public campaigns when they did.[6] In addition to shifting justifications for their deployments, members of the U.S. military underwent demographic reconfigurations after the 1973 end of conscription that saw more than two hundred thousand women on active duty by 1989, more than 10 percent of total personnel.[7]

The 1990s deserve special attention not only for being understudied but also for historic changes in how nation-states successfully incorporated feminist rhetoric without undergoing legitimately feminist transformations. The intensification of transnational feminist activism made significant inroads into patriarchal institutions by this decade, opening up debates about sexual harassment, women in combat, and other forms of discrimination by the U.S. state as well as spreading outcry and international legal action on rape during times of war. These efforts culminated in the October 2000 passage of UN Security Council Resolution 1325 on women, peace, and security, which called upon warring parties "to take special measures to protect women and girls from gender-based violence, particularly rape and other forms of sexual abuse," among other key reforms.[8] Ultimately, though, these feminist-inspired reforms were repurposed by nation-states, especially the United States, to resist demilitarization and gender equity. This work confirms those of other scholars who have noted the ascendancy of neoliberalism and humanitarian imperialism during the 1990s.[9]

Throughout this chapter, I stage a series of encounters between quotidian forms of media produced through transnational corporations (newspapers, trade paperbacks, and film) and transnational feminist activists pushing back against these narratives in less well-circulated but equally significant interventions. While I focus on the development of militarized rhetoric and practices relating to sexual violence, I simultaneously demonstrate how this force was met at every step with doubt and resistance, especially emanating from feminists outside of the United States. I explicate this process in order to facilitate its reversal. Taken together, the rhetoric professed by state officials aided by the makers of certain mainstream cultural artifacts produced new meanings and understandings of sexual violence that privileged militarized solutions and obscured problems within the military. Both of these factors bore positively on the ability of the U.S. government and military to wage a global War on Terror in the wake of these events, as the media-consuming public was primed to accept both military action as a tenable response to rape and widespread rape within the military as an affordable sacrifice. No person should have to suffer sexual violence during war, nor should anyone be forced to bear the risk of sexual assault to participate equally in a public institution, but addressing both of these issues at once has, so far, proven to be a profound challenge.

"JUST CAUSE" IN PANAMA

In his "Address to the Nation on Panama," aired live hours after U.S. troops began attacking forces loyal to Noriega, President George H. W. Bush provided a number of reasons why the time for U.S. action had arrived. Bush laid a groundwork accusing the Panamanian government of allowing drug trafficking and endangering U.S. citizens, democracy, and the Canal Treaty before moving to the events of December 16, when, he claimed, Noriega's soldiers had shot two U.S. servicemen at a roadblock before they "arrested and brutally beat a third American serviceman; and then brutally interrogated his wife, threatening her with sexual abuse."[10]

Bush was not the only one impressed by the story of the naval officer and his wife detained in Panama City.[11] Military historian Lawrence Yates, who was present in Panama at the time, wrote that "there was no visible sense of outrage" about the roadblock shooting, but "the outrage came on Sunday" when officers heard that "at least one Panamanian officer made sexual threats and fondled [the officer's wife] until she ultimately passed out."[12] Journalist Malcolm McConnell used it as the climax for the prologue to his 1991 triumphant account *Just Cause: The Real Story of America's High-Tech Invasion of Panama*. McConnell elaborated, writing that the "American Navy lieutenant and his attractive young wife" were "manhandled" by the Panamanian soldiers, who "kicked him savagely in the groin" and "pulled up her knit cotton jumper and thrust his hand inside. . . . 'I'll fuck her tonight,' he added."[13] Another journalist, Kevin Buckley, used the story in an equally dramatic fashion, as the culminating event before the invasion in the chapter "Pulling the Trigger" in his more restrained *Panama: The Whole Story*. Buckley had several details different than McConnell—his Panamanian soldiers "appeared to be drunk," drove a pickup instead of a van, threw the wife against the wall instead of groping her, and dropped the couple off in a different place—but the multiple blows to the man's groin and threat of sexually assaulting the woman remained consistent.[14]

The to-this-day-unnamed "officer's wife"—outside of the military but always hailed in relation to it—made for a compelling victim of hypersexual men of color unprofessionally playing at soldiering. The women of Panama proved to be of much less interest to the U.S. military and media. As Gavrielle Gemma and Teresa Gutiérrez, the Panamanian project directors of an independent commission on the invasion, wrote, "The media, every television station, every major newspaper participated in a virtual orgy of applause while covering up what was really taking place in Panama."[15] As they described it, it was "a story not of liberators being welcomed, but of death and destruction."[16] Other Panamanian women, such as Edilma Icaza, organized active resistance to the U.S. invasion in the form of all-women "dignity battalions," and prominent Black Panamanian jurist Graciela Dixon took to the radio waves to decry the racism inherent in the U.S. invasion and its disproportionate impacts on Panamanians of color.[17]

At least five hundred, and possibly five thousand, civilians were killed during the invasion; many residential areas were bombed, leaving almost twenty thousand homeless; and thousands were left with visible and invisible scars from explosions, bullets, captivity, and other traumas.[18] Reflecting on the mixture of racism, sexism, and classism with which the U.S. media regarded Panama and its people, Black feminist scholar Joy James writes, "Sensationalized as a safari hunt, with international law and state violence treated as no more than factors in a game between the romanticized hunter and animalized hunted, the invasion of Panama and the devastating effects on its people, democratic law, and policies were trivialized."[19] In the aftermath, Olga Mejía, president of the National Human Rights Commission of Panama, claimed, "One hundred days after the invasion, the occupying army continues to operate with impunity and the high cost in human life still remains to be brought to light."[20] She went on to describe the horrors experienced by civilians in the Chorrillo neighborhood during the U.S. bombardment and subsequent mass graves that included everyone from young mothers to six-year-old boys, asking for special consideration for "all of the mothers who know what life is and know what it is to lose their most precious loved ones."[21] Meanwhile, in July 1991 Congress held hearings on the

"Current Situation in Panama" that consisted entirely of congress-
men interviewing men from the military and state department who
found no need to mention women from the U.S. or Panama or sexual
violence committed by Panamanian or U.S. troops.[22]

Despite their deadly consequences, the tropes deployed alongside
the troops in the U.S. war on Panama would not be demobilized after
Noriega's ouster and extradition to the United States. No efforts were
made to reduce the prevalence of sexual violence against women in
Panama, and no attempts were made to hold the naval lieutenant's
wife's alleged attackers accountable or even to identify them. Rather
than address the wrong they supposedly invaded to right, the proponents of U.S. militarism set their sights elsewhere. The 1990–91 Gulf
War, addressed in more detail in chapter 2, also relied on accusations
of sexual assault to mobilize citizens for war.

THE RAPE OF KUWAIT

Interventionists celebrated the U.S. invasion of Panama as a welcome
contrast to their failures in Vietnam, "but George Bush remained
troubled by America's Vietnam experience" and would not be able to
declare, "By God, we've kicked the Vietnam Syndrome once and for
all" until after the U.S. intervention in Kuwait.[23] Several early reports
documenting the crises triggered by Iraq's August invasion of Kuwait
drew specific attention to an alleged epidemic of sexual assault by
Iraqis. In the opening weeks of the conflict, reporter Robert McFadden wrote of how refugees "spoke of rape, looting, and violence by
the invasion troops"; the editors of the New York Times borrowed
heavily from Washington Post coverage and wrote of "several confirmed instances of rape" without obtaining any external confirma-
tion; Barbara Crossette reported on "Thai and Filipina maids being
sought out for rape by Iraqi soldiers"; and William Safire claimed that
any delay in invading Iraq would simply give Saddam Hussein "the
time he needs to rape and repopulate a nation."[24]

No doubt, women in Kuwait were forced to endure sexual violence throughout the war. However, the visibility of violence against
Kuwaiti women and immigrant women in Kuwait did not translate
into a pushback against local or transnational forms of patriarchy.

Instead, men used this visibility to justify military intervention and the spectacular light cast on wartime rape served to obscure the ever-presence of rape during times of "peace." As antimilitarist feminists have documented across the world, women experience sexual violence across the continuum of war and peace in a way that troubles any clear boundary between the two.[25]

The invasion of Kuwait became inescapably linked to accusations of sexual assault by October, when President Bush began calling the invasion "the rape of Kuwait."[26] Within a month, the phrase appeared without quotation marks in *USA Today*, *Los Angeles Times*, *Chicago Tribune*, *Wall Street Journal*, and countless smaller newspapers with increasing frequency in the new year.[27] In January 1991, author Jean Sasson capitalized on this convenient shorthand by publishing a best-selling "nonfiction" book titled *The Rape of Kuwait*. In it, Sasson claimed to relay the stories of survivors, including a Filipina migrant maid, who had Kuwaiti employers with a "really sweet nature" that "never mistreated her in any way" before her brutal group assault by Iraqi soldiers. Sasson described a young survivor who "hates all men now, except for her father of course," and "is determined to kill the Iraqi rapist," whereas the older Kuwaiti woman she described "hopes the army of Saudi Arabia drops nuclear bombs on the country and kills every Iraqi."[28]

Given Sasson's deification of the Kuwaiti upper class, her tendency to define women as male possessions and her eagerness to indulge in revenge fantasies about the Iraqis she portrays as reprehensible, her endorsement of U.S. military intervention and the restoration of the undemocratic Kuwaiti monarchy was unsurprising.[29] The reach of the book was enhanced by the publisher's shipping two hundred thousand copies to U.S. soldiers in the Gulf, funded by the Kuwaiti Embassy, and the publisher still sold more than 1 million copies more, hitting number two on the paperback best sellers list, where it spent seven weeks.[30] Even Sasson had to acknowledge the appearance of opportunism in the confluence of capitalist, militarist, pro-Bush, and pro-Kuwait sentiments in her work, complaining to reporters, "I've been accused of war profiteering . . . of being a lobbyist for President Bush and . . . of being a propagandist for the Kuwaiti government."[31]

Even before Sasson's book, journalists had raised questions about the veracity of accusations of mass rape in Kuwait. On December 16 Judith Miller, whose journalistic career ended later due to her poorly sourced reporting in favor of the second war on Iraq, wrote that the contrasting statistics and stories provided by different sources within Kuwait had "given rise to suspicions among some human rights monitors that abuses are being exaggerated, consciously or not, for political purpose." Although the numbers were disputed, Miller continued, "what is not disputed is the propaganda value of Iraqi atrocities in Kuwait."[32] As one Saudi monitor from Middle East Watch put it, "What's happening in Kuwait is terrible . . . but we simply cannot find persuasive evidence of the thousands of deaths and mass rapes and many of the other abuses on a scale that have been reported in the press."[33] While unsubstantiated accusations of sexual assault by individuals are extraordinarily rare, recent U.S. history demonstrates how proponents of war make such claims for survivors without an attendant commitment to providing justice for those survivors. Whether one or one thousand women were assaulted does not change that such violence is unacceptable, nor does it change the fact that U.S. intervention exacerbates experiences of violence for women rather than diffusing such violence.

During the conflict, U.S. bases took on a tradition of playing country singer Lee Greenwood's "God Bless the U.S.A." at noon every day.[34] The song, originally released several years earlier, found renewed popularity through radio airplay and a popular music video produced by MCA Records featuring images of both the war and soldiers returning home.[35] The song is especially appropriate for understanding this moment because the refrain indicates the predominant gendered misconceptions underlying the militarization of sexual violence. Greenwood repeatedly assures the listener that he "won't forget the men who died" before promising to "defend her still today." This chorus erases women's labor within and outside of the military by crediting only "men who died" for their service before indicating that a feminized nation is in some sort of peril from which Greenwood must "defend her," even though Iraq never posed any sort of direct threat to territory claimed by the United States. Greenwood's song provided a powerful tool to reproduce notions of women in need of rescue, foreign men as threats, and U.S. soldiers as unimpeachable protectors under the cover of pop banality.

The Gulf War officially ended on February 28, 1991, but as members of the African Women's Anti-War Coalition have written, "there is no aftermath for women." Rather, "in the aftermath, men use violence against women and women's fear of violence to reinforce their hold on women."[36] In Kuwait those who survived rape during the war and were so precious for a moment to those in favor of war found little support as they dealt with the stress and stigma of surviving sexual assault. In Iraq interpersonal violence was difficult to measure, but structural violence against women was obvious. Women suffered ideologically from Hussein's repositioning of himself as a traditionalist and materially from sanctions that lowered women's wages and rates of education while dramatically increasing their care burdens.[37] As Iraqi activist Haifa Zangana put it, "The suffering of Iraqi women extended from the physical to the psychological. . . . Iraqi women suffered from depression, insomnia, weight loss, and headaches due to shock caused by military bombardment, the death of their children, anxiety, and uncertainty about the future."[38]

Men's violence against women remained relevant after the cessation of formal hostilities for the United States as well. A July 1992 report revealed that the U.S. soldiers sent to the Persian Gulf, in part to defend Kuwaiti women from sexual assault, were "accused of committing at least 31 sex crimes against female soldiers in the Persian Gulf."[39] The gap between the U.S. government's professed outrage at sexual assaults by foreign men and the practice of sexual assault within the U.S. military received little attention in the U.S. media. The *New York Times* neglected to even give the story its own headline, not because the topic of sexual assault in the military was off the agenda but instead because another more lurid tale of sexual assault in the military had already taken top billing.

"BOYS WILL BE BOYS": TAILHOOK

At the 1991 annual conference for naval pilots, "flush from their victory in the Persian Gulf" and "encouraged by strippers and scantily

clad female bartenders," more than one hundred naval officers created a hallway gauntlet in which dozens of women and a few men,
military and civilian, were sexually assaulted.[40] In addition to the
gauntlet, naval officers engaged in a range of activities infused with
violent sexuality during that year's Tailhook Convention, including
the public shaving of a woman's lower body and biting unsuspecting
individuals on the buttocks ("sharking").[41] The abuse at the event
was subsequently compounded by the efforts of senior naval officers to minimize or cover up this sexual abuse in a manner that the
U.S. Court of Military Appeals later called "curiously careless and
amateurish."[42] Coverage of the Tailhook scandal at once produced
revelations about the consequences of the military's patriarchal values and simultaneously refused to engage in analysis of the affini-
ties between these sexist values and military culture itself. That is,
although most reporters and officials were quick to condemn sexual
assault, they condemned these assaults as deviations from militaristic values rather than products of those values.

Perhaps no statement better sums up the feckless attitude of military commanders toward those whom they lead than "boys will be
boys": a model of masculinity as both juvenile and fixed. Simultaneously too kind and too harsh toward "boys," it excuses their worst
behavior while sentencing them to a narrow model of masculinity
from which they are incapable of escaping. Rather than seeing men
in the military as prisoners of an essential masculinity, it is more
useful to see their behavior as a product of their conditions. As the
naval inspector general explained, "inappropriate sexual behavior . . .
had been accepted, tolerated, and even condoned over the years"
by naval leadership, "making it now the norm."[43] According to the
same report, "a common thread running through the overwhelming
majority of interviews" with those who were present for the abuses
at Tailhook was: "What's the big deal?"[44]

The navy's highest officers modeled sexually abusive behavior not
only at their yearly soirees but also in their attempts to stymie investigations into this behavior. The first indication of a coverup was
when Navy Secretary Lawrence Garrett III conceded that he "came
by" during the assaults and that the pages containing this informa-

tion had been redacted from the initial Naval Investigative Services report.[45] Following Garrett's subsequent resignation, the Defense Department's inspector general's office took over to correct the "fumbles" of the previous two internal naval investigations, which were not able to penetrate the "wall of silence put up by pilots and their commanders" or even get an accurate count of assailants *or* victims.[46] In addition to investigative failures, more doubts arose when the Pentagon revealed, "Fearful of angering the public, senior Navy officials tried to alter the language of a report concerning the assault . . . apparently to make the incidents seem less offensive."[47] Some naval investigators seemed incompetent, while others reproduced the attitudes that motivated sexual abuse at Tailhook, including one who revictimized a survivor of the assaults with unwanted pressure "to establish something other than a professional relationship with her."[48]

As a few individuals began to face the possibility of accountability, no one mounted a more spirited defense of a militarized vision of sexual violence than former marine and future senator James Webb. In an October 1992 editorial, Webb wrote that a "botched" (not sabotaged) investigation and "revelations of inexcusable harassment" (not sexual assault) had "left in their wake a witch hunt that threatens to swamp the entire naval service." He went on to lament that the navy "used to have a spine" and was "being maligned and diminished before our eyes" by a combination of "ardent feminists" and government leaders who were "at best passive and most often downright fearful."[49] Webb's message was simple: maintaining the effectiveness of the military meant maintaining its culture, however toxic, and a few women getting harmed along the way was a worthwhile sacrifice. While politicians may not have been able to afford women coming home in body bags, they would have to find ways to contain the political costs of women returning from the military as survivors of sexual assault.

During the second year of the scandal, focus shifted from what happened at the convention to questions of how high in the command structure accountability should reach. Chief naval officer Admiral Frank Kelso II had initially appeared in the media as an advocate for women, initiating an investigation into sexual harassment at the

United States Naval Academy in September 1990 and backing full integration of women into the navy's combat forces in April 1993.[50] What was not revealed until the publication of the Defense Department's final inquiry on Tailhook was that Kelso not only participated in the infamous convention but that he also may have orchestrated the coverup. Following pretrial testimony in a court martial related to the convention, a military judge determined that "Kelso witnessed misconduct and tried to shield himself from blame," and furthermore, the judge dismissed the charges against the officers brought up for court martial because "it was unfair for them to be charged with what they say Admiral Kelso did and got away with: failing to stop assaults on women."[51] A week later, Kelso accepted early retirement, though only after petulantly demanding that the secretary of the navy publicly call him "a man of highest honor and integrity" in direct contradiction of the military judge's findings.[52] Some officers received administrative punishments ranging from early retirement to reduction of rank, but none faced trial.[53]

Reflecting on the opening of naval combat pilot jobs to women that followed Tailhook in her extended study of the scandal, *Tailspin*, Jean Zimmerman wrote, "Giving American women the right to prove themselves as warfighters establishes them on a new footing, as fully participatory, first-class citizens."[54] As later events demonstrate, the concessions made to female participation in combat did little to address violence against women in the military. Zimmerman went on to celebrate that the navy's decision to let women pilot fighter jets "serves to dismantle the divided, hegemonic culture of two classes— the protectors and the protected."[55] What Zimmerman and others who share her triumphant perspective on women's integration failed to appreciate is that this move did not dismantle but reinforced the divided and hegemonic relations between women in the United States and people living in countries suffering from U.S. military interventions. The privileges associated with "protecting" their nation required raining destruction on other nations. Lest anyone doubt the continuity of certain traditions in the military during the changing circumstances of the 1990s, the United States deployed their increasingly female armed forces to Haiti, a place all too familiar with U.S. occupation.

When U.S. troops deployed to Haiti in the summer of 1994, they marched in the footsteps of U.S. troops who had occupied the country from 1915 to 1934. In 1990, eight months after the elections that brought him to power, President Jean-Bertrand Aristide was ousted by his U.S.-trained army commander-in-chief, Raoul Cédras, in a military coup that drew international censure and resulted in a United Nations mission in Haiti to shepherd the transition back toward democracy beginning in September 1993.[56]

The following spring, journalist Amy Wilentz described the situation as a "spasm of terror . . . convulsing Haiti" and wrote of the "grotesque" practices of the military regime including "facial scalping," defiling corpses, and "rape used as an instrument of political violence."[57] Wilentz conjured the Haiti that consumers of U.S. media had come to expect, replete with "smoking, monumental pyramids of trash," run by individuals afflicted with the same sorts of racialized pathologies Europeans projected onto nineteenth-century Haitians ("monstrous," "thugs," "gangsterism") and garnished with the obligatory references to voodoo ("Haiti's Death Mask") and Haitians' supposed propensity for spreading HIV. Despite this unfavorable portrait, Wilentz assured her readers that rape was "a new phenomenon for Haiti" and "used to be exceedingly rare"; rather, it was the spontaneous invention of Cédras's junta, unrelated to the long history of foreign military occupation or ongoing contestations over gender roles in Haiti. Soon, other foreign correspondents traveled to Haiti to file similar stories. One piece eschewed context to open with a description of a funeral in which "women wailed and writhed on the ground, choking on dust and chanting incoherently in the traditional Haitian ritual of mourning."[58] Three days later, another piece focused specifically on rape as a political weapon opened with the equally lurid image "in Haiti, naked boys are a common sight" before assuring readers that tradition "kept rape in Haiti to a minimum" before the 1990s.[59]

The military regime carried out many sexual assaults and other acts of brutality, but the militarized understanding of sexual violence predominating in U.S. media and policies demanded that the response focus on punishing perpetrators rather than addressing the needs of survivors. Rose Margui Lormil's story, reported in a June 1994 *New York Times* piece, lays bare this prioritization.[60] Lormil, a member of the pro-democracy Comme Il Faut group, survived a brutal sexual assault by policemen in Port-Au-Prince that led her to believe she had only one option: "I must get out of my country now." She was far from the only Haitian to have made such a decision; on July 4, 1994, alone, the U.S. Coast Guard intercepted 3,247 refugees attempting to flee the conflict by sea.[61] At the same moment U.S. officials professed sympathy for the plight of Haitians, the U.S. military was actively engaged in a campaign to stop refugees from reaching the United States, detaining fourteen thousand refugees at Guantanamo Bay while showing reckless indifference to hundreds of drownings.[62] Reports of rapes committed in the camp were ignored by the most widely distributed sources.[63] No follow-up was written about Rose Margui Lormil in any English-language publication, and her fate is unknown.

Conditions in Haiti had not improved significantly by September, when President Clinton's talk of a U.S. invasion grew louder, despite the administration's being "keenly aware that it does not enjoy broad public or Congressional support for an invasion of Haiti."[64] In response to the public unwillingness to consider a military solution, "the White House decided to highlight human rights abuses in laying out the reasons it contends an invasion may be necessary."[65] Hence, when Clinton took to live television to make his case for intervening in Haiti, he spoke of "a horrible intimidation campaign of rape, torture, and mutilation," "a reign of terror, executing children, raping women, killing priests," and "a terrifying pattern of soldiers and policemen raping the wives and daughters of suspected political dissidents," as well as other graphic tales of women, youths, and clergy members in peril.[66] Finally, Clinton also promised that the military's project in Haiti would be strictly punitive, claiming soldiers would depose the military dictatorship but would "not be involved in rebuilding Haiti or its economy."[67]

On September 18, 1994, with U.S. paratroopers inbound, General Cédras agreed to step down and allow Aristide to return to the country that had elected him. Aristide immediately expressed reservations about granting amnesty to those the United States supposedly sought to punish and about the lack of parallel guarantees of protection for supporters of Aristide and the democratic process in Haiti.[68] In the United States, doubts about whether the agreement could produce stable peace focused more on the inherent flaws of the Haitian people rather than self-reflexivity about the role of the United States in creating these conditions. The *New York Times*'s Washington bureau chief, R. W. Apple, called Haiti "a complex and violent society with no history of democracy," in which multiple factions "retain their homicidal tendencies, to say nothing of their weapons."[69] Quite predictably, Apple could not finish his assessment of Haiti's future without reference to how said future was "vastly complicated by the influence of the voodoo priests and secret societies."[70] Following the arrival of U.S. troops, fears of a voodoo coup were never corroborated, but stability and security remained uncommon for most Haitians.

Haiti's postintervention future was also complicated by the lack of commitment from both the United States and the international community to the women they claimed to defend. Haitian feminist economist Myriam Merlet writes that, far from waiting for foreigners to rescue them during the crisis, "women's organization brought the struggle against violence directed at women to the forefront of the nation's political agenda." They provided direct services to survivors, documented episodes of violence, organized national meetings and an international tribunal, and developed a platform for national legal reform. "Unfortunately," Merlet explains, "the vicissitudes of Haitian political life did not permit the enactment of these laws," and worse, "the situation of impunity that currently prevails in the judicial system exposes women even more to the risks of conjugal and sexual violence."[71] Once again, intervention premised on the mission of saving women from rape failed to be accountable to survivors, to hold perpetrators responsible for their actions, and to reduce sexual violence, all while creating the potential for more sexual violence.

Anyone proposing military intervention as a solution to sexual violence must contend with the long history of sexual violence committed by soldiers against the people whose land they occupy. Imbalances in authority and resources combined with the displacements and vulnerabilities produced by conflict create a ripe environment for sexual exploitation and violence by so-called peacekeepers in post-conflict societies. In addition to countless undocumented assaults in Haiti, UN peacekeepers from Sri Lanka, Uruguay, and Pakistan were returned to their home countries following documented sexual assaults in 2007, 2011, and 2012, respectively.[72] Long before these assaults came to light, however, the United States military was forced to contend with the fallout from a sexual assault committed by their forces on another island eight thousand miles away.

"FOR THE PRICE THEY PAID TO RENT THE CAR": OKINAWA

On September 4, 1995, on the southern Japanese island of Okinawa, three U.S. servicemen—Rodrico Harp and Kendrick Ledet, both marines, and naval seaman Marcus Gill—abducted a twelve-year-old Okinawan girl, drove her out into a rural area, and raped her, sparking mass protests by Okinawans directed at the thousands of U.S. troops stationed on the island.[73] The situation stood in contrast to the much rosier portrait painted three months earlier by Nicholas Kristof in his *New York Times* piece on the fiftieth anniversary of the U.S. occupation of Okinawa. The then Tokyo correspondent and future advocate for "women worldwide" framed his piece around the story of a teenaged Okinawan girl who, during the 1945 battle, "pleaded with the American soldiers to shoot her in the head immediately instead of raping and torturing her first" before realizing that they were there to rescue her. Anxieties about sexual assaults by U.S. military personnel on Okinawa stalked even those attempting to portray them as heroic saviors, but Kristof's ultimate assessment was that "most Okinawans do not mind the 55,000 Americans . . . who live on the island."[74] In the wake of the September 1995 rape, no serious observer could make such a claim.

Against the stated desires of the indigenous population, Japanese-occupied Okinawa is one of the most militarized places in the world, a place where military imperatives take precedence over all other concerns.[75] Japanese activists have organized and protested against the presence of U.S. bases since at least the 1950s, and a crescendo of protests grew in the 1990s.[76] Not only did residents have to endure hundred-decibel flyovers, but they also had little control over the hundreds of crimes committed every year by U.S. servicemen who were protected by a Status of Forces Agreement between Japan and the United States that essentially allowed the military to police itself.[77] As Okinawan feminist Nobuko Karimata explained in an interview, "What angered us Okinawans the most was that the GIs used to get away with a lot of the crimes. . . . Everything from a traffic violation to rape resulted in the same verdict: innocent."[78]

Events in which U.S. soldiers evaded Japanese prosecution ranged from the 1955 rape of a six-year-old girl known as Yumiko-chan to a 1993 rape by a marine who escaped confinement on his base to take a commercial flight back to the United States.[79] One commentator said that this "child's rape echoes [the] rape of Okinawa itself," whereas another drew upon an even longer history in calling Okinawa's circumstances the "thousand-year rape of an entire people."[80] In 1995 feminist organizers from Okinawa Women Act against Military Violence arrived home from the Fourth UN Forum on Women to the news of the rape and "then became the spearhead that mobilized the Okinawan people and government," leading to "the largest protest demonstration in Okinawa's history" at which the organizers "repeatedly quoted from the speech of Hillary Rodham Clinton . . . that 'women's rights are human rights' and that military rape is a war crime."[81] Feeling the pressure of tens of thousands of protesting Okinawans, the U.S. military elected to not exercise its right under the Status of Forces Agreement to hold the servicemen and transferred them to the Japanese authorities.[82]

On November 7, 1995, Gill pleaded guilty to rape, abduction, and assault, while Harp and Ledet both pleaded guilty to participating but denied they actually raped the girl.[83] Despite the servicemen's admissions, some of their family back home remained convinced that their confessions were coerced and wondered aloud if racism against Black servicemen might have played a role in the military's willingness to expose them to prosecution.[84] While the soldiers' violence against women precluded coalition building between Okinawan women and

Black soldiers, both were united in being seen by the white-dominated military leadership as expendable in comparison to the occupation.

No individual seemed more oblivious to the culture of sexual assault in the military, or the resentment Okinawans felt toward their occupiers, than the commander of the U.S. forces in the Pacific, Admiral Richard Macke. At a meeting with reporters on November 17, Macke expressed his view that the rape by the three men under his command was "absolutely stupid" because "for the price they paid to rent the car they could have had a girl."[85] Macke failed to see the commodification of women's sexualities in Okinawa and the desire expressed by many soldiers there to dominate and violate women as inextricable from the white supremacist stereotypes about sexually available Asian women produced during the long history of military occupation and hypersexualized "rest and recreation" in East Asia. The admiral could not understand how his belief that women were objects available for purchase modeled the sort of violent sexual behaviors practiced by the servicemen he oversaw. Macke's comments were immediately panned as not only sexist but also damaging to already strained U.S.-Japanese relations, which resulted in the admiral's almost immediate resignation.[86] A few months after Macke's departure, in March 1996, an Okinawan court convicted Gill, Harp, and Ledet of rape and sentenced them to prison terms. Unfortunately for the people of Okinawa, neither the servicemen's imprisonment nor the departure of a leader indifferent to the military rape culture that encouraged violence against women would solve the consequences of U.S. occupation.

Writing thirteen years later about the island's response to the rape, Linda Isako Angst claims, "The discourse has been transformed from protests voiced largely by women concerning human rights and headed by an outspoken local feminist human rights activist, Takazato Suzuyo, to protests by (male) landowners about rights to land."[87] Not only did this serve to insulate Okinawan men from critiques of local gender inequity and their use of violence against women, but it also kept focus on the national-level negotiations between Japan and the U.S. military rather than on the local impacts of violence against women. Assaults on women in Okinawa by U.S. soldiers continued unabated. Following the convictions of Harp, Ledet, and Gill, in Okinawa, a naval seaman slashed a woman's throat in July 1996, a marine corporal attempted to rape a woman in January 2000, and an air force sergeant was accused of raping a woman in June 2001.[88] Although the U.S. military appeared embarrassed by the propensity for sexual assault among many of its servicemen, the institution also appeared uninterested in substantively addressing the crisis, a fact that would become all too clear following allegations emerging from a Maryland army base in late 1996.

RAPE AND RACISM: ABERDEEN

The U.S. military's Combat Exclusion Policy, which stipulated the limitations on women's participation within the military, formed a bridge between the need for high rates of female participation in the all-volunteer military and the gendered anxieties about women in peril. Unfortunately for women in the U.S. military, peril has never been limited to the battlefield. Investigation into the 1991 Tailhook Convention revealed how the sexual politics of the U.S. Navy could produce an environment of depersonalized mass sexual assaults. Five years after Tailhook, critics and survivors questioned how the culture of the U.S. Army's Aberdeen Proving Ground allowed for relationships between trainers and recruits characterized by abuse of power, harassment, death threats, and rape. The so-called Aberdeen sex scandal opened public inquiry into sexual assault within the military like never before, but the lack of substantive change in the wake of the scandal revealed the progress of the militarization of sexual violence.

On November 8, 1996, multiple reports asserted that the army had charged two trainers at Aberdeen with a number of offenses, including rape, forced sodomy, and having an improper relationship with a recruit.[89] Another trainer was indicted for a related obstruction of justice charge, and as Matthew Wald's article warned, the army was "investigating accusations that an unspecified number of other men at the center engaged in sexual harassment." A military spokesman quickly attempted to contain the incipient scandal, alleging that there had been no rape allegations at Aberdeen for years and that the investigation was revealing mere harassment or "fraternization," not sexual assault: "verbal harassment, maybe touching, some consensual sex, which is not allowed, that kind of thing."[90]

Placing the burden upon survivors to advocate for themselves within a hostile system, the army responded by "strengthening its 'buddy system' at the Aberdeen Proving Ground" and opening an 800 number to field complaints from women trained at the center.[91] Within a week the scandal had widened significantly: the hotline received thousands of calls resulting in hundreds of investigations, two more sergeants were charged with indecent assault, and details emerged about one telling a recruit, "If anyone finds out about me having sex with you, I'll kill you."[92] By the end of the year, more than twenty-five drill sergeants at Aberdeen were under investigation, and public voices had "rekindled a fundamental debate over how far the military should integrate women into its male-dominated forces."[93]

A Department of Defense panel led by former Senator Nancy Kassebaum went so far as to recommend "that the Army, Navy and Air Force significantly roll back the integration of men and women in basic and advanced training."[94] Although the secretary of defense later rejected this recommendation, he conceded at the time that he had no choice, as the all-volunteer military "cannot meet its obligations without the continued strong contribution of men and women working together."[95] This debate had already been brought to the public in the summer of 1996 through the film *Courage Under Fire*, which depicts a fictional inquiry into whether a deceased female U.S. Army captain, played by Jodie Foster, had acted with bravery or cowardice during the Gulf War. The film opens with a discussion pointing toward the public relations boost provided by awarding a woman the Medal of Honor and is filled with discussions of the relative fitness of men and women for combat duty but, adhering to a "good soldier" narrative, completely ignores the subject of sexual violence in order to provide a triumphant arc of militarized glory for Foster's character and servicewomen in general.

The army's investigations into sexual assault at Aberdeen concluded within a year; ultimately, they charged twelve male soldiers with misconduct and sentenced four to incarceration, including a captain who had sex with a cadet who "had come to him to complain of sexual harassment by her drill sergeant."[96] Of the more than fifty complainants, all were women. Considering the long history in the United States of Black men enduring corporal punishment for perceived sexual unruliness and white men's probable impunity in the commission of sexual assault, it is unsurprising that all twelve of the punished soldiers were Black, a fact that did not escape the attention of advocates for racial justice.

Members of the NAACP and Congressional Black Caucus called for an investigation into anti-Black racism in the Aberdeen investigation by March 1997.[97] Ian Fischer reported in June that year on the "tones entwined with deep love and distrust" with which Black soldiers regarded the military's approach to justice. Fischer noted that "black soldiers are charged with sex crimes disproportionately more often than whites" but attempted to provide ostensibly nonracist justifications for these facts, ranging from civilian Black men's higher incarceration rate to the combination of the army's attempts to advance Black soldiers into leadership positions while confronting sexual harassment in favor of women.[98] Again, the extensive focus on men of color's violence against women served to obscure the overall system of militarized and sexualized violence that privileges white men most of all.

The *New York Times* alone provided ample evidence from outside Aberdeen to diagnose a pandemic of sexual violence in the U.S. military during the late 1990s. Five days after the Aberdeen allegations were first reported, a sergeant at Fort Leonard Wood pleaded guilty to having sex with trainees.[99] Over the next year a West Point cadet was court martialed for the rape of a fellow cadet; three trainers at an army base in Germany were court martialed for raping trainees; multiple generals were relieved of duty following allegations of adultery and sexual harassment; two marines assaulted campers in Oregon, raping one of them; two drill sergeants at Fort Jackson were convicted of multiple charges of sexual misconduct; and countless other assaults went unreported because, as an army investigation acknowledged, "most female troops were unwilling to report instances of sexual misconduct out of a well-justified fear that they would be punished instead of their tormenters."[100] Despite their obvious inability to prevent or properly address sexual violence within the organization, the U.S. military continued to be deployed with the stated goal of addressing sexual violence in the wake of Aberdeen. No amount of evidence demonstrating how men in the military were among the most prolific perpetrators of sexual assault in the nation would stop the U.S. state from representing its violences as the ultimate hope for addressing sexual assault transnationally.

"A LICENSE TO KILL": KOSOVO

War-related sexual violence was disturbingly commonplace through-out the 1990s, occurring on every populated continent. While many of these atrocities received attention, none garnered as much as those in the former Yugoslavia. The series of wars through which Yugoslavia dissolved served as a postscript to the Cold War in which practices and standards of transnational warfare were reshaped for a new era, none more so than understandings of rape as a weapon of war.[101]

Quantitative data cannot transmit the horrors visited upon women during the Yugoslav Wars, but the United Nations estimates that twenty thousand to fifty thousand women, mostly Muslim Bosniaks, survived sexual assaults, committed for the most part by militias affiliated with the Republika Srpska. The 1996 decision by the International Criminal Tribunal for the former Yugoslavia to prosecute rapes committed during the wars and their subsequent ability to do so were products of decades of feminist activism.[102] Sexual assault has historically accompanied warfare, and proponents of war have often successfully argued for a militarized hierarchy of needs that placed combatants beyond accountability. Defining rape as a war crime emanated from the antimilitarist idea that participants in armed conflict have no right to commit atrocities against civilians and then claim that they were merely following orders or swept up in the "fog of war." In the militarizing environment of the 1990s, however, even antimilitarist feminist initiatives were subject to appropriation by those favoring the perpetual deployment of U.S. troops abroad.

The first reports of brutalities occurring in Bosnia grabbed head-lines in summer 1992, when John Burns reported from Sarajevo about grenades tossed into a bus full of civilians, desecration of children's corpses, and "rape and other abuse of women."[103] From 1992 to 1995, paramilitaries killed, raped, and displaced tens of thousands of civilians in plain view of global media producers. Reporters documented extensive brutalities, from organized programs of rape to the devastating siege that left the city of Sarajevo a bombed-out hulk. The stories provoked much outrage and a limited international intervention, but stability was short-lived.[104]

In Kosovo, a province in southern Serbia with an ethnic Albanian majority, tensions between Serbs and Kosovars grew during the dissolution of Yugoslavia before exploding in the wake of neighboring Albania's chaotic 1996 transition away from communism. The mid-1990s crises across the western Balkans created conditions for an insurgency led by the Kosovar Liberation Front against the Serbian government, which alternated between ceasefires and hostilities throughout 1998.[105] Both sides committed atrocities, and even when not considered an atrocity, deadly force was used unethically against the most vulnerable, but there was no evidence of a systematic campaign of rape or gender-based executions as in Bosnia. Unlike in the early 1990s when the U.S. military charged into Iraq and Haiti, it remained primarily an observer in the former Yugoslavia; however, the United States sought to take the initiative on Kosovo.

On March 20, 1999, President Clinton made his case for U.S. military intervention at a White House press conference. "In dealing with aggressors in the Balkans," Clinton claimed, "hesitation is a license to kill."[106] Despite his intent to focus on the misdeeds of men from Serbia, one reporter forced Clinton to dodge a question about Juanita Broaddrick, who had recently accused the president of raping her in the 1970s. Ultimately, Clinton was able to push some military action against Serbia through the clouds of assorted sex-related scandals that surrounded his administration. The United States initiated a bombing campaign that at first triggered a more vigorous campaign of ethnic cleansing in Kosovo but did, along with Milosevic's indictment for war crimes and declining support from Russia, push the Serbian government to agree to a ceasefire with the Kosovar Liberation Front and an international peacekeeping force in Kosovo.[107]

When the bombing campaign began, Lepa Mladjenovic, a Serbian feminist counselor, sprang into action. Refusing to side with the militarized violence unleashed by their own government or that of the governments at war with Serbia, Mladjenovic and her fellow feminists at Belgrade's Autonomous Women's Center against Sexual Violence (AWCASV) "started from the fact that during the seventy-seven days of bombing and ethnic cleansing almost everyone was living in a state of fear . . . and that it was our duty as feminists and counselors to try to take care of the different groups of women living in fear."[108] AWCASV functioned as a communications hub, counseling and giving news to women in both Serbia and Kosovo through phone, fax, and email while also providing bike deliveries of necessary goods to women afraid or unable to leave their homes, weekly workshops on coping with war trauma, and the *Feminist Notebooks* newsletter. Directly inspired by the dual implications of Audre Lorde's revelation that "I am not my sister's keeper, I am my sister," the women of AWCASV rejected both a paternalistic mode of "keeping" the survivors of violence as well as a self-abnegating mode of femininity that demands women always put themselves last.[109]

An optimistic viewpoint might regard the Kosovo War as a model for post–Cold War success in intervention and state building. Kosovars have a de facto state, have made incremental steps toward sovereignty, and are mostly safe from Serbian aggression. Another assessment would point toward the continuing low-intensity conflicts in the Preševo Valley and northern Macedonia, the tens of thousands of UN troops still present and the absence of a clear path toward full independence for Kosovo as serious obstacles to sustainable peace.[110] This more sober assessment also requires accounting for the continued violence against women after the formal end of hostilities.

On January 17, 2000, the U.S. military indicted Staff Sergeant Frank Ronghi, who also served in Iraq and Haiti, for abducting, raping, and murdering an eleven-year-old Kosovar girl and then disposing of her body with the help of another soldier. During Ronghi's trial, complaints emerged about U.S. soldiers assaulting Kosovar women during searches and stops. Although Kosovars had many positive things to say about the foreigners who assisted them in pushing out their Serbian oppressors, some began to see the gendered consequences of military occupation. As one neighbor of the murdered girl's family put it, "We don't want them here to give us security if they are going to do this."[111] Unfortunately, when defined in militarized terms, security cannot center on the needs of eleven-year-old girls, address violence against women in a way that does not produce more violence, or attend to the ways in which militarism encourages sexual violence. Thus, reporting from the dawn of the millennium with a militarized understanding of sexual violence as something that militaries are suited to address rather than something that militaries produce, the U.S. media was able to portray the military as more protector than perpetrator, despite all evidence to the contrary.

DEMOBILIZING G.I. JANE

The plot of the 1997 movie *G.I. Jane* encapsulates much of what the militarization of sexual violence seeks to accomplish. In the film, Demi Moore plays a naval officer seeking to be the first woman to join the elite (and fictional) Combined Reconnaissance Team by passing an intensive course. Throughout her training, Moore's character is sexually harassed by her fellow trainees and a harsh trainer played by Viggo Mortensen, in addition to becoming a pawn of politicians embroiled in debates over combat exclusion, base closures, and Don't Ask, Don't Tell. Training culminates with a brutal hostage simulation in which Mortensen's character assaults Moore's, bends her over a table, cuts her pants and belt off with a knife, and attempts to rape her before she fights him off. In her moment of triumph, she delights her fellow recruits by claiming phallic potency and telling the trainer, "Suck my dick." Following her success at enduring harassment and simulated rape, Moore's character then performs valiantly during an intervention into Libya, saving her fellow trainees and receiving the respect of Mortensen's character, who gifts Moore's character a prized medal in the closing scene.

Moore's character strikes a disturbing bargain with the military, tolerating sexual violence by her ostensible allies in exchange for inclusion in a fraternity with the privilege of visiting enormous violence upon men of color. Such a deal elevates the interests of the military over justice for survivors, civilian models of accountability, and transnational human rights. It is exactly the deal to which women were asked to assent for inclusion in the privileges distributed through full participation in the U.S. armed forces. Politicians remained anxious about the deaths of female soldiers, but the post–Cold War military requires that they bear a disproportionate risk of sexual assault if they wish to be treated as equals. Had the intervention in *G.I. Jane* been predicated on rescuing imperiled women rather than a downed spy satellite, the film would have painted an even fuller portrait of the militarization of sexual violence during the 1990s. Ultimately, the militarization of sexual violence allowed for the incorporation of feminist concerns about women's rights to serve equally in the military and to be free from sexual assault during wartime into the military-industrial complex with deleterious effects for many in and outside of the United States.

Movements led by women of color in the United States and elsewhere have been at the forefront of developing methods of confronting sexual violence without asking for the intervention of a violent state apparatus. A joint statement by INCITE! Women of Color Against Violence and the prison abolition organization Critical Resistance provides a clear window into such work: "We call social justice movements to develop strategies and analyses that address both state *and* interpersonal violence, particularly violence against women. . . . To live violence-free lives, we must develop holistic strategies for addressing violence that speak to the intersection of all forms of oppression."[112]

Feminists like Olga Mejía in Panama, Haifa Zangana in Iraq, Myriam Merlet in Haiti, Takazato Suzuyo in Okinawa, and Lepa Mladjenovic in Serbia have all been doing just that since at least the 1990s. Their analyses recognize the complex intersections of gender, race, and other forms of identity in shaping women's lives; their work centers the concerns of the most vulnerable and does not seek to correct violence with the application of more violence. These women need academic feminists to develop strategies for them as much as they needed U.S. military intervention. A transnational feminist perspective suggests that U.S. scholars, rather than concocting solutions to violence against women in distant countries, would do better by attempting to understand and undermine the nexus of heteropatriarchy, white supremacy, and militarism that produces gender-based violence in our own country—the subject of the next chapter.

2

Confronting an Enemy Abroad, Transforming a Nation at Home

HETEROSEXUALITY AND DOMESTIC MILITARISM

In a 1991 speech at the end of the "Desert Storm" operation against Iraq, U.S. president George H. W. Bush told Congress that those who fought "set out to confront an enemy abroad, and in the process, they transformed a nation at home." But what sort of transformation at home arose out of this confrontation abroad? Here, taking the former president at his word, I ask how this war against Iraq "transformed a nation at home," recognizing home as a metaphor for both the land within the borders claimed by the United States and the space occupied by a heteronormative family.[1]

Beginning with the claim of protecting children as the underlying justification for the Gulf War, I connect the transnational militarism of U.S. intervention abroad to subsequent episodes of militarized violence within the borders of the United States, including the Los Angeles Uprising, Waco siege, and Oklahoma City bombing. Through a reading of government declarations and documents, print media, and cultural production, I develop the concept of domestic militarism, a term encompassing the double meaning of *domestic* by exploring episodes of state violence exercised within national borders and in enforcing a particular vision of the family. Domestic militarism is an ideology that justifies this state violence through circular logics of heteronormativity and settler nationalism, manufacturing perceptions of sexualized threats and helpless victims while preventing the articulation of connections between violence abroad and violence at home. Ultimately, this chapter points toward a series of 1996 laws amending regulations on marriage, public assistance, immigration, and the death penalty to trace the concrete effects of this new, post–Cold War militarized heterosexuality, which manifests in spectacular and structural forms of violence ranging from state-sanctioned killing to racial inequity in child malnutrition.

Scholars including Chandan Reddy, Jasbir Puar, and Scott Morgensen have identified the increasingly convivial relationship between militaristic nationalism and certain gay and lesbian constituencies during the 1990s, but few scholars have shown interest in the intertwining of militarism and heterosexuality.[2] Even Lisa Duggan's *The Twilight of Equality*, one of the few works connecting heterosexuality to state violence, remains much more widely cited for the concept of homonormativity than for her analysis of heterosexuality.[3] Recent work by Ariana Vigil has begun to establish how the U.S. state increasingly used heterosexuality to bulwark its legitimacy in the closing decade of the Cold War.[4] I expand this work by tracing the reassertion of a reproductive heterosexuality complicit with state violence in the face of epochal change brought on by the end of the Cold War and the gains of feminist and LGBTQ movements. This chapter historicizes problems emblematic of the age of the War on Terror, such as police brutality, state-sanctioned killings, and the reintegration of combat veterans into civilian society, by demonstrating how militarized responses to these issues became normative during the 1990s.

The often convivial relationship between heterosexuality and militarism, as well as the normalization of heterosexuality in twentieth-century U.S. culture and politics, complicate the project of analyzing militarized heterosexuality. Such a project must begin from an understanding that the relationship between heterosexuality, the state, and its violences has been constructed through historical struggles and cannot be taken for granted. Jonathan Ned Katz explains that heterosexuality transcends neither history nor culture; rather, it "signifies one particular historical arrangement of the sexes and their pleasures."[5] The state has been and remains enormously invested in this arrangement and consequentially works to regulate these arrangements and simultaneously to erase the mark of its influence upon them. As Margot Canaday writes in regards to homosexuality, states did not "simply encounter homosexual citizens, fully formed and waiting to be counted, classified, administered, or disciplined." Instead the state "was a catalyst in the formation of homosexual identity"; she writes, "To uncover those processes is to challenge the law's own tendency to authorize homosexuality as somehow pregiven or even natural in its constitution."[6] Analogously, I dissect the ongoing construction of the heterosexual citizen to denaturalize the relationship between heterosexuality and militarism—a project Canaday's work implies but does not pursue.

The primary dissonance in a specifically heterosexual form of militarism is that war produces death while heterosexuality, through the institutionalization of heteronormativity, claims a monopoly on the production of life.[7] Domestic militarism soothes the tension between these strange bedfellows by justifying the death-making of war as a necessary feature of the way in which the nation-state fosters life. This framing functions by characterizing those outside of the domestic both as imminent threats to what Judith Butler calls "grievable life" and as ungrievable should they face death at the hands of the state.[8] More concretely, one need only to reflect on the implications of the popular antiwar slogan "make love, not war"—or the more troubling "girls say yes to boys who say no"—to understand the potential for conflict between (hetero)sexual and militaristic imperatives. The potential for raising children in a world free of the threat of nuclear annihilation made possible by end of the Cold War, a topic addressed further in chapter 4, produced a new disconnect between militarism and heterosexual domesticity in the early 1990s.

As in the previous chapter, my central concern here is to demonstrate how proponents of and apologists for state violence increasingly relied on appeals to sexuality in the last decade of the twentieth century. The tireless efforts of feminist and LGBTQ activists and thinkers had already significantly transformed the landscape of U.S. sexualities leading up to the closing moments of the Cold War and the opening years of the 1990s. Recognizing that both heterosexuality and militarism faced significant challenges in the late twentieth century that threatened their decentering, I characterize the post–Gulf War transformation of the United States as a cultural and material reinvestment in two institutions in crisis. I argue that as anticommunism and blatant white supremacy became less acceptable justifications for state violence, officials increasingly turned toward justifications for state violence grounded in underexamined assumptions about heterosexuality as natural, normal, and moral. This is not a break with the militarism and heterosexualization of Cold War ideology but a reformed continuation of it in response to the collapse of its primary justification.

Scholars such as Edward Said, Steven Salaita, and Haunani-Kay Trask have demonstrated how the proponents of this reinvestment cited white supremacist tactics of racializing indigenous, Black, and East Asian people to produce evidence of a threat in the form of Arab, Muslim, and "Middle Eastern" people.[9] Recentering the heteronormative nuclear family rather than individual citizens or the broader public polity as the unit for which the state acts proved equally important in creating the ambiance of peril underlying U.S. policy before, during, and after the Gulf War. Furthermore, the state and media reasserted a commitment to the conventions of heterosexuality in defiance of increasingly louder calls for sexual equity and pluralism. Understanding how this transformation amounted to a militarization of heterosexuality allows for clearer understandings not only of state violence wielded domestically in the 1990s but also of state violence wielded transnationally in the 2000s.

PROTECTING CHILDREN IN THE PERSIAN GULF

On August 2, 1990, the *New York Times* reported that the Iraqi military had attacked Kuwait and "penetrated deeply into the country." Relations between Iraq and the United States had been declining for months.[10] In July Senator Nancy Kassebaum argued for sanctions on Iraq, claiming, "I can't believe any farmer in this nation would want to send his products . . . to a country that has used chemical weapons and a country that has tortured and executed its children."[11] Kassebaum did not mention that the United States was the world's largest producer of chemical weapons—technology used against children in Vietnam and shared with Iraq during its war with Iran—and had only recently begun to move some of its chemical weapons stockpile toward destruction.[12] Additionally, Kassebaum's casting of the United States as defender of children belied the government's resistance to ratifying the UN Convention of the Rights of the Child; a resistance arguably related to the fact that United States continued to recruit children for the military and execute individuals for crimes committed as juveniles.[13] Children provided justifications for military intervention in three ways: as hostages caught in the middle of the conflict, as the victims of Iraqi brutality, and as the domestic beneficiaries of transnational militarism.

At the outset of war, thousands of foreign oil workers lived in Kuwait. Joseph Treaster's September 8, 1990, article about the first U.S. citizens to depart after the invasion staged the story as a gendered drama in which "the American men hoped that some military action would be taken" while "the women burst into tears when they were asked about the husbands they had left behind in hiding."[14] The hostages existed in a clear binary of masculine doers and feminine sobbers. In this same article, the phrase "women and children" appears eight times in ten sentences. According to Cynthia Enloe, news media unselfconsciously use a breathless phrase like "womenandchildren" "because in network minds women are family members rather than independent actors, presumed to be almost childlike in their innocence about international *realpolitik*."[15] Television critic Walter Goodman's mid-September 1990 article presumed as much in claiming, "The confrontation with Iraq has become a war of the innocents. The screen is dominated not by warriors but by wives, not men but boys, not armor but infants."[16] Thus, even before the United States officially intervened in Kuwait, the media had constructed a dichotomy contrasting the passive role of womenandchildren in the conflict with an active militarized masculinity that could not escape gendered tropes, even as many women and young people contributed to both sides. To incite support for that intervention against Iraq, the U.S. government then sought to make this foreign conflict domestic through producing evidence of Iraqi violations of heterosexual domesticity in the form of infanticide.

As the occupation of Kuwait stretched into months, many remained unconvinced that distant Iraq posed any sort of threat to the United States.[17] Allegations of murders committed by Iraqi troops' ejecting Kuwaiti infants from their incubators provided a vivid rationale for anyone seeking to justify U.S. military action. Beginning in September 1990 with stories in the *Washington Post*, *New York Times*, and *USA Today*, multiple sources accused Iraqi soldiers of killing fifteen, twenty-two, three hundred, or some other number of infants in a variety of fashions, usually completing their alleged crimes by absconding to Iraq with the incubators.[18] The testimony of "Nurse Nayirah" to the Congressional Human Rights Caucus on October 10 increased interest in these stories. The widely broadcasted testimony shows a young Arab woman tearfully claiming, "I volunteered at the al-Addan hospital. . . . While I was there I saw the Iraqi soldiers come into the hospital with guns. They took the babies out of the incubators, took the incubators and left the babies on the cold floor to die."[19]

A month later President Bush further embellished Nayirah's story, claiming that "babies [were] pulled from incubators and scattered like firewood across the floor."[20] In December Amnesty International issued a report confirming that "300 premature babies . . . died because incubators were stolen." Anyone who had been reading the news would have understood the reference Bush made on the eve of the U.S. invasion when he said "innocent children" were "among those maimed and murdered" by Saddam Hussein.[21] The U.S. Senate voted to authorize war by only a five-vote majority, and seven senators cited Nayirah's testimony in their voting statements.[22]

Despite its impact, Nayirah's story was not all it had been made out to be.[23] Not only had the public relations firm Hill and Knowlton written Nayirah's testimony, but the "nurse" was a daughter of the Kuwaiti ambassador and a member of the royal family. Furthermore, no one who was actually at a Kuwaiti hospital corroborated her claims. The truth was unimportant, however, as the U.S. war on Iraq was balanced on a fulcrum of narrative. With no threat of dominos falling to global communism to point toward, officials needed to find new ways to bring a sense of peril home from confrontations abroad.

Nayirah's story was so compelling in large part because it hinged on the violation of the most valued product of heterosexuality: children. War is the production of death but is best justified as the protection of life, and no symbol appears more useful for making that bait-and-switch than a child in danger. Recent work by Kathryn Bond Stockton, Margaret Peacock, and Lee Edelman, though divergent in methods and results, concurs that definitions of childhood trace highly contentious power struggles and that children have been symbolically and rhetorically crucial to disguising oppression as innocence.[24] Stockton demonstrates how adult discourse attempts to confine the messiness of childhood into clear categories that comply with hegemonic power, while Edelman argues that investments in protecting children mask a deeper investment in reproducing heteronormativity. Peacock shows how Cold War governments used representations of children to starkly differentiate substantially similar militaristic projects. In the case of the Gulf War, imagining that the war's purpose was to defend children served to obscure the war's negative consequences *for* children.

Within a month of the initial U.S. assault, the Iraqi government began negotiating for an end to the conflict. Remarking on his view of the fires raging across southern Iraq from his helicopter trip to negotiate the ceasefire, U.S. commander Norman Schwarzkopf said, "It looked like hell."[25] A month later the Iraqi foreign minister took to Baghdad radio to lament "the deliberate destruction of Iraq's infrastructure, including power and water plants, irrigation dams, bridges, telephone exchanges and factories producing infant formula and medicine."[26] The ensuing thirteen years of sanctions, known as the siege, caused even more harm. "The siege touched every aspect of Iraqi life, causing death, disease, rapid economic decline, and nearly an end to any sort of human development," Haifa Zangana, an Iraqi activist, explains. "By the mid-nineties, half a million children died."[27] As Nadje Al-Ali and Nicola Pratt write, the postwar years proved especially devastating for women: "Aside from the most obvious and devastating effects, related to dramatically increased child mortality rates, widespread malnutrition, deteriorating health care and general infrastructure, unprecedented poverty, and an economic crisis, women were particularly hit by a changing social climate."[28] They detail how women and girls increasingly lost access to the job market and education while being forced to take on increased economic and cultural burdens.

As family life disintegrated in Iraq, President Bush sought to recenter it in the United States. In his 1992 State of the Union address, Bush connected tales of his own progeny to stories of his wife's charitable work with HIV-positive children and a letter from a grateful Gulf War widow in order to insist that, despite the many challenges they may face, individuals "have responsibilities to the taxpayer . . . to hold their families together and refrain from having children out of wedlock."[29] In this framing, the transnational politics of militarized heterosexuality merge seamlessly with the politics of white supremacy and heteropatriarchy in the domestic context; whether the problem is geopolitical disorder or blood-borne infection, the only solution is a reinvestment in the nuclear family. Presented with a diverse range of threats to security and potential solutions, Bush asserted, "We must strengthen the family because it is the family that has the greatest bearing on our future."

What this rhetoric masks is that neither "family" (one kinship group) nor "families" (kinship groups collectively) are homogenous or identical in interests. Furthermore, the task of "strengthening families" functions without the consent of those least empowered by the culturally specific forms the family takes (in this case, womenandchildren). The project of strengthening families implies that they are threatened and in need of the sort of protection the state offers: militarized violence. Whereas Vietnam War–era organizations like Another Mother for Peace were able to use parenthood as a culturally sanctioned perspective from which to make an argument against sending their children to fight in war, the domestic militarism of the 1990s militarized parenthood. Being a "good mother" or a "family man" came to rely increasingly on support for militarized violence; consequently, the rhetoric of family became militarized through a perception that state violence is necessary to strengthen families.

When making his call for more aggressive military action against Iraq to a Joint Session of Congress in September 1990, President Bush veered into the topic of how "our ability to function effectively as a great power abroad depends on how we conduct ourselves at home." He further explained that, for the United States, "world leadership and domestic strength are mutual and reinforcing; a woven piece, strongly bound as Old Glory."[30] Rather than dismissing this metaphor as another hackneyed bit of prose, we gain insight into the changing conditions of the 1990s by taking seriously Bush's contention that transnational militarism ("world leadership") structures the conditions of oppression within the borders of the nation ("domestic strength"). Furthermore, this leadership and strength are inextricable from practices of sexuality, or "how we conduct ourselves at home."

Three days after Bush declared, "Kuwait is liberated," a Los Angeles man named Rodney King was brutally beaten by group of police officers.[31] That night's events may have lapsed into obscurity, like so many other instances of anti-Black violence, were it not for a nearby resident sharing a videotape of the beating with a local news station. The state's subsequent failure to secure convictions against the offending officers sparked a series of civil conflicts centered in Los Angeles during late April and early May 1992. The LA Uprising, more commonly referred to by the racialized term the "LA Riots," was a "coming out" for the new post–Gulf War domestic militarism that sought to justify the use of state violence within the borders of the United States through appeals to heterosexual normativity. This set the stage for further militarization of heterosexuality as the decade continued.

Within hours of the "not guilty" verdicts, outrage fanned across the country and reactions ranged from orderly protests to concerted attempts at property destruction. By April 30 thousands of police officers and the California National Guard had been mobilized, soon to be joined by U.S. Army and marines deployed by President Bush. These forces arrived not to protect the mostly Black and Latino neighborhoods of south-central Los Angeles but to wage war on them. Bush's Executive Order 12804, federalizing the California National Guard and ordering the marines and army into the city to suppress "the conditions of domestic violence and disorder," drew its constitutional legitimacy from the Chapter 15 of Title 10 of the United States code, which only applies to insurrection and rebellion against the government, demonstrating the political and antistate nature of the actions depoliticized and pathologized by the term *riots*. The conflict provided an opportunity to display the effectiveness of the army's newly reorganized Seventh Division light infantry units, which had recently been deployed to both Honduras and Panama and were designed with a post–Cold War mission "to react quickly to emergencies around the world."[32] As Ruth Wilson Gilmore writes, the LA Uprising "democratically domesticated" the "state terror" of U.S. interventions abroad in service of "the rehabilitation of white, male heterosexuality."[33]

From the opening hours of the uprising, television viewers across the globe were invited to witness scenes of violence from news helicopters circling overhead. Reflecting on the continuities between "helicopter airmobilities" in Vietnam and Hawaiʻi, Vernadette Vicuna Gonzalez writes, helicopters "generate mobilities, fields of vision, and structures of feeling" that are "profoundly interconnected with past and present military violence."[34] Viewing Los Angeles from the sky exoticized the urban landscape, making the ostensibly domestic space of California appear more foreign and encouraging viewers to adopt the perspective of the military force that sought to first surveil, then suppress the uprising. On May 10 most of these troops withdrew, leaving the city with more than fifty dead and more than $1 billion in property damage in the largest-scale armed civil conflict in the United States since the 1960s.[35] Producing distance from the scene for readers while citing uprisings past, *Newsweek* accompanied a photo of a Korean American man standing in front of a burning store wearing a Malcolm X shirt and holding a rifle with the caption "This is not America."[36] The persistence of applying a Gulf War metaphor to the urban uprising was made most clear by a reporter who observed "what had been scattered pillars of smoke" on the first day of rioting morphing into "a huge black cloud reminiscent of the burning oil wells of Kuwait during the Persian Gulf war."[37]

In the wake of the uprising, loud criticism of rioters drowned out critiques of the police and National Guard killing ten civilians. The post-uprising debate instead focused on the underlying causes, and while loud debates fumed over race and class, many promoted domestic militarism by attributing the uprising to a Moynihanian culture of poverty. Vice President Dan Quayle stated that "the lawless social anarchy which we saw is directly related to the breakdown of family structure, personal responsibility and social order in too many areas of our society."[38] Quayle located the source of rioters' oppositional actions and politics in their nonnormative sexualities and implied that a militarized response functioned to correct both. Right-wing commentator Midge Decter went further, revealing a deep fixation on deviant heterosexuality contra class politics in asking, "How is it possible to go on declaring that what will save the young men of South-Central LA, and the young girls they impregnate, and the illegitimate babies they sire, is jobs?"[39]

President Bush best summarized the intersection of militarized policing and heteronormative orderliness in a speech at the South-Central Boys and Girls Club, where he said, "Families can't thrive, children can't learn, jobs can't flourish in a climate of fear, however. And so first is our responsibility to preserve the domestic order."[40] Here, the dual modalities of the domestic as internal to a household and internal to a nation-state become inseparable because in Bush's estimation the acceptable form of both is the same hierarchical order. Domestic militarism offers the patriarchal family as the only response to the disruptions of capital and demands state violence against those who refuse to conform. As Rod Ferguson has argued, urban strife has been "narrated as an instability rooted in nonheteronormative intimate relations among blacks, relations whose alleged potential to generated social instability had national implications."[41]

The uprising revealed a new post–Cold War terrain in which the external threat of communism receded to be overtaken by anxieties about internal threats provoked by racial and sexual disorder. Concomitantly, the state abdicated the interventionist promises of the New Deal and Great Society, moving toward a leaner neoliberal state that militarized by shedding functions not related to a narrow concept of national security. Both cultural anxieties and structural adjustments relied upon seemingly neutral descriptive terms like *structure, responsibility*, and *order* to mask the raced and gendered components of both policies and their unequal effects. Some of the same soldiers who went to Kuwait to avenge Iraqi depravations against children there battled "gangs of armed youths" and supposedly broken families in the streets of urban America to distribute the violence of the state in a way that maintained the internal security of suburban white nuclear families.

Long before the uprising, hierarchies of sexual shame and the projection of aggression onto the oppressed consistently characterized anti-Blackness across many historical disjunctures. The poet Sapphire makes as much clear in the 1993 poem "Strange Juice (or the Murder of Latasha Harlins)," which links the 1991 shooting death of Black teenager Latasha Harlins, an often forgotten aggravating factor in the uprising marginalized like the deaths of so many Black girls and women, to Billie Holiday's classic song about lynching, the African American Civil Rights struggle, and the colonization of the Americas. Rather than flattening these events into a homogenous tale of Black pain, Sapphire draws these connections to the past in order to point toward the future. Without infantilizing Harlins as a figure of childhood innocence, Sapphire makes an impassioned case for seeing Harlins as part of a solid intergenerational network "birthed by black people's struggle" in which she *"wasn't* pregnant, but . . . was gonna have a baby, definitely, one day."[42] African American cultural production in response to the uprising established a clear precedent that Black lives matter two decades before Alicia Garza, Patrisse Cullors, and Opal Tometi brilliantly applied the phrase to the movement against another intensification of anti-Black violence in 2013.

Different sentiments arose in popular responses to the uprising by white artists, even those who claimed a close relationship to it. The self-titled record the California band Sublime released in 1996 sold more than 5 million copies, spent 122 weeks on the Billboard charts, and depicted a domestically militarized vision of the uprising

in "April 29, 1992 (Miami)."⁴³ The song's first-person narrator partic-
ipates in the uprising by looting liquor, music, and furniture stores
before declaring that "it wasn't about Rodney King" but instead a
transracial problem with police brutality. The only woman to appear
in the story is the mother of a family taking diapers from a looted
store; the song then ends with a refrain of "Let it burn" directed at
cities across the United States. This account of the uprising, certainly
the only artistic response many white audiences have encountered,
operates within the framework of domestic militarism by using the
frame of property crime to understand political rebellion, accepting the borders claimed by the United States as the widest possible
frame for solidarity, and reducing women's role to biological and
social reproductive functions.

Although I now turn toward locating the ideological underpin-
nings of state violence directed against a predominantly white group
of people in the United States, the constitutive nature of anti-Black
violence remains an instructive example in assessing the meaning
of domestic militarism in the 1990s. Just as Black-majority neighborhoods were used as a laboratory for more militaristic styles of
police intervention that later became a national phenomenon, the
United States would continue to visit violence upon its citizens in
the name of children and the heteronormative family throughout
the decade.⁴⁴ At the same time, the state forged formal connections
between transnational militarism and domestic policing through
the Defense Logistics Agency Disposition Services, which increasingly distributed surplus military hardware to police forces around
the country. Ideas about proper sexuality would be equally crucial
to defending the use of this hardware against civilians as the decade
continued.

CHILDREN IN PERIL AT THE WACO SIEGE

In March and April of 1993, the U.S. public focused raptly on the
headquarters of the Branch Davidians just outside of Waco, Texas,
watching a series of events unfold that would leave eighty-six people
dead. Here, I connect the Branch Davidians to the people of Iraq and
Los Angeles through their common relationship to domestic milita-

rism without suggesting any equivalence between these communities. The militarized violence experienced by Iraqis, Angelenos, and Branch Davidians is by no means the same but is certainly linked. I demonstrate the contrast between the state's professed actions "in the interests of children" and the mass immolation of children at Waco, again highlighting the power of domestic militarism to disguise hypocrisy as normalcy.

On the morning of February 28, agents of the Bureau of Alcohol, Tobacco, and Firearms raided the Mount Carmel Center to arrest David Koresh on a weapons charge. Those who saw him as their spiritual leader were known as Branch Davidians, an offshoot of the Davidians, itself a breakaway segment of Seventh-day Adventism, a Protestant Christian denomination. The exact theology of the group shifted depending on the teachings of successive leaders, but all shared with Adventists a focus on an apocalyptic second coming of Jesus.[45] Of the more than one hundred members who were present, almost as many were from the United Kingdom as from the United States, and while majority white, about one-third of them were Black.[46] Once the siege began, newspapers across the country had no reservations about referring to the group as a cult and characterizing members through such a lens.[47]

The Branch Davidians repelled the government raid, initiating a fifty-one-day standoff that provided ample opportunities for news media to speculate on the character of all involved, particularly Koresh. The "big figure in this drama[,] ... in fact the only interesting character," was "an odd mix of religious zealot and frustrated rock performer" with a "rootless and fatherless childhood" who was comparable to "Jim Jones and Manson" or "Hitler and Stalin" and had a "history of learning disabilities."[48] Despite a seemingly bottomless supply of negative traits, Koresh "proved himself attractive" and "whatever his religious convictions, they did not preclude him from having sex ... even after he married a 14-year-old girl."[49] Such fascination with Koresh's sexual practices became the primary route through which he was characterized as "deviant" and, consequently, deserving of state violence.

The first quote the New York Times provided from Koresh encapsulates much of the ensuing coverage: "I've had a lot of babies these past two years. It's true that I do have a lot of children and I do have a lot of wives." This same article includes reports based on hearsay of "sexually abused girls" as well as rumors that "Mr. Koresh might have abused children of group members and . . . claimed to have at least 15 wives."[50] The number of wives grew to nineteen by the next day, alongside reports of his "abusive tendencies, including sexual relations with young girls."[51] He was so thoroughly saturated in nonnormative heterosexuality that even his rise to power was predicated on uncommon sexual relations: Koresh supposedly became a prophet by having sex with his predecessor Lois Roden, five decades his senior.[52] Reporters characterized Koresh as "a madman" and "David Death," but the accusations most instrumental to the standoff all focused on how Koresh acted toward his presumed dependents, the womenandchildren of the Mount Carmel Center.[53]

Domestic militarism assumes a system in which certain men present a sexualized threat and only militarized violence can save innocent children and women from them. Whether the threat rests in the body of an individual like Koresh or Saddam Hussein or in the faceless "thugs" accused of violating the domestic order in Los Angeles, the state diverts attention from its violence by positioning itself as protector and savior. The raid that sparked the Waco conflict operated on the assumption that the Branch Davidians consisted of dangerous men and helpless womenandchildren. Stephen Labaton and Sam Howe Verhovek's special report on the raid explains that the Bureau of Alcohol, Tobacco, and Firearms "timed the raid to take advantage of a period when . . . the cult's routine would separate the men from both the weapons and the women and children."[54] The raid also relied upon surveillance, tactical training, and an aerial diversion by Army Special Forces and National Guard units from Texas and Alabama.[55] Even though women participated actively on both sides of the raid, reducing them to their supposed helplessness served to cast militarized violence as benevolent protection.

On April 13 Verhovek reported that the government had no intention of assaulting the Mount Carmel Center "largely because of fears that such action could harm the 17 children inside."[56] Soon, though, the government began to execute "a plan of slowly stepping up the pressure" through the use of tear gas. To justify their escalation, officials relied upon accusations of escalating child abuse inside the compound. Attorney General Janet Reno defended the decision as such: "We had information that babies were being beaten. . . . I specifically asked, 'You really mean babies[?]' 'Yes, that he's slapping babies around.'"[57] Here, violence against infants, just as in the story of the Kuwaiti incubators, functioned as the ultimate transgression of heterosexual domesticity and a last resort to justify militarized violence.

Thus, on April 19 the same Bradley model tanks used in the Gulf War "pumped tear gas through holes punched in the walls of the compound," smoke appeared in several parts of the complex, and within an hour "David Koresh and more than 80 followers—including at least 17 children—apparently perished . . . when flames engulfed the sprawling wooden complex on the Texas prairie."[58] Immediately after these deaths, government officials asserted that it had been done with the best intentions—that is, for the womenandchildren. *Newsday* reported that while FBI agents were concerned with "restoring order," Reno "had different concerns—primarily the plight of the 17 children at the compound."[59] Similarly, a spokesman for the Justice Department insisted on the maternal instincts of his boss, saying the factor "that drove her the most was her concern about the children."[60] President Bill Clinton also stuck to the story about ongoing child abuse ("the children who were still inside the compound were being abused significantly"), blamed the deaths on the Branch Davidians ("they made the decision to immolate themselves"), and assured his audience that what mattered most was the children ("I feel awful about the children").[61]

While federal officials insisted on the legitimacy of their conjectures about ongoing child abuse, the Justice Department's October report on the siege conceded that "there was no direct evidence indicating that Koresh engaged in any physical or sexual abuse of children during the standoff."[62] Sam Howe Verhovek's reporting on the children during the siege revealed that "none show any signs of physical abuse, and most seem consumed with a wish to see their parents."[63] Furthermore, "cult members have disputed that there was any child abuse or beatings at the compound, and Texas authorities who had looked into such accusations before the Feb. 28 raid had never found any proof."[64] Although the Justice Department report conceded that Reno "had made an inaccurate statement" in regards to the child abuse, it insisted that unsubstantiated innuendo was "sufficient to be relevant to the decision making process."[65] Commentator William Safire was less charitable; he went so far as to claim that Reno "misled the public after the attack (and probably the President before the attack) by arguing that the children were being 'abused' inside."[66] While questions remain about how children were treated within the Mount Carmel Center, the inferno that killed its residents rendered some details permanent mysteries.

The fire's exact origin also remains a mystery, but both the U.S. government and media outlets settled on the assumption of a mass suicide by the Branch Davidians. What is clearer from accounts of the Waco siege is that the U.S. government sought to solve problems with overwhelming force, which it attempted to justify to the public through the logic of domestic militarism. The perception that tanks ramming into a building and spitting noxious gas "represent[s] the best way to resolve the standoff without catastrophic loss of life" concedes significant ground to militarization by depicting this sort of professionally administered violence as a life-saving measure. While one reporter claimed that a "confusing swirl of political, practical, and psychological forces inevitably steered officials toward the plan," the most pertinent fact is that "no alternatives were formally presented to Attorney General Janet Reno" besides a tank and tear gas assault.[67] Domestic militarism was the driving force that steered officials toward the plan, not *inevitably*, but *ideologically*. As other standoffs, like the 1994 Justus Township siege in Montana, revealed, loss of life is not inevitable when citizens clash with their government, but assumptions about the dangers of nonnormative kinship arrangements and the utility of militarized violence make loss of life more likely.

Many surviving Branch Davidians gather at the ruins of the Mount Carmel Center every April 19 to commemorate the deaths that occurred there. By 1995 the site had become a rallying point for "a political crusade, albeit one that the survivors haven't joined and don't even approve of."[68] The ranks of these crusaders, who "called themselves constitutionalists or patriots or militiamen," grew throughout the early 1990s, rallying around citizen-state conflicts like Waco and Ruby Ridge with their own militaristic fervor, brandishing firearms, and peppering federal authorities with bellicose rhetoric.[69] The Branch Davidians, by contrast, stood a skeptical distance from the militiamen, "perplexed, and even offended," wary of the gun-toting militia, and totally unarmed.[70] At the same time, three hundred miles due north of Waco, one of those self-described militiamen turned April 19 into a day that would both eclipse the Waco siege in losses of human life and link the siege into a larger chain of militarized violence.

THE "BABY KILLER" IN OKLAHOMA CITY

Just after 9:00 a.m. on April 19, 1995, an ammonium nitrate and fertilizer oil bomb exploded in front of the Alfred P. Murrah Federal Building in downtown Oklahoma City. Hundreds of millions of dollars of property damage was overshadowed by 168 deaths. Representations of the space of the bombing, its youngest victims, and the bomber's motives for his violent act all demonstrate the historical linkages between state violence and heteronormativity, or domestic militarism.

In the aftermath of the bombing, many Oklahomans appeared most disoriented not by the tragedy of bombing itself but rather by the place in which it occurred. "One by one they said the same thing," journalist Rick Bragg reported: "this does not happen here."[71] Locals had plenty of ideas about where these things *do* happen: "Beirut," "Bosnia . . . Jerusalem . . . Baghdad . . . Bolivia," and "countries so far away, so different they might as well be on the dark side of the moon."[72] The belief that Oklahoma existed as part of "America's heretofore invulnerable and innocent heartland . . . whose uncorrupted values and innocence were beyond the reach of such violence" required effacing the racialized violence that contours the history of Oklahoma as well as the transnational exportation of that violence by the United States.[73]

Mass-casualty incidents were uncommon but by no means unprecedented in Oklahoma's history. In a defining moment of U.S.-indigenous relations, the federal government began a systematic forcible displacement of the Cherokee, Seminole, Chickasaw, Creek-Muscogee, Choctaw and other indigenous nations to contemporary Oklahoma in 1830, resulting in thousands of deaths on multiple Trails of Tears. Furthermore, not only was the state a scene of the quotidian violence of Jim Crow, but it also was the scene of more spectacular forms of white supremacist violence like the 1921 assault on Tulsa's "Black Wall Street" that left hundreds dead and thousands more homeless. When those at the scene of the 1995 bombing claimed, "It's hard to imagine this happening in the heartland," they participated in a collective forgetting of tragedies like the Tulsa race riot that justified ongoing violence against people of color.[74] Domestic militarism requires effacing the suffering that was necessary to establish a seemingly benign domestic order, or as Chandra Mohanty and Biddy Martin claim in reference to the concept of "being home," it requires "an illusion of coherence and safety based on the exclusion of specific histories of oppression and resistance."[75]

Histories of transnational militarism were also denied through representations of innocent Okies "newly burdened with an unfortunate sense of connection to the rest of the world."[76] The normalization of dozens of sudden deaths by explosion abroad—whether in Beirut, Baghdad, or Bolivia—arises out of the logic of domestic militarism that says the burden of violence should be borne *out there* and not within the domestic space of the United States. The idea that violence must be suffered in foreign countries existed in a mutually reinforcing relationship with the idea that violence must also originate from foreign countries, placing immediate scrutiny upon Arabs and Muslims as the search began for the bomb suspect. As a *Wall Street Journal* article two days after the bombing that neatly segregates the foreign and domestic claimed, "The mere prospect of a link to international terrorism has the potential for elevating . . . foreign policy . . . which lately has taken a backseat to domestic reform."[77]

A. M. Rosenthal encapsulated the dominant attitude of the moment: "Police do not know for certain whether the bombing is foreign terrorism or domestic. Either way . . . whatever we are doing to destroy Mideast terrorism, the chief terrorist threat against Americans, has not been working."[78] This is to say, regardless of who is responsible for the bombing, Arabs or Muslims (it's rarely clear) should be punished for it. Even after the U.S. government stopped pursuing Arab suspects and focused on a cadre of white men, Walter Goodman hedged his critique of how televised news cast "Arab-Americans" as "the suspects of first choice in terrorist attacks" when he said, this "suspicion is understandable."[79]

While many were immediately occupied with scrutinizing their neighbors, the victims of the bombing transfixed many more, and both government and media represented children at the apex of victimhood in order to promote domestic militarism. Before any details about the bomb emerged, Rick Bragg asserted that "it was intended to murder on a grand scale: women, children, old people coming to complain about their Social Security checks."[80] Little mention was made of the Drug Enforcement Administration, Secret Service, Marine Corps, Army Recruiting Battalion, or Defense Security Service in the same building. Instead, "the enduring image of this tragedy" was that of bloodied one-year-old Baylee Almon being carried away from the rubble by a firefighter.[81] Photos of Almon "pierced the heart" of millions who saw the pictures through the Associated Press Wire and "prompted a flood of calls to newspapers from people concerned about the child's fate."[82] Sadly, Baylee Almon died as a result of the bombing and, like the eighteen other children killed in the blast, became a filter through which to look at domestic terrorism without seeing domestic militarism.

While 168 people died that day, the nineteen children became "the focus, the epicenter, of the nation's bereavement over the blast and its rage and loathing at the bomber" because their unquestionable innocence made the bombing appear, as President Clinton put it, like "an attack on innocent children and defenseless civilians" rather than an attack on a centralized node of repressive state power.[83] Furthermore, centering the youngest victims facilitated an image of a national family bound together by the strength of fathers and the vulnerability of dependents. The first responders did not just pull Baylee Almon from the wreckage; as the New York Times reported, they "called [her] 'my baby,' adopting [her] on the spot, as did the entire nation."[84] The state also rhetorically adopted Almon, using her very real pain as a rhetorical resource to assuage concerns about the real pain the U.S. government would continue to inflict upon many children.

There was no shortage of familial metaphors in response to the bombing. Journalist Todd Purdum claimed, "A disaster or security threat transforms the President instantly into a national paterfamilias," and prolific child psychiatrist Robert Coles described the attack as "against our own family."[85] Clinton, the "national father figure," seemed to relish the role, surrounding himself and First Lady Hillary Clinton with children of federal workers for "a brief national teach-in on anxiety and reassurance" in which he promised that the governmental response would be "putting our children first."[86] With no foreign enemy to punish for provoking this anxiety, the United States turned toward the bombing's primary perpetrator to make sense of the tragedy, but domestic militarism obscured the most important explanations.

Timothy McVeigh, the man charged with and executed for bombing the Murrah building in Oklahoma City, recalibrated the scale through which negative representations could be judged. Journalists called him a "lunatic," the "most detested of pariahs," "so sick," "Satan," an "evil person," "a demon," and a "monster," but no invective stuck like "baby killer."[87] McVeigh's widely broadcast "perp walk" in Perry, Oklahoma, featured a crowd screaming, "Baby killer! Burn him!"[88] The *New York Times* fed the image of McVeigh as baby killer, speculating that "the Murrah building may have been chosen specifically because its layout insured that a bomb could be placed so close to children" and claiming that "McVeigh had displayed no reaction even when he had been shown photographs of maimed and dead children."[89]

In addition to the title of "baby killer," a portrait emerged of Timothy McVeigh that emphasized his failed heterosexuality. McVeigh apparently was "a supremely dedicated soldier" who was "well on his way to . . . a brilliant military career" but also a "loner" who "could not imagine settling down, working, marrying, becoming 'domesticated.'"[90] According to some of the men who served with him, McVeigh "embraced the solitude of his pillow night after night" and "never had a date."[91] Lou Michel and Dan Herbeck, who McVeigh selected to write his biography, related tales of him failing to woo potential girlfriends, skipping family weddings out of discomfort, and silently blushing when Barbara Walters asked him about his social life.[92] McVeigh's hyposexuality, his failure to be appropriately "domestic," functioned to pathologize him and mark his militaristic violence as improper. The creation of such a distinction is critically important because of the way he blurred the division between his "legitimate" violence as a soldier for the state and his "illegitimate" bombing.

In a letter written a few months before his execution, McVeigh connected his military training to his actions in Oklahoma City: "Bombing the Murrah Federal Building was morally and strategically equivalent to the United States hitting a government building in Serbia, Iraq, or other nations." He claimed the bombing was "no different than what Americans rain on the heads of others all the time, and subsequently, my mindset was and is one of clinical detachment."[93] The technical content of McVeigh's actions, from his familiarity with explosives to his composure under pressure, arose out of his training and attachment to militarism. McVeigh's struggle to reckon with his combat experience in Iraq, his revulsion at seeing the sort of tank he manned there used against the Branch Davidians in Texas, and his sense of himself as protecting domestic order, each a highly politicized perception, were completely evacuated before they could even be examined. As Pam Belluck wrote a few weeks after the bombing, "Any argument that Mr. McVeigh had been motivated by political opposition to some drastic Government action or injustice would be very difficult to advance, *since the bombing killed innocent women and children.*"[94] Domestic militarism maintains the cognitive dissonance necessary to disarticulate domestic terrorism from its roots in transnational militarism; it provides a framework for interpreting kinship, nation, and violence in ways that insulate the state from critique. In this way, the connections between McVeigh's combat history in Iraq and the bombing were actively avoided, as many of the same people eager to punish McVeigh for the murders he committed in Oklahoma City enthusiastically encouraged the murders he committed in Iraq.

The 104th Congress and President Clinton created a series of laws in 1996 that reflected the changes wrought over the first half of the 1990s and helped to codify a new post–Gulf War domestic militarism. Four pieces of legislation reflect both the progress and the fragility of militarized heterosexuality in the 1990s, affirming the values of domestic militarism, while also suggesting that the relationship between heterosexuality and militarism did not arise from the nature of either but rather was an active construction of the state.

I have argued that representations of and responses to state violence militarized heterosexuality in the early 1990s. I refer to this as domestic militarism in that these events were militarized violence used both within the borders claimed by the United States and to enforce a particular vision of the family. The U.S. government advanced and media regularly endorsed justifications for this violence grounded in binary gender roles, hegemonic whiteness, and genocidal ideas about indigenous people. In this final section, I provide one final demonstration of how the imagined interests of children provided a convenient excuse for regressive social change that ultimately increased the suffering of many children.

The Antiterrorism and Effective Death Penalty Act of 1996 (AEDPA) transformed from "a snail into a race horse" due to the "domestic terrorism" of the Oklahoma City bombing but focused its definition of terrorism almost exclusively on what it called "international terrorism."[95] In addition to tightening restrictions on contributions to foreign organizations designated as terrorists and opening up foreign governments to suit in U.S. courts, AEDPA created new procedures for deporting immigrants suspected of terrorism through secret trials and limited the ability of people accused of terrorism to seek asylum in the United States.[96] Along with the Illegal Immigration Reform and Immigrant Responsibility Act of 1996, which increased both the authority of the Immigration and Naturalization Services to imprison people indefinitely and the speed with which they could deport migrants, the AEDPA reshaped the legal regime governing immigration, separated countless families from each other, and reflected contemporaneous conceptions of security and national identity.[97] These laws drew upon and reinforced white supremacist conceptions of Euro-Americans as the rightful arbiters of the land within the borders claimed by the United States while projecting the threat of violence regularly committed by the U.S. state—at home and abroad—onto racialized, "foreign" threats.

The Illegal Immigration Reform and Immigrant Responsibility Act also sought to eliminate immigrants' access to the limited social safety in the United States, a goal more effectively achieved by the Personal Responsibility and Work Opportunity Reconciliation Act of 1996 (PRWORA).[98] The law begins with two findings: "marriage is the foundation of a successful society," and "marriage is an essential institution of a successful society which promotes the interests of children."[99] Lest the exact sort of marriage to which this Congress referred be misconstrued, it is worth noting that a week earlier it had passed the Defense of Marriage Act, which defined *marriage* as "only a legal union between one man and one woman as husband and wife."[100] This aggressive promotion of heterosexuality evident in PRWORA went hand-in-hand with the anti-Black racism and classism identified by Dorothy Roberts in her work on race and reproduction in the United States. Roberts sees PRWORA as driven by "a set of myths about the connections between family structure, welfare, race, and poverty" toward the goal of "modifying poor people's behavior."[101]

How, then, did this law passed "to promote the interests of children" modify their lives? Quantitatively, less than half the number of children receiving Aid to Families with Dependent Children benefits in 1995 were receiving the post-PRWORA Temporary Assistance for Needy Families benefits by 2000, despite a growing population and a child poverty rate of more than 17 percent.[102] The Center for Popular Economics reported that the new welfare regime "offers no guarantee that families with young children under the poverty line will receive public assistance," even though children in poverty "are more likely to have behavioral problems[,] . . . are more likely than other children to be overweight and suffer from other chronic health problems . . . [and] are far more vulnerable to neglect and abuse."[103] Clearly, serving children, particularly children of color and working-class children, was not the number one priority of PRWORA. As Roberts claims, "How we interpret child maltreatment is a political issue."[104]

The politics of interpreting what constitutes child maltreatment and the interests of children emerged concurrently with domestic militarism in the 1990s. Heterosexuality, through its claim of producing life, became the mechanism to excuse militarism's destruction of life. The government and media contributed to the structural power and power-evasiveness of patriarchal, Euro-American heterosexuality in the way the way they framed outrage at the alleged maltreatment of children by the Iraqi military and the Branch Davidians. In Los Angeles officials and commentators attempted to excuse deploying military units within the borders of the United States by proposing that as the only tenable solution to the pathologies of the Black community. In the cases of Waco, immigration reform, and welfare reform, the U.S. government positioned itself as operating "in the interests of children," and in each case children suffered and died. The Oklahoma City bombing, in which Timothy McVeigh used the training he received abroad from the U.S. military to kill a great number of people within the United States, showed the perverse yet inevitable results of this logic.

The symbolic use of children—bound up in the dynamics of sexuality, gender, race, and other forms of identity—allows for the rhetorical elision of the pain and death experienced by real, live children. The "transformation at home" heralded by Bush amounted to a militarization of heterosexuality through the ideology of domestic militarism. Critically examining representations of domestic militarism allows us to better understand how the logics used to rationalize state violence against people outside of U.S.-claimed borders inevitably comes home to be applied unevenly within those borders. Understanding the militarization of hegemonic sexualities during the 1990s, furthermore, prepares us better to understand the militarization of queer sexualities during the same time period.

3

The Propensity or Intent to Engage in Homosexual Acts

MILITANT QUEERNESS AND MILITARIZED HOMOSEXUALITY

In early 1991, with news of the Gulf War still dominating the headlines, a Black high school student named Tracey Harris enlisted in the U.S. Army. She served for twelve years, including tours in Afghanistan and Iraq and rose to the rank of sergeant before leaving the military because leadership had made it clear to her that "being gay was a far more serious offense in the military than sexually harassing a fellow service member." In 2010 Tracey Cooper-Harris wrote of the "constant fear" she experienced as a lesbian soldier and explained, "I was always looking over my shoulder, censoring what I said and keeping as much physical distance as possible between my military life and my personal life."[1] While Cooper-Harris labored to keep her military and personal lives separate, military regulations and social movements had set these spheres on a collision course out of which new formations of militarism and sexuality emerged. Cooper-Harris emerged as an advocate for lesbians in the early 2000s and sought neither a broad set of rights based on sexual orientation nor a more transformative agenda of liberation; rather, her advocacy focused on ensuring that lesbian, gay, and bisexual people had equal access to veteran benefits and the military.

This chapter tracks contentious debates and significant trans-formations within the multiple, diverging, and overlapping movements of lesbian, gay, bisexual, and transgender people during the late 1980s and early 1990s.[2] I focus on the collision between two competing tendencies that, drawing upon phraseology from that time, I refer to as "militant queerness" and "militarized homosexuality." This conflict shaped, responded to, and reshaped a separate but related conflict between the U.S. military and those pressuring that institution to end its ban on gay and lesbian service members. That clash produced an ambivalent transformation in 1993 when a policy that would come to be known as "Don't Ask, Don't Tell" came into effect. This policy spoke of the "propensity or intent to engage in homosexual acts," defining "homosexual act" as solely a form of bodily contact with a sexual aim. Here, I am concerned with a much more capacious definition of what it might mean to have such a propensity or intent, one that accounts for significant and substantive differences in how LGBT people define their relationships with the nation-state and their identities more broadly.

In the early 1980s, self-described "Black feminist, lesbian, poet, mother, warrior" Audre Lorde, in defining lesbianism, said, "The true feminist deals out of a lesbian consciousness whether or not she ever sleeps with women. I can't really define it in sexual terms alone although our sexuality is so energizing why not enjoy it too?"[3] Sexual identities not only relate to erotic gratification, but they also shape the definitions and boundaries of social collectivities. Larry Kramer, like Lorde a gay writer but otherwise dramatically different in thought and style, said around the same time, "We have a sense of self and identity and relating as exists in any religion or philosophy or ethnic background, and in which sex plays no more a role than it does in heterosexual identity."[4] More recently, David Halperin has argued that "homosexuality, itself, even as an erotic orientation, even as a specifically sexual subjectivity, consists in a dissident way of feeling and relating to the world." That is to say, queer people do not simply experience queer desires and exhibit queer sexual practices; they also occupy a culturally and historically specific "queer subjectivity," which "expresses itself through a peculiar, dissident *way of relating* to cultural objects . . . and cultural forms in general."[5]

My analysis of the militarization of homosexuality tracks a shift in that way of relating between the U.S. military and queer subjectivities in the late twentieth century. As LGBTQ movements grew in size and strength throughout this time period, the stakes and visibility of contestations over the definitions and boundaries of the gay community also rose. Lorde's vision of feminist solidarity, Kramer's desire for a distinctive cultural brotherhood, and Halperin's shared sensibility of arch reappropriation were joined by many other competing definitions of what it means to be lesbian or gay during this period, including assimilationists, who argued that there was little difference between gay and straight people besides how they have sex, and anti-assimilationist queers, who rejected the invitations certain queer people received to integrate into dominant institutions. The late eighties and early nineties also marked the rise of queer theory and queer studies as outsider ways of reading desire and bodies, soon mired in contentious debate over how well they could and how much they should integrate into heteronormative academia.

In the United States, where militarism has the potential to reach into any aspect of social and cultural order, competing queer subjectivities were compelled to establish a way of relating to the military and militarism by the national policy debate over the rights of gay and lesbian people to serve openly in the military. As Cathy Cohen's work on HIV and Black sexualities shows, more work must be done to "understand how marginal group members define and redefine themselves" because "contestation over identity . . . has tangible effects, influencing the distribution of resources, services, access, and legitimacy within communities."[6] The drive for more LGB access to the military consumed a great deal of activist, nonprofit, personal, and media resources that could have been applied to addressing youth homelessness, criminalization, transgender health, HIV/AIDS, street violence, or other issues affecting many LGBTQ people in the United States had priorities been different. At the same time, due to the transnational nature of contemporary militarism, contestations over participation in the U.S. military have tangible effects reaching far beyond the gay community in the United States.

I begin by framing LGBT politics in the late 1980s, focusing on the developing schism between those who would push intently for access to the U.S. military and those who would steer LGBT politics toward other goals. Then I shift focus to some events that kept debates over gays and lesbians in the military in the national consciousness into the early 1990s. After that, I detail how the Don't Ask, Don't Tell policy emerged out of the 1992 presidential elections, analyze the policy itself, and follow some of its effects over its short lifespan. Then I return to the continued intragroup struggles of LGBTQ people in the United States as the 1990s wore on. I conclude by reflecting on the importance of understanding these conflicts today in the wake of Don't Ask, Don't Tell's demise and the ongoing debate over transgender service members.

LGBT history, the history of sexuality in general, and queer ways of interpreting the world have not always found a welcome home in the academy. Those of us who work on this sort of history owe a great debt to the people and communities who preserved and promoted this history in addition to developing the perspectives and interpretations that let us understand it. At the same time, I work in the frame of peace and conflict studies, which cautions us to not excuse violence due to our empathy for the perpetrators. I seek to propel the movements out of which my methodology arises forward with all their contradictions preserved. Leonard Matlovich, who in 1975 appeared on the cover of *Time* magazine in his air force uniform, with the text "'I Am a Homosexual': The Gay Drive for Acceptance," had carved on his headstone the message "When I was in the military, they gave me a medal for killing two men and a discharge for loving one."[7] I seek to chart a path that at once honors the love for which the military persecuted Matlovich and Cooper-Harris without glorifying the violence for which the military honored them.

FRAMING LGBT POLITICS

The platform from 1987's Second National March on Washington for Lesbian and Gay Rights provides a snapshot of LGBT politics at the national level in the late 1980s. Alongside planks calling for legal recognition of lesbian and gay relationships and a lesbian and gay civil rights bill were more intersectional calls for reproductive freedom, an end to sexist oppression, and "an end to racism in this country and apartheid in South Africa." Significantly, in the plank addressing the HIV/AIDS crisis, the organizers articulated the fight against AIDS as hampered by the federal government's focus on a militarized vision of national security. The demand "money for AIDS, not for war" most clearly articulated the inseparability of progay and antimilitarist politics in the late eighties, but the centrality of this affinity would soon be in jeopardy.[8]

In 1993 the next national mobilization added "bisexual" to the constituents and "liberation" to the goals but demonstrated significant militarization by dropping the reference to war in the plank on AIDS and adding a call for an "end to discrimination by state and federal governments including the military" to the first plank. Seven years after that, for the Millennium March on Washington, ballots for the platform offered the "right to serve our country" as an option while excluding any critiques of state violence and the commitment to gaining access to military service ultimately expanded to warrant its very own plank.[9] Though there has not been another national march since, there are many signs that this transformation has continued. The 2013 statement by the organizers of San Francisco Pride disavowing transgender soldier and whistleblower Chelsea Manning, in which they asserted that "even the hint of support for actions which placed in harms way the lives of our men and women in uniform . . . will not be tolerated," reflected a dogmatic support for militarism deeply transformed from the long tradition of radicalism in San Francisco's queer community.[10]

Emily Hobson, Christina Hanhardt, and Deborah Gould, among others, have extensively documented the anti-imperialist, antistate, and radical tendencies that often predominated in LGBT movements between the 1960s and 1980s.[11] Each of their works follow these tendencies into dissipation, cooptation, or fracture in the late eighties and early nineties, where this study picks up. How was the militarization of homosexuality so successful during this period? How did it so deeply overshadow the militant queerness of the late 1980s that drew deep connections between homophobia and militarism? How does that structure relationships between LGBTQ people and the state today? The degree to which homosexuality militarized over the course of the 1990s and the rancor with which many heterosexuals resisted the calls for tolerating openly gay service members can obscure just how contentious the process was. So before explaining how promilitary voices came to speak for the LGBT community at large, it is crucial to understand how the conditions of the late 1980s initially produced an LGBT discourse better described as militant than militarized.

The use of *militant*, a term affiliated with radicals of color in the 1960s and subsequently applied to feminists and others who stridently questioned the orthodoxy of their context, increased in reference to gay activists in late 1980s, especially as the AIDS crisis worsened and attention-grabbing activism spread across the nation. As Deborah Gould explains, some were driven to an increasingly militant analysis and posture after the 1986 *Bowers v. Hardwick* decision that upheld antisodomy laws in effect across much of the country.[12] Soon, many formerly politically inactive and even conservative or patriotic gay activists were openly questioning loyalty to the U.S. government.

Larry Kramer declared at a September 1987 Constitution Day celebration, "I am ashamed to be an American today. . . . I hate this country I once loved so much."[13] Many of the men who wrote to Kramer at the time appeared to share his sentiments. A man from New Jersey wrote of how researching the AIDS epidemic had caused him to "get rid of some very childlike notions about this country," and another man from New York explained, "We have two enemies now: the disease and the government."[14] In an essay connecting the experiences of African Americans to Black South Africans, Lorde countered a perennial justification for U.S. military activity abroad, asserting that the United States "stands upon the wrong side of every liberation struggle on earth."[15] Within the context of growing panic around AIDS and hostility toward the U.S. government, particularly on the cusp of the early post–Cold War demobilizations, few prominent lesbian or gay activists were vocally concerned with access to the military, but that does not mean war was not on their minds.

The language of late 1980s gay and lesbian activism was saturated with the language and metaphors of war. Especially after the spring of 1987, countless sources referred to, called for, or asserted that gay groups were calling for a "War on AIDS."[16] In 1988 alone the national summit of lesbian and gay activists met under the name "The War Conference," safe sex innovator Michael Callen released a record titled *Purple Heart* that included refrains of "We are living in wartime" and "This is war," and film historian Vito Russo delivered a celebrated speech in which he explained that his life as a gay man with AIDS "is like living through a war which is happening only for those people who happen to be in the trenches."[17] It is important to recognize that, regardless of their comfort with war metaphors and despite several threats to engage in warfare, militant queer activism never slipped into the militarized mode of drills, uniforms, or armed struggle evinced by many heterosexual radicals and remained a thoroughly demilitarized militancy throughout the era.[18]

Probably the most visible group in the trenches of late eighties gay struggle was the AIDS Coalition to Unleash Power (ACT UP). ACT UP coalesced in 1987 as panic around the epidemic and a spirit of direct action spread through LGBT communities. The headline of a 1990 profile on the group, "Rude, Rash, Effective," neatly encapsulates their confrontational attitudes toward those in power, urgent focus on immediate media attention over long-term coalition building, and ability to push drug companies, the federal government, and other institutions to unprecedented action on the HIV/AIDS crisis.[19] Emily Hobson has detailed how San Francisco's ACT UP chapter grew out of the work of Central American solidarity organization Lesbians and Gays against Intervention.[20] Chapters in Philadelphia, Chicago, and New York also benefited from the leadership of anti–Vietnam War activists of color such as Kiyoshi Kuromiya and Ortez Alderson. Kuromiya heralded the effectiveness of blending sexually explicit and antimilitarist messages almost two decades before ACT UP with his provocative, anti–Vietnam War "Fuck the Draft" poster series, and Alderson was practiced at direct action targeting the federal government, having spent a year in prison for burning draft cards as part of the Pontiac Four.[21]

Homophobic critics, curious journalists, and ACT UP members alike all used the term *militant* to describe the organization and the attitude embodied by its members, but agreement tended to end there. From the start, many ACT UP chapters were divided into one camp focused almost exclusively on AIDS (sometimes known as the "drugs in bodies" people) and another camp with a broader intersectional agenda of confronting injustice against queer people. Such tensions are reflected in a summer 1988 letter to Kramer, who was instrumental to the founding of ACT UP NY, from three members named Thomas, Neal, and Robert. "A typical Monday night general meeting," they contended, "spends at least as much, if not more, time devoted to women's rights and sexism, the problem of racism, preventing nuclear war . . . etc. as is spent on the actual subject of AIDS."[22] As militants took to the streets, many treatment advocates professionalized and, in a parallel move to gay activists who drew closer to the government as they advocated for access to the military, found pathways toward assimilating into the late-blooming federal response to AIDS.

More militant members of the LGBT community may have advocated for confrontation but represented a current in the movement much more likely to criticize the U.S. military than seek access to it. This became particularly clear on January 22, 1991, when ACT UP members snuck into CBS Studios to disrupt the opening minutes of the *Evening News* and *MacNeil/Lehrer NewsHour*. Protestors briefly got on camera, shouting, "Fight AIDS, not Arabs" before being subdued. Once outside, a reporter asked them, "Don't you think this is an immature and silly way to get your point across to the country?" to which the ACT UPers responded, "No, we think spending hundreds of billions of dollars bombing people in another continent is a silly and immature way to get a point across."[23] The next day, other members of ACT UP used balloons to raise a massive banner in Grand Central Station that shouted the chorus of the moment: "MONEY FOR AIDS NOT WAR."[24]

In the early nineties, *militant* became increasingly synonymous with the former slur *queer*, which was increasingly being reclaimed by members of the LGBT community and is now one of the more common identity labels embraced today. The widespread popularity of the term *queer* can be traced to a pamphlet titled *Queers Read This* distributed anonymously at the 1990 New York City Pride Parade. The pamphlet asserts that "lesbians and gays live in a war zone" and calls for forming an "army of lovers" to confront the rising tide of open homophobia emboldened by the AIDS crisis as well as the well-intentioned but patronizing voices that facilitated invisibility by envisioning LGBT people assimilating into heteronormativity. Two years later, a less widely circulated broadside with the same aesthetic titled *Wake Up Queers or We're All Through* appeared. It touted lesbians' contributions to both the AIDS movement and Central American solidarity, criticized the growing for-profit AIDS industry, and called for political funerals, letting "rats loose in the halls of Congress," and "storming the White House with pitchforks and torches."[25] The organization Queer Nation emerged around the same time, heeding the pamphlet's call to reject the goal of expanding privacy rights and instead embrace the queering of public space. Queer Nation, which hyperbolically appropriated the language of nationalism and lived by the motto "We're here, we're queer, get used to it," drew broad attention with public actions ranging from their storied "kiss-ins" to demonstrations against the Gulf War.

Prominent critics of queer militancy pushed back even during the crest of antimilitarist organizing in the community. Randy Shilts, one of the only openly gay journalists writing about gay issues in straight newspapers at the time, lamented in 1989 that "militants already have had a major impact on policy," but "their methods are becoming so confrontational that they are beginning to backfire." While "militancy undoubtedly will fester further," he regarded militant queer activists as "infantile . . . counterproductive" and perhaps even "among the forces of death."[26] Death claimed many on every side of debates within the community during these years, interrupting intergenerational transmission of radical values and disproportionately impacting low-income, racialized, and other marginalized communities out of which much queer radicalism grew. Such ideas also lost ground in LGBT spaces like pride parades and publications like *The Advocate* as the growth of an identifiable gay market brought more potential for profit and concerns about attracting corporate advertisers. HIV activism encouraged some to emphasize how gay and bisexual men were "just like everyone else" and focus on examples of monogamy, physical prowess, nationalistic heroism, wealth accumulation, and other markers of whiteness that normalized certain queer bodies for the straight community. Large foundations like the Human Rights Campaign Fund and Gill Foundation increasingly backed their vision of a gay agenda focused on assimilation and integration into dominant institutions. Regressive gay thinkers such as Andrew Sullivan quickly moved to center stage; Sullivan was made editor of the *New Republic* in 1991 and soon after solicited controversial contributions from anti-Black neo-eugenicist Charles Murray.

Simultaneously, militant antiwar queers were increasingly replaced on the evening news and in mainstream media with images of strapping, patriotic, assimilationist gay men and lesbians seeking to maintain their positions in the military and participate fully in the interests of the nation-state. Douglas Crimp described these leading activists as exchanging "the image of the healthy body for that of the sick body," which may have been tactically effective in improving heterosexual perceptions of gay people while unstrategically conceding to the militarization of homosexuality and the exclusion of certain nonconforming bodies.[27] At the same time, Crimp's critique of representation cannot be taken too literally, as in the case of Leonard Matlovich, who was both an energetic and militarized icon of gay masculinity and a person with AIDS. The most circulated image of Matlovich lying infirm was not of his final days before succumbing to AIDS but of him with his Purple Heart shortly after stepping on a land mine in Vietnam. These contradictions helped to subsume the broad agendas of ACT UP and Queer Nation, which sought economic justice, demilitarization, and redress for the concerns of the growing number of queer people identifying as transgender under a national gay and lesbian civil rights agenda focused narrowly on accessing institutions rather than transforming them and exclusively on the axis of sexual orientation rather than the full range of identities within the community. And though this shift has been recognized in queer theory as homonormativity or homonationalism, few scholars have located the historical dimensions of this shift or placed it into the context provided by feminist scholars of gender and militarism.[28]

By the early nineties, countries including the Netherlands, France, and Japan allowed, on paper if not always in practice, lesbian and gay people to serve openly. Canada ended the prohibition on lesbian and gay soldiers in October 1991 and Australia in November 1992, but the United States remained resolute in separating from service any service member determined to have committed a "homosexual act."[29] While the resources devoted to identifying and discharging sexually suspect service members had ebbed and flowed in inverse proportion to the ebb and flow of new recruits, the gains made in gay and lesbian visibility during the late twentieth century provoked greater scrutiny of potentially gay soldiers. The need for personnel of the post-1973 all-volunteer military also required the enlistment of many individuals, particularly women, who would have been previously rejected by the military, and forced recruiters and administrators into a delicate balancing act between fulfilling enlistment needs and screening out recruits they did not desire.

Given that homosexuality is not a fact ascertainable through any known scientific test and that discretion is a skill many people with nonnormative sexual desires learn to use in a heteronormative society, the U.S. government has gone to great lengths to devise methods through which to accurately identify gay people. During World War II, the military harnessed the purported skills of psychologists and social scientists to screen for potential or actualized homosexuality among recruits, but the tried and true method took a less empirical approach. Beginning with then undersecretary of the navy Franklin D. Roosevelt's search for men who have sex with men among sailors in 1920s Rhode Island, the U.S. military pursued a strategy of treating homosexuality as a crime and sending investigators to contact and expose suspect individuals—the "gay witch hunt."[30]

Two gay witch hunts of the late 1980s set the stage for the struggles of LGB people in the U.S. military during the 1990s. For women suspected of lesbianism, the Parris Island scandal revealed how patriarchal values mixed with homophobia made women particularly vulnerable to accusations of improper conduct for merely associating too closely with a suspected lesbian. For men suspected of homosexuality, the postmortem defamation of navy sailor Clayton Hartwig in the wake of an explosion aboard the uss *Iowa* provided a vivid example of the innuendo, shaming, and homophobia of military policy and practice. Both cases sent clear messages to those inside the military, as well as those in civilian life, that the U.S. military held lesbian and gay soldiers in the lowest regard and actively sought to separate them from the service.

On Parris Island, South Carolina—the swampy ground on which recruits of the United States Marine Corps receive basic training— "about 10 percent of the 120 women who were drill instructors" were "discharged or imprisoned for homosexual behavior" over the course of a 1988 investigation.[31] The investigation appeared to begin when Lance Corporal Diana Maldonado's ex-boyfriend claimed he found her in bed with Corporal Barbara Baum.[32] As consensual lesbian encounters are clearly a victimless crime, the Marine Corps used the threat of harsh prosecution to secure the women's cooperation as confidential informants and then used their testimony to ferret out other potential lesbians and discharge them from the marines. These also created ripe conditions for lesbian-baiting, blackmail, and sexual assault; as Tracey Cooper-Harris explained, "I was found out by some male 'friends' at my first duty assignment. . . . I let these men have their way with me in exchange for their silence."[33]

The Parris Island Scandal highlighted the double-bind military women faced in terms of their gender expression. As one female marine under investigation for lesbianism explained, "The qualities and traits that we demand and are supposed to be training our recruits are the same traits that they're saying make us look homosexual."[34] The strong association of soldiering with masculinity, coupled with the assumption that gender-nonconforming behavior signals non-conformity to heterosexuality, placed almost any woman in the military under suspicion. Furthermore, the scandal led to the revelation that in the 1980s the military discharged women under suspicion of homosexuality at ten times the rate at which men were discharged.[35] Later on, Pentagon data made clear that African American women, contending with intersectional oppression and the history of stereotypes about Black women's sexualities, were discharged at an even higher rate than the non-Black women they served with.[36] As James Woodward, cofounder of the nonprofit Gay, Lesbian, and Bisexual Veterans of America, said, "Very seldom does the military go after gay men in the kind of coordinated, full-out way that they go after women. . . . The Parris Island investigation has been the epitome of the old McCarthy witch-hunts."[37] Much as lesbian issues have been historically marginalized in gay movements and as women's health remained a marginal concern in mainstream AIDS activism, women suffered the impacts of antigay sentiment in relative obscurity while (mostly handsome and white) men remained the face of suffering.

Although being a woman increased a soldier's vulnerability to accusations of improper sexuality, being a man of course provided no defense. Following the April 1989 explosion of a gun turret aboard the USS *Iowa* that killed forty-seven men, naval investigators suggested to the public that Clayton Hartwig had committed sabotage after the dissolution of his relationship with fellow sailor Kendall Truitt.[38] Echoing the investigators, reporters described Hartwig—in a parade of stereotypes about overly emotional, damaged gay men who pine fruitlessly for the affections of straight men—as "a troubled man," "deeply despondent and excessively dependent on a few people," and driven to suicide after his "sexual advances had been rejected by other sailors."[39] Though navy investigators concluded the explosion was "probably an intentional act" and blamed Hartwig, soon everyone from the captain of the ship and sailors who survived the explosion to family members of sailors who died and members of Congress began to publicly express their doubts.[40] A second investigation commissioned by the Senate Armed Services Committee confirmed that incompetence or an accident could have caused the explosion and that the evidence in no way indicated sabotage. However, the damage had been done. Mere innuendo about improper sexuality was enough to render Hartwig unfit for service and a chilling message had been sent to soldiers about what might happen were they even suspected of homosexuality.

These scandals, along with the October 1992 homophobic murder of naval officer Allen Schindler by enlisted sailors and the public advocacy of openly gay service members like Joseph Steffan, Dusty Pruitt, Keith Meinhold, and Marguerite Cammermeyer, forced debates over gay and lesbian service in the military to the center of the 1992 U.S. presidential elections. As Jeffrey Schmalz wrote in his lengthy piece "Gay Politics Goes Mainstream," published a month before the election: "For the first time in a race for the White House . . . gay and lesbian issues are being raised—and fought over."[41] At the family values–centric Republican National Convention, in what was later dubbed the "culture war speech," Pat Buchanan called July's Democratic National Convention the "greatest single exhibition of cross-dressing in American political history," fumed about "homosexual rights," and railed "against the amoral idea that gay and lesbian couples should have the same standing in law as married men and women."[42] Elsewhere, Urvashi Vaid, director of the National Gay and Lesbian Task Force, called the Bush-Quayle campaign "the most explicitly anti-gay campaign we've ever seen."[43]

The distinctions between the candidates' positions on lesbian and gay rights served to elide their profound similarities on other issues, particularly investment in the military-industrial complex. During the campaign, President Bush proposed spending $1.42 trillion on the military during his next term, while his Democratic rival Bill Clinton advocated for $1.36 trillion in spending.[44] Here, we can see that loud debates over sexuality served as convenient camouflage for the topic of militarism to pass without debate and cleaved cultural politics from material politics, a split that Lisa Duggan has called a "ruse" to "obscure redistributive aims" and "hide . . . investments in identity-based hierarchies."[45] That is to say, the militarization of homosexuality divided lesbian and gay movements from a broader critique of dominant power, allowing for an argument about equality around sexuality to disguise the regressive class and race politics of gay assimilation. The process allowed for the integration of certain gay, lesbian, and bisexual constituencies into an exploitative system that points to its integration of sexual minorities as evidence of how it is not exploitative.

Upon Clinton's victory, reports emerged of people flooding onto the street "in gay enclaves like San Francisco and West Hollywood, weeping, dancing and hugging to celebrate the victory."[46] The next week, on Veterans Day, Clinton announced his intention to rescind the military's ban on gay and lesbian service members, but in the wake of opposition from the Joints Chief of Staff, he hedged his promise of rapid action and appealed to gay and lesbian constituents for patience as he consulted military and political officials.[47] Thus began a year of studies, debates, legal challenges, and compromises that would ultimately result in Don't Ask, Don't Tell.

UNDERSTANDING DON'T ASK, DON'T TELL

In January 1993 congressional disapproval for Clinton's plan to rescind the gay ban "broke into open revolt," and Clinton backed away from his fabled executive order overturning the ban, instead asking the military to pause ongoing discharges under the gay ban and to temporarily not ask new recruits about their sexuality.[48] This six-month interim policy, ostensibly to be ended with a repeal of the ban, closely resembled the eventual permanent policy adopted in July after contentious hearings in Congress and closed-door deliberations of a panel of Pentagon-appointed officers and enlisted personnel. Ordered to find an alternative to the gay ban, the panel presented two options, neither of which actually sought to end discrimination. The first option, favored by Clinton, would permit "declared homosexuals" to serve but continue to criminalize "homosexual conduct." Another option would ban "declared homosexuals" for their identity regardless of their practice of or abstinence from "homosexual conduct"; Senate Armed Services Committee chair Sam Nunn called it "Don't Ask, Don't Tell."[49]

The notoriously antigay Nunn proffered the phrase "don't ask, don't tell" as a simple shorthand for a complex policy developed by military sociologist and intellectual homophobia apologist Charles Moskos, but it would go on to have a life of its own.[50] Within a decade, "don't ask, don't tell" had become an endlessly adaptable cultural reference, appearing in the *New York Times* as a metaphor for the underground organ transplant market, the (hetero)sexual behavior of President Clinton, the finances of a New Jersey candidate for Senate, and even the question of whether light is a particle or wave, just to name a few.[51] Before becoming a flexible meme, by the end of July 1993, this idea had become the official policy of the U.S. military: technically, "don't ask, don't tell, don't pursue, don't harass," but much more commonly known as Don't Ask, Don't Tell.

Section 654 of Title X of the United States Code, in effect from December 1993 until September 2011, elucidated the "policy concerning homosexuality in the armed forces." The policy was based on the finding that "the presence in the armed forces of persons who demonstrate a propensity or intent to engage in homosexual acts would create an unacceptable risk to the high standards of moral, good order and discipline, and unit cohesion that are the essence of military capability."[52] Consequently, it required that an individual would be "separated from the armed forces" if she or he met any of three criteria: having "engaged in, attempted to engage in, or solicited another to engage in a homosexual act"; having "stated that he or she is a homosexual or bisexual"; or having "attempted to marry a person known to be of the same biological sex."[53]

Working from these criteria, Don't Ask, Don't Tell actually represented a significant expansion of the military's ability to separate people from service, given that it added particular speech acts and the pursuit of same-sex marriage to the list of procedural justifications. Whereas one once had to violate the Uniform Code of Military Justice by committing a particular sex act in order to be discharged as homosexual, post-1993 policy lowered the bar to include past statements, present status, and future intent. Just as heterosexual scientists had moved from the surface of the body to interior physiology to psychology to microscopic abstractions of brain waves and DNA in search of the proof of homosexuality, the military attempted to fix a contingent social identity to verifiable universals. While the policy provided exacting detail in some areas, the "don't pursue" element was lost in the process, and it ultimately provided no regulations for how officials would go about investigations and discharges, regulating only the sexual behavior and "propensities" of personnel and giving leaders wide latitude to search for gay, lesbian, and bisexual service members as they saw fit.

Four important effects of Don't Ask, Don't Tell include the militarization of civil rights, the conflation of sex acts with sexual identity, the reification of a particular conception of "the closet," and the foreshadowing of the then incipient movement for same-sex marriage equality. A legal category, such as civil rights, is militarized when it prioritizes the needs and goals of the military over the consistency and impartiality professed by the Constitution, civil rights law, and executive orders on nondiscrimination.[54] In allowing the argument that "military life is fundamentally different from civilian life in that . . . [it] is characterized by its own laws, rules, customs, and traditions" to override the civil rights of lesbian and gay citizens, the U.S. government abdicated the power over the military delegated to it by the Constitution and accepted the militarized assumption that the military should be a sovereign fiefdom run by officers rather than one arm of a democratic state. This assumption transformed discussions about sexuality by shifting conversations about the relationships between public and private spheres so central to liberal thought into a different context dominated by the supreme needs of the military itself, rather than the rule of law.[55] While the policy is correct in stating that "the primary purpose of the armed forces is to prepare for and to prevail in combat should the need arise," militarism (tinged with homophobia) provides the only rationale for this purpose to take primacy over the imperatives of a supposedly nondiscriminating government.

Understanding how Don't Ask, Don't Tell both distinguished and blurred distinctions between homosexual identity, homosexual acts, and the propensity or intent to perform them illuminates a central confusion of the dominant epistemology about sexuality in the 1990s United States. What constitutes a propensity to commit to certain sexual act? How much advanced planning or proximity to the act is required to demonstrate intent? Sexuality is best understood as the complex mediation between one's erotic desires, practices, and identities, or what one wants, what one does, and the collectivities in which these things occur. Desires, practices, and identities are interrelated but distinct and do not always line up in neat or conventional ways. In this policy, identity is defined as committing a certain act, tautologically defined as constitutive of that identity. That is, one is lesbian or gay because one takes a particular action that is defined as lesbian or gay because it is an action undertaken by lesbians and gay men. This circularity precludes the necessity of defining a heterosexual person or act (even though such a definition is actually necessary to precisely define who the policy considers to be bisexual) because heterosexuals are heterosexual by virtue of doing heterosexuality. Although Clinton had vowed to make policy that regulated "conduct, not status," Don't Ask, Don't Tell made either act (conduct) or identity (status) sufficient for dismissal while simultaneously reducing the complex social realities of lesbian and gay identities solely to sex acts.

The only people formerly barred from military service allowed to serve under Don't Ask, Don't Tell were those individuals who personally acknowledged their homosexuality but actively sought to hide it. As Senator John Warner put it to Marguerite Cammermeyer, "Give up the right to actively profess your sexuality among your fellow soldiers. . . . Then we'll let you serve quietly and patriotically in every other way."[56] The idea that one can separate one's private sexual identity from one's participation in the public sphere animates militarized homosexuality, which argues that nonnormative sexualities should be practiced independent of the politics emerging out of them, but is an anathema to militant queerness, which sees any attempt to unqueer the public as a profound violation. Mobilizing gay, lesbian, and bisexual people for war simultaneously worked to demobilize emergent LGBTQ movements that refused to go quietly into reproducing either the white, middle-class nuclear family or the white, middle-class-dominated nation-state. As Warner indicated, the only recruits welcomed into this mobilization were those who were willing to quietly keep their sexuality in the closet.

The closet and coming out as metaphors for LGBT experience have a long history tied to the tradition of young community members "coming out" à la the tradition of cotillions and the 1987 March on Washington's call to "Come Out, Come Out, Wherever You Are" that spawned National Coming Out Day. These metaphors took on new meanings in the early nineties as scholars like Eve Sedgwick critiqued the "epistemology of the closet," an unstable framework in which gay identity is both minoritized and universalized, and as activists like Michelangelo Signorile outed closeted supporters of homophobic policies like Undersecretary for Defense Peter Williams in the pages of *OutWeek*.[57] While Sedgwick demonstrated the dissonance of a culture in which same-sex bonds are both revered and feared through nineteenth-century literature, Signorile used contemporary celebrities and newsmakers from Malcolm Forbes to Jodie Foster in order to demonstrate the impossibility of fully sorting the sexual into the private and the political into the public. Like "don't ask, don't tell," in the early nineties "the closet" became a flexible meme referring to a range of revelations about the self from HIV and alcoholism to religious and political beliefs.[58] The popular dichotomy of confinement (the closet) and hypervisibility (coming out or being outed) also had particular consequences for African Americans, leading to the erasure of certain Black queer identities and the pathologizing of others, according to C. Riley Snorton.[59] Don't Ask, Don't Tell raised the stakes of the closet by demarcating it as a safe space in which gay and lesbian soldiers could hide while acknowledging that the military could fling open the closet doors at any moment and invalidate the security that some sought in there.

Finally, in addition to regulating erotic desires and behavior, Don't Ask, Don't Tell represented a preemptive stance by the U.S. military against a then almost inconsequential but soon sometimes successful movement for same-sex marriage equality. Don't Ask, Don't Tell changed military policy, singling out successful or attempted same-sex marriage as grounds for discharge only months after the Supreme Court of Hawai'i ruled in May of 1993 that marriage is a civil right and that bans on same-sex marriage may constitute discrimination on the basis of sex.[60] The mere possibility that the ultimately unsuccessful legal challenge to Hawai'i's policy of recognizing only mixed-sex marriage, *Baehr v. Miike*, would plant a sprouting seed of same-sex marriages in the United States led to national backlash culminating in the 1996 Defense of Marriage Act (DOMA). Far from resolving the struggle, DOMA, which defined marriage as only "one man and one woman as husband and wife," set off a series of struggles at the state level that increasingly turned in favor of treating same-sex marriage as indistinguishable from the mixed-sex variant after 2004 and culminated in 2015's *Obergefell v. Hodges*.[61] Same-sex marriage also produced a political split in the contemporary moment that is reminiscent of the divide between militant queers and militarized homosexuality, with one side calling for LGBTQ movements to reject straight institutions and the other calling for straight institutions to accept LGB people, reflecting some of the broader consequences of the conflict over military service.

The issues of military service and marriage, assimilationist goals of an agenda set more by wealthy donors and heterosexuals in public office than by the grassroots of LGBTQ communities, came to define the most visible formations of lesbian and gay politics after 1993. A militarized, mostly white, mostly male, mostly upwardly mobile member of the community would be the front face of a conciliatory gay and lesbian civil rights movement focused on equal participation in the system rather than liberation from it. Militant queers were put in an unenviable position: enervated from decades of struggle, numbers depleted by HIV/AIDS, and split between the winnable goal of achieving formal equality around sexual orientation and the more ambitious goal of dismantling the structures that produce intersecting inequalities. Many militant queers were forced into harm reduction mode by the changing circumstances, reserving their critiques of organizations that emerged in the wake of Don't Ask, Don't Tell like the Servicemembers Legal Defense Network because, in spite of their militarized politics, thousands of queer service members desperately needed their support. Others refocused their energy on addressing horizontal oppression within the community as well as struggles against medicalized violence in an array of emerging groups, including Transgender Nation (1992), Intersex Society of North America (1993), Audre Lorde Project (1994), and Gender PAC (1995). The tradition of militant queerness never disappeared, though militarized homosexuality came to overshadow it during Don't Ask, Don't Tell's lifetime. Perhaps it is ripe for resurgence in the wake of the policy's demise.

AFTERMATH OF THE REPEAL

On September 20, 2011, the Don't Ask, Don't Tell policy ended, and soldiers like Josh Seefried, the founder of an organization for LGBT soldiers called OutServe, expressed relief that they could finally "be part of the military family."[62] From a post–Don't Ask, Don't Tell vantage point, the policy appears like a finger stuck in a cracked dam to hold back a flood. For all the intransigence of military and government officials, the tide of movements for lesbian and gay civil rights only rose higher during and following the nineties, drowning the gay ban, however slowly. While the 1996 passage of the federal same-sex marriage ban was a significant win for antigay forces, their victories became smaller and increasingly rare. Widespread attention and disgust at the violent murders of college student Matthew Shepard in Wyoming in 1998 and Barry Winchell, a soldier targeted by his fellow soldiers in 1999 after his girlfriend was outed as a transwoman, had significant impact on public opinion about both bias-motivated violence against LGBTQ people and their right to serve openly in the military.[63] In August of 1999, the Pentagon "decided to issue broad new guidelines intended to end abuses of the 'don't ask, don't tell' policy . . . including limits on investigations [and] anti-gay-harassment training."[64] Four months later President Clinton, reflecting on Winchell's death, said of the policy, "It's out of whack, and I don't think any serious person could say it's not."[65] Clinton, as in 1993, failed to live up to these words, however, and left the policy intact as he passed the office of president on to eight years of explicitly antigay leadership by George W. Bush.

Despite Bush's advocacy against LGBTQ communities, discharges under Don't Ask, Don't Tell dropped once the War on Terror began, peaking in both total discharges and discharges as a percent of active duty forces in 2001.[66] SLDN and other advocacy organizations stepped up their efforts to repeal the policy once Barack Obama took office in 2009. The documentary *The Strange History of Don't Ask, Don't Tell* follows their successful lobbying effort and crystalizes some of the assumptions of militarized homosexuality with statements like, "The emergence of gay identities in cities is directly attributable to our military" and, "The story of 'Don't Ask, Don't Tell' is the story of gay rights in this country."[67] Alternate histories of the community, queer antimilitarism, and opposition to state violence disappear in their moment of triumph. Despite the major victory, veterans like Tracey

Cooper-Harris found the military to be a continued adversary after the repeal when in 2013 she was forced to sue the Department of Veteran's Affairs for her and her partner Maggie's disability benefits.[68]

While the U.S. military is yet to be described as a particularly gay-friendly workplace, service by openly lesbian, gay, and bisexual soldiers is not only allowed but is also perhaps more importantly touted both as a measure of the progressive attitudes toward sexuality espoused by the military *and* as representative of broader shifts toward these progressive attitudes in the United States itself. In this formation, where the military becomes a mimesis of the broader U.S. nation-state, the militarization of homosexuality is evident in the way that the supposedly independent military structure comes to be understood not only as part of but wholly representative of U.S. national culture. This imagined evidence of the violence of the U.S. state as more enlightened or progressive through the inclusion of diverse service members remains crucial to the perpetuation of U.S. military engagements abroad during the War on Terror.

Openly transgender people remained barred from service due to the discriminatory application of medical policies after Don't Ask, Don't Tell's repeal, but transgender veterans and advocates led by transgender billionaire and veteran Jennifer Pritzker almost immediately began to push for reform.[69] At the same time, prominent transgender leaders such as Dean Spade, Mattilda Bernstein Sycamore, and the organization Against Equality all engaged in campaigns to advocate for transgender people, including service members and veterans, from a militant, antimilitarist position without contributing to the legitimacy of this historically exclusionary institution.[70] While the military technically rescinded its ban on transgender soldiers in the summer of 2016, by the summer of 2017 the chief executive announced his intention to reinstate the ban.[71] Once again, crucial conversations occurring within a segment of the queer community have been disrupted, distorted, and unevenly amplified by cisgender and heterosexual policies, voices, and material support.

It is much easier to write critically of the drive to repeal policies preventing LGB people from being open about their sexual identities when serving in the military in 2018 than it would have been ten years ago. The stakes are also lower for those of us who have not historically been excluded from the military due to gender, race, or (dis)ability. For queer people within the military and without, however, the stakes could not be higher. The road to a world without heterosexism and cisgenderism does not have to go through the U.S. military, and the decision to take that path has consequences inside and outside the United States. Understanding how this conflict within the LGBT community played out in the early 1990s provides crucial perspective for understanding how it functions today while also elucidating the deep connection between histories of militarism and sexuality in the United States. Leonard Matlovich can rest knowing that he would no longer face a discharge for loving another man, but we are no closer to getting justice for the two men he killed.

For Tracey Cooper-Harris, lesbianism would no longer expose her to the same institutional vulnerabilities she once experienced, but the military has rarely been successful at addressing the intersecting oppressions of race and gender that conditioned her experiences of homophobia. While one could make a case for claiming significant progress in rights around sexual orientation during the post–Cold War era, relatively little has been done to deviate from the long-established path of exploiting and devaluing the sexualities of women of color. In the following chapter, I foreground questions of reproductive sexuality to demonstrate how the transition out of the Cold War failed to ease the impacts of militarism on indigenous women at the edge of U.S. empire.

4

A Close and Mutually Beneficial Relationship

THE UNITED STATES, MARSHALL ISLANDS, AND MILITARIZATION OF REPRODUCTION

Darlene Keju, a woman from the island of Ebeye in what is now the Republic of the Marshall Islands (RMI), described the effects of militarization on human reproduction in her community to a Vancouver audience in 1983: "Since then we have had endless health problems. For example, we have hundreds of women who have miscarriages, we have leukemia cancers, we have thyroid cancers, we have stillbirth babies. . . . We have babies we call jellyfish babies. . . . It's a colorful, ugly thing that's not shaped like a human being."[1]

The "then" to which she refers is a series of nuclear tests conducted between 1946 and 1962 by the U.S. government at the Pacific Proving Grounds, slightly north of the equator and west of the international date line in the Pacific Ocean. This area, while often depicted as a sort of terra nullius in the U.S. national imaginary, has been home for thousands of years to indigenous nations known collectively by outsiders as Micronesians.[2] U.S. Cold War strategy built upon a long history of Euro-Americans sexually exploiting indigenous people of the Pacific when federal weapons testing programs received priority over the reproductive capabilities of many Ri Majol (indigenous Marshallese) people and of their nation as a whole. This chapter addresses the *militarization of reproduction* in the post–Cold War United States through an analysis of Marshallese-U.S. relations and the impacts of nuclear testing. I focus particularly on the two decades since both governments agreed in 1983 on the Compact of Free Association (COFA), which led to an independence process culminating in UN membership in 1991 and was subsequently renewed in 2003.

The militarization of reproduction is my term for the process through which the needs and desires of the military dictate when, how, and how often humans express their capability to reproduce. Reproduction became increasingly militarized in the Marshall Islands as the ability of Ri Majol people to create new generations and ensure their health has been subordinated to the U.S. military's ability to produce effective weapons of mass destruction. Reproduction can be and is militarized in many other ways, from military policies about service members' childbearing choices to policies of cross-ethnic forced impregnation carried out during wartime, whenever the desires of military leadership take priority over how and when people elect to (or not to) reproduce.[3] The connections between nuclear weapons and human reproduction have been made elsewhere, but many of these accounts have marginalized the experiences of Marshallese people.[4] In this chapter, I focus on the harm done to Ri Majol reproductive capabilities by the U.S. military to demonstrate both the importance of foregrounding sexuality in analyzing militarism during the post–Cold War period and the way in which Cold War paradigms of transnational engagement persisted in the 1990s in spite of its declared end.

My approach draws primarily upon three paradigms: reproductive justice, indigenous feminisms of Turtle Island, and indigenous Pacific voices, particularly those of the Marshallese. Reproductive justice revises the highly individualistic model of reproductive freedom or choice into a community-centered concept prioritizing access and equity while centering the needs and perspectives of women of color.[5] Indigenous feminisms recenter the struggle for gender equality around the struggle for Native sovereignty and are crucial for understanding how contemporary efforts by the United States to relocate Ri Majol people relate to a long history of sexual violence against indigenous people.[6] Lastly but most importantly, as a non-Marshallese person and more specifically as a white U.S. citizen, I foreground the testimonies and statements of Ri Majol people in this chapter because their analyses of these circumstances are the most significant and valid way to apprehend both the enormity of these problems and possibilities for solutions.

I begin with a brief sketch of the history of the United States' engagement in the Pacific leading up to the establishment of U.S. control in the Marshall Islands through the Trust Territory of the Pacific relationship, followed by an overview of the United States' nuclear test program and attempts at mediating some of its impacts on Marshallese people. Second, I detail some of the long-term reproductive impacts of this program that are still playing out across the generations in the Marshall Islands. Next, I use these histories to frame my reading of the COFA that establishes the post–Cold War relationship between the United States and the Republic of the Marshall Islands with a focus on how it enacts reproductive violence through policies that resemble past attempts at Indian relocation. Finally, I highlight the survivance demonstrated by Ri Majol people, who have become savvy actors on a global stage and remain committed to their people, land, and water despite persistent attempts to place U.S. military needs over their lives and futures.[7]

The Compact of Free Association speaks of a "close and mutually beneficial relationship" between the United States and the Marshall Islands, but critical analysis of the history of this relationship reveals a great deal of dysfunction and abuse.[8] The COFA sought not only to usher Marshallese-U.S. relations out of a Cold War paradigm but also to effect a break with a recent history of imperial dominance through textual declaration. During the 1990s, the impacts of past malfeasance and incompetence on the part of those conducting the U.S. nuclear testing program became increasingly apparent; at the same time, the changing terms of this relationship attempted to seal away both the physical debris and financial liabilities related to these militarized activities. This chapter demonstrates the continuity of these impacts across eras through a focus on sexuality and refuses the closure of accounting for this harm until, in the estimation of the Ri Majol people, both their environment and their bodies are healed.

Stretching across millions of square miles of the Pacific Ocean between the Philippines and Hawai'i, Micronesia consists of a series of archipelagoes and atolls including Palau, the Marianas (including Guam), the four island groups that make up the Federated States of Micronesia, the sixteen island groups that compose Kiribati, and the twenty-four inhabited atolls collectively known as the Marshall Islands. The indigenous inhabitants of these islands developed dynamic cultures in harmony with their limited landmasses and seemingly unlimited stretches of sea. Despite distance, these societies were rarely isolated and regularly interacted across vast stretches of water for millennia. In a sense, these Micronesian islands' path to the heart of U.S. geostrategy began with the arrival of Spanish explorers in the sixteenth century but only took shape in the early nineteenth century as the then nascent United States began to tentatively search for a Pacific empire.

U.S.-based literary scholar Paul Lyons coined the term *American pacificism* to describe "the double logic that the islands are imagined at once as placed to be civilized and as escapes from civilization," a sort of U.S.-centric Orientalism about the people of the Pacific.[9] Simultaneously imagining the Marshallese as in need of the civilizing influence of the U.S.-trustee relationship and their islands as an empty testing ground for radioactive bombs required an ideological structure that could resolve such contradictions. Lyons locates the origins of this structure that "at once naturalizes and neutralizes knowledge of the effects of U.S. trajectories into Oceania" in the official and literary texts authored by early North American travelers in Polynesia, Melanesia, and Micronesia. These often commercial operations, first whalers in the early 1800s and then those seeking sandalwood, bêche-de-mer, and sugar in the 1860s, laid crucial groundwork alongside Christian missionaries for the U.S. takeover of both Hawai'i and the eastern portion of Samoa in the 1890s.[10] These seizures of territory occurred in tandem with further expansion of U.S. power in the Pacific through the transfer of Guam and the Philippines (along with Puerto Rico and Cuba) from Spain to the United States through the 1899 Treaty of Paris.

For the purposes of my study, it is necessary to understand the specifically sexual nature of U.S. encounters in the Pacific and how these violent nineteenth-century encounters resonate in later exoticisms. As Lyons writes, "Encounter in Oceania is always at some level potentially a sexual event."[11] In addition to seeking safe harbors, extractable natural resources, and control over territory, early Euro-American visitors to the Pacific also sought access to indigenous women's bodies. Within a decade of the first European arrival, Hawaiian women were being trafficked by foreign seafarers, and the Kingdom of Hawai'i made diplomatic overtures and enacted laws in response to the kidnapping of Kanaka Maoli women by the 1820s.[12] In the 1850s Ri Majol warriors overcame sailing crews and then burned multiple ships that had been kidnapping Marshallese women as part of the "blackbirding" practice of Euro-American slavers in the Pacific.[13] Still, islands in the Pacific remained sites for Euro-Americans to project their sexualized fantasies, from the South Seas adventure novels of Herman Melville to the Impressionistic paintings of Tahitian women by Paul Gauguin, and from the anthropological studies conducted by Margaret Mead to Louis Réard's new two-piece swimsuit, the bikini, unveiled only four days after the first U.S. nuclear test on Bikini Atoll in 1946.[14]

As Teresia Teaiwa explains, "The bikini-clad woman is exotic and malleable to the same colonial gaze that coded Bikini Atoll and its Islanders as exotic, malleable, and most of all, dispensable."[15] Imagining Micronesians as sexually available by nature quickly slid into both the sexual exploitation of their bodies and a devaluation of the residents as having neither sovereignty over the land and water nor sovereignty over themselves. It remains important to recognize how this narrative recapitulates multiple histories of colonial encounter where sexual availability becomes linked to political conquest and at the same time bears a Ri Majol specificity in the particular impacts of nuclear fallout and climate change that threaten their very existence. Teaiwa, an I-Kiribati and Black Micronesian American who identified several links between sexuality and militarism in her groundbreaking 1992 presentation "Bikinis and Other S/Pacific N/Oceans," coined the term *s/pacific body* to recognize the dual possibilities of understanding the bodies of Pacific Islanders as "a site for comprehending specific social and physical environments and for apprehending generic colonial technologies of marginalization and erasure."[16] While the Marshallese spent three centuries after first contact figured as genericized Pacific Islander bodies on the most distant edge of the European imagination, their futures became more closely tied to specific foreign empires as the nineteenth century progressed.

At the dawn of the twentieth century, excepting the significant U.S. naval presence on Guam, most of Micronesia was administered as part of the German empire's New Guinea colony. After only about twenty years of occupation, these colonies were taken over at the end of World War I by the Japanese empire under a League of Nations mandate. Japan took a more active stance toward its South Pacific Mandate, transporting thousands of settlers to the islands and instituting public education in Japanese while also fortifying many islands as the likelihood of confrontation with other imperial powers in the Pacific grew. Soon, Micronesia implanted even deeper in the cultural memory of the United States through a series of battles beginning on Wake Island in 1941 and continuing through the U.S. "stepping stones" campaign across Tarawa, Makin, Kwajalein, Enewetak, Saipan, Guam, Tinian, and Palau, on their way to reconquer the Philippines.[17] The islands became scattered with the graves of U.S. and Japanese servicemen as well as the ecological devastation of war, and ideas about the islands spread across North America through letters, the memories of returning service members, and the construction of memorials to the Pacific War.

With the end of World War II, the United States sought to consolidate its control over Micronesia through the United Nations' creation of the Trust Territory of the Pacific Islands in 1947. UN Security Council Resolution 21 gave the United States "full powers of administration, legislation, and jurisdiction" over the former Japanese South Pacific Mandate with the expectation that it "promote the development of the inhabitants[,] . . . protect the inhabitants against loss of their lands and resources[,] . . . protect the health of the inhabitants," and guarantee "freedom of migration and movement."[18] An entire year before the formal legitimation of paternalistic U.S. rule over this area, however, the U.S. military had already undermined the long-term development, ecology, public health, and freedom of movement for Ri Majol people by dropping two atomic bombs on Bikini Atoll in 1946. As Bikinian Kilon Bauno explained to the documentarians making the 1988 film *Radio Bikini*: "An American came to Bikini. . . . He said America wanted to use Bikini and that we would have to leave. . . . As we left, a great sadness came over us. . . . There is nothing in my life I want more than to go home to Bikini. The reason I can't go back is because the Americans tell me there is 'poison' there."[19] One also cannot ignore this project's related impacts on long-term development, ecology, public health, and freedom of movement for the Yakima Nation and other Columbia River tribes, on whose territory plutonium was produced at the Hanford Reactor, and the Mescalero Apaches, on whose land the first nuclear test took place.[20]

Over the next twelve years, the United States conducted twenty-one more nuclear tests at Bikini and forty-three on the atoll of Enewetak, displacing the populations of both. The fallout from one of these tests, March 1954's Castle Bravo, known locally as the Day of Two Suns, spread from Bikini to the atolls of Rongelap and Utirik, prompting evacuations that have kept people off their home islands for decades.[21] These dislocations have been further compounded by a lack of support for the relocated, contradictory scientific evidence leading to aborted resettlements, minimal efforts at environmental remediation, and the continuing presence of the U.S. military that tested chemical weapons in Enewetak during the 1970s and continues to test missiles at Kwajalein Atoll to this day.[22] The overall effect is that of a militarization of reproduction, in that both the ability to bear children and to rear the next generation have been devastated by military activities, but accountability remains subordinate to what the military declares necessary.

"WE NEVER EXPERIENCED THESE TYPES OF BIRTHS BEFORE"

During the 1980s, the negative repercussions of nuclear testing on future generations had become clear to many residents of the Marshall Islands, despite the denials of U.S. officials. As RMI Foreign Minister Tony deBrum claimed, U.S. government agencies had "shown great reluctance to assist us in identifying and treating the medical problems present in the exposed atolls."[23] Other statements from the Marshallese pointed to the health of future generations as their highest priority, highlighted the emerging threats through which nuclear testing had imperiled these future generations, and made the world aware of the precarity their people endured. At the same time as they used their voices, Ri Majol people also acted: disrupting U.S. missile tests with "sail-ins" and, with help from the environmental organization Greenpeace but no support from the U.S. government, fleeing the contaminated atoll of Rongelap in 1985.[24]

Leaders from Rongelap spoke in front of the U.S. Senate in 1991, reading a statement collectively written by local residents that indicated both threats to reproduction and the high value the Marshallese placed on generations to come. Of the evacuation of their home island, they wrote, "Our people knew that it might mean they and their children would never again know life on their ancestral homeland of the last 4,000 years. But the safety of our children and the unborn was more important; so we moved. . . . We were only trying to protect our children—and nothing more."[25] Senator Jeton Anjain went on to say, "The people of Rongelap decided to move from their homeland for the sake of their children. . . . The life of their children they think will be shortened by staying longer in a contaminated environment."[26] The fears of the Marshallese, however vociferously denied by representatives from the United States, could find support in scientific studies emerging in the United States at the time that described reproductive issues caused by radiation including delayed pubescence, altered hormonal levels, higher rates of sterility, uterine changes that complicate pregnancy, and variations in the ability to lactate.[27] For the Marshallese, the most common long-term side effects of radiation were thyroid tumors, but many women experienced symptoms ranging from hormone imbalances and sterility to miscarriages and birth defects that amounted to reproductive violence.[28]

Reproductive violence, by which I mean the manifold ways in which reproductive potential can be altered without consent, has a particularly devastating effect on indigenous people because they contend with the reduction of both population and genetic diversity through colonialism. While that quote attributed to Henry Kissinger—"There are only 90,000 people out there. Who gives a damn?"—was intended to minimize the value of the Micronesians to the world, it actually highlights how crucial it is to ensure them reproductive justice.[29] Indigenous people maintain cultural and genetic legacies that ongoing settler colonial perspectives both ideologically devalue and materially harm. Even a relatively small reduction in the fertility of members of an indigenous nation can threaten the future of the group overall, as happened to some Native nations from Turtle Island due to Bureau of Indian Affairs–sponsored forced sterilization programs.[30] As a sovereign nation, Ri Majol people should largely control their own future, but when their ability to reproduce is harmed in favor of protecting the U.S. military from culpability, reproduction is militarized.

The militarization of reproduction is most disturbingly illustrated by the phenomenon of "jellyfish babies," mentioned in the opening quote. U.S. government studies documented the disproportionately high rates of radioactive materials in the bodies of young Marshallese women in the 1980s, which placed them at risk for bearing these short-lived offspring and encouraged many of them to speak out in public forums.[31] Lemeyo Abon from Rongelap elaborated on this phenomenon to a UN Panel in 2012:

> To this day women in the Marshall Islands give birth to jellyfish babies, or babies born with no bones in their bodies and translucent skin. . . . We never experienced these types of births before the U.S. testing program. We have complained about these births for decades and we are always told by the U.S. Government that they are not the result of radiation exposure. Yet, our language, our history, our stories have no record of these births before the testing program. After the testing program we've had to create new words to describe the creatures we give birth to.[32]

The testing program alienated Ri Majol women from their special role as transmitters of a matrilineal culture, from the products of their reproductive labor that Abon can only refer to as "creatures," and from their own bodies, which became repositories for reproductive stigma as the United States continued to refuse to accept culpability.

As Marshallese poet Kathy Jetñil-Kijiner writes in her poem "History Project," in the voice of a woman hiding miscarriages from her husband, "I thought / there must be something wrong / inside me."[33]

Because of the long-term effects of radiation on reproduction and the propagation of genetic material, these impacts have no clear expiration date. As James Yamazaki, a Japanese American physician who began working with survivors of nuclear blasts in the 1940s, wrote in the 1990s, "Research was demonstrating how vulnerable the human fetus and children are to radiation," and "no one can say how much longer it might take for defects to show up in succeeding generations."[34] Thus Ri Majol women must not only contend with the realities of fallout-induced birth defects but also the anxiety that consequently stalks every reproductive decision. Just as militarization is a process that extends the effects of the military outward beyond enlisted ranks, the U.S. nuclear test program reverberates through every aspect of Marshallese life long after the 1963 Partial Nuclear Test Ban Treaty ended the nuclear program in the Pacific (which continued in the U.S. Southwest until 1992; France continued to test nuclear weapons in Polynesia until 1996).

The consequences of reproductive violence to Ri Majol women had become clear to outside observers by the end of the 1990s. Robert Barclay, a white U.S. citizen who grew up in the U.S. military reservation on Kwajalein Atoll, authored *Melal: A Novel of the Pacific*, a story about Kwajalein that takes place on Good Friday 1981. The novel focuses primarily on a Marshallese man and his two sons and also includes some decidedly masculine characters from Ri Majol lore and a trio of boys from the United States, to the almost complete exclusion of women speaking or acting. The only significant female character is Iia, a wife and mother who has several miscarriages before, between, and after the births of her two sons, the last one fatal. Barclay explains: "She was one of the lucky ones, she said, never suffering from the thyroid cancers that eventually grew in most of the other children exposed that day, but then she always had that trouble having babies, and sometimes . . . she had jellyfish babies, what some Marshallese women called monster babies because they looked inside-out, and finally it killed her."[35]

Quantitative data on health outcomes in the Marshall Islands is limited due to the U.S. government's historical control over the flow of information coming from the islands, the modest resources of the RMI government, the low rate of professionalized care on the outer islands, and the reluctance of some Ri Majol people to discuss reproductive health issues or traumas with medical professionals. The United Nations places the Marshall Islands' contemporary maternal mortality ratio as 140 deaths per 100,000 live births: lower than Papua New Guinea but otherwise higher than all other Pacific Island nations and ten times that of the United States.[36] A private study by the Institute for Health Metrics found that in 1990 preterm birth complications were the second greatest cause of years of life lost in the Marshall Islands. While this has improved somewhat over the past twenty years (to the fifth greatest cause), those gains have been more than offset by dramatic increases in diabetes and heart disease that have impacted middle-aged women especially hard.[37]

Damage from testing, remaining nuclear fallout, and the hyper-concentration of the Marshallese population has also led to profound alienation from the environment, which compounds these negative impacts on reproduction. As Abacca Anjain-Maddison explained to the same UN panel to which Abon spoke, "Women and newborn infants after birth undergo herbal baths that require the drinking of concentrated herbs for at least three months. Older women will pound and touch the contaminated leaves and fetch wood for fire to prepare the herbs. The best foods are always local foods that will be given to mothers in order to produce breast milk. Not to mention, every birthday, funeral, church activity requires people to gather and celebrate the Marshallese way, using many local resources."[38]

The use of local flora and fauna, which not only promotes good health in general but also plays a crucial role in cultural practices around reproduction, is especially fraught for Ri Majol people because, decades after the end of the testing program, ingesting locally grown plants or animals that feed on them remains the primary source of radiation contamination.[39] Coconuts and the coconut crabs that feed off of them were a major source of nutrition for islanders for millennia before the testing program, especially when they lacked access to reliable fishing vessels, as they often do now. Traditional foods like coconuts represent a material link to the past deeds of the both indigenous and imperial residents, allowing the Ri Majol people to enact the practices of their ancestors while at the same time poisoning them with radiation that threatens their descendants. This is a particularly pernicious aspect of how reproduction can be militarized in that ties to ancestry, rather than descent, are damaged.

A group of Marshallese children wrote in their collective text *Life in the Marshall Islands: Then and Now*, "We are very fortunate because we have coconuts in our homeland. . . . To this day, the coconut is still very important to us."[40] Contrast that with Teresia Teaiwa's poetic response to the high level of radiation in coconuts, in which she wrote, "An apple a day / Keeps the doctor away / But a coconut a day / Will kill you." Western medicine and products shipped from outside the islands retain the authority of early nuclear scientists to aid, reshape, or deeply harm Ri Majol life. Doctors have recommended to many Marshallese that they subsist off of a primarily imported diet, which encourages some of the previously mentioned health issues and increases food insecurity.[41] Even when Ri Majol people are able to reproduce in their desired fashion, their ability to transmit and reproduce their culture has been damaged by militarized institutions that remain unaccountable.

The militarization of reproduction, like all forms of militarization, is a step-by-step process that does not arise out of a single moment of hubris or desperation. The Marshallese experienced centuries of vulnerability to sexualized exploitation that provoked little outcry because they were regarded as too few in number, too simplistic in their means of production, and too racialized in Euro-American representations. This vulnerability continued in the twentieth century with nuclear tests on their lands and in their waters, but the negative externalities of military tests alone may not constitute a militarization of reproduction. Militarization, the practices through which the ideology of militarism comes to dominate civilian politics, requires the impunity with which the military has acted to find sanction from civilian sources. The Compact of Free Association negotiated in the 1980s just did that.

The lack of accountability characterizing the ongoing relationship between the RMI and the United States is enacted and allegedly justified through the Compact of Free Association, initially signed in 1983, put into force in 1987, and renewed with minor amendments in 2003. This agreement was negotiated at the confluence of three major geopolitical forces: global pressure to either make colonial possessions like the Pacific Trust Territory independent nations or to fully integrate them into the colonizing nation, the United States' desire to maintain access to crucial weapons testing facilities and Pacific territory, and demands for independence among many Ri Majol people and other Micronesians.[42] In its preamble, the COFA frames itself in as expressing a "common desire" on the part of both the United States and the Marshall Islands to "continue and strengthen their relationship of free association," but close reading and contextualization reveals the document to be a tremendously imbalanced agreement that ensures the continuation of a U.S. military presence and impunity for the consequences of its nuclear testing program while funneling the Marshallese away from a sustainable future in their homeland and toward second-class citizenship in the United States.[43] The "close and mutually beneficial relationship" to which the COFA refers is undoubtedly intimate but dubiously mutual in its benefits.

The COFA ended the trust relationship between the United States and the Marshall Islands and established the RMI as a self-governing entity but with many restrictions.[44] Most prominently, Title III on "Security and Defense Relations" specifies that the United States "has full authority and responsibility for security and defense matters" and that the RMI "shall refrain from actions" that the United States determines "to be incompatible with its authority and responsibility for security and defense matters."[45] Such a hierarchal relationship is neither a free form of association nor properly described as expressing a "common desire," given the paternalistic nature of the relationship. In addition to subjecting the Ri Majol people to militarized foreign authority, the agreement secured the islands' status as a testing ground for weapons of mass destruction more than twenty years after the end of atmospheric nuclear testing. Kwajalein Atoll has hosted the impact and recovery area for testing intercontinental ballistic missiles (without nuclear warheads attached) launched from the U.S. mainland since 1960, and the COFA ensures this program's access to Marshallese land and labor for the foreseeable future.[46]

Despite assuring a long-term relationship between the United States and the RMI, the COFA also sought to seal away obligations generated through that relationship and reestablish terms that would reduce the U.S. government's liabilities. Article VII on "General Legal Provisions" provides both governments with immunity in each other's courts but also establishes a special Nuclear Claims Tribunal to provide a final reckoning of the United States' obligations to those harmed by the testing program.[47] While the Nuclear Claims Tribunal has awarded survivors over $2 billion in judgments, the U.S. government never adequately funded the tribunal, and less than 0.2 percent of that money has actually been paid out to Marshallese people.[48] The United States also handed over liability to the RMI for sites like Cactus Dome on Runit in Enewetak, where in 1979 the military dumped thousands of tons of radioactive waste in a nuclear test crater and covered it with a concrete cap that is now reported to be leaking profusely.[49] Thus, people in the Marshall Islands face a degraded environment that produces ongoing threats to their health and reproduction while also restricting their economic options to either low-wage labor in the "Pacific slum" of Ebeye near the Kwajalein testing facility or outmigration to the United States. Once again, from an indigenous feminist viewpoint, one can see that even when individual Ri Majol people retain the physiological capability for healthy reproduction, the reproduction of their nation as a whole is categorically threatened by the conditions produced through the COFA.

Relocation to the United States is abetted by Article IV of the COFA, which provides citizens of the RMI with authorization to work within the United States as "nonimmigrant residents" who enjoy none of the rights of citizenship beyond selling their labor and are given no path toward obtaining these rights.[50] With agriculture rendered untenable by nuclear tests, little tourist development, and almost no industry, Marshallese people have been forced to tend to their

immediate existence even as they remain focused on future generations. This has resulted in a steady flow of Ri Majol people, especially
to (relatively) nearby Hawai'i and to an enclave based around long-
term employment by the Tyson corporation in Springdale, Arkansas.
By 2010 more than twenty-two thousand Marshallese were living in
the United States, as compared to about fifty-two thousand living in
the RMI.[51] Like U.S. immigration policy overall at the time, the provisions of Article IV privilege heterosexual marriage and relations
as the basis of "chain migration," but unlike policies seeking "highly
skilled" migrants from other countries, the enticement of labor from
the Marshall Islands focuses on low-wage, "unskilled" labor with no
attempts to prepare Marshallese people for maximizing their utility
in the competitive U.S. market.

The relocation of Ri Majol people echoes past U.S. policies of dislo-
cating Native people from their traditional territories through multiple means. From the arrival of the earliest European settlers well
into the nineteenth century, many Native nations were removed from
their land without consent by the military, just as the indigenous
people of Bikini and Enewetak were forcibly evacuated in the 1940s.
Euro-American settlers have also displaced Native people through
violence against the land, ranging from dam and canal building to
mining and other extractive activities, just as the people of Bikini and
Enewetak cannot return to their homelands because of the level of
nuclear fallout. In the mid-twentieth century, the Indian Relocation
Act sought to transfer Native populations off reservations into urban
areas with the promise of job incentives. Similar to how Article IV of
the COFA has functioned for the Marshallese, this law succeeded at
population transfer but provided little support through that process,
producing new vulnerabilities in both the newly diasporic communities as well as among those left on traditional territories.

Muscogee (Creek) legal scholar and activist Sarah Deer reassessed
the legacy of the 1950s relocation policies and found that "in practice, 'relocation' is a continuation of the colonial determination to
destroy the inherent protection offered by one's relative in one's
own homeland and apathy toward the conditions in which the relocated people find themselves. . . . Indeed, these relocations ensured

that yet another generation of Native women would be exposed to sexual abuse and degradation and the genocide of Native peoples would be advanced."[52]

Ri Majol people continue to experience the sexualized threats initiated during early European contact, which are exacerbated by transnational mobilities and the disruption of kinship networks. A 2016 U.S. State Department Office to Monitor and Combat Trafficking in Persons report suggests that "some Marshallese searching for work in the United States experience indicators of trafficking, such as passport confiscation, excessive work hours, and fraudulent recruitment." Furthermore, it reports, "Marshallese children are transported to the United States where they are subjected to situations of sexual abuse with indicators of sex trafficking."[53] Adding to that, and again echoing past policies in regard to indigenous people of Turtle Island, hundreds of Ri Majol children were adopted by non-Marshallese families in the United States at a rapidly increasing pace in the late 1990s until the RMI instituted a moratorium on foreign adoptions in 1999.[54]

The health impacts of nuclear testing, migration, and other risk factors were compounded by neoliberal reforms in the mid-1990s, previously discussed as ushering in a form of domestic militarism that redrew the lines of national sexuality. As the COFA defined Marshallese people in the United States as nonimmigrant aliens, the Personal Responsibility and Work Opportunity Reconciliation Act excluded them from Medicaid, Medicare, Social Security, and other federal public benefits, even when they paid into these programs.[55] While the stated goal of such a reform was "to remove the incentive for illegal immigration provided by the availability of public benefits" and "to assure that aliens be self-reliant," neither goal applies here.[56] The COFA essentially eliminated the possibility of illegal migration by a Marshallese person, given that they each have the right to reside within the United States without regard to the Immigration and Nationality Act, and denial of healthcare actually harms self-reliance among Marshallese migrants by limiting their access to preventative care and forcing them to delay treatment for debilitating injuries and diseases.[57] A lack of health care also directly affects rates of infant and maternal mortality and provides another pathway through which the militarization of Ri Majol lives continues apace, perpetuating into future generations.

The sum of these assaults on biological and cultural reproduction has placed the people of the Marshall Islands in an exceptionally precarious set of circumstances made even more precarious by the effects of climate change. Since at least 1989, governments of island nations in the Pacific have called for global action to arrest sea level rise caused by climate change, which threaten their nations with not simply disruption but destruction.[58] Most of the Marshall Islands sits only a few feet above sea level with its highest hill reaching to only thirty-three feet, making it more immediately imperiled by sea level rise than almost any country in the world. It is in addressing this existential threat, however, that the Marshallese have most demonstrated their active survival and vocal commitment to producing and protecting the next generation while also making the links between demilitarization and the reproduction of their precious nation.

"HOW THE NEXT GENERATION WILL SOAR"

Micronesians have a long and admirable history of resisting foreign oppression against the longest odds. Spanish, German, and Japanese rule were not accepted willingly across the region, and every colonial power struggled to reconcile its conceptions of Pacific islanders as languid savages with the realities of their active and sophisticated resistance.[59] The United States faced similar circumstances, initially operating from the assumption that the Ri Majol people would be docile and malleable in the face of U.S. military might, technological superiority, and assertions of displacement as Christian duty, then learning that their colonial subjects were not so docile and malleable after all. In 1967 displaced Enewetakese protested in front of U.S. administration buildings in Majuro; Bikinians soon followed with statements of protest, though most could not join physically as they were trapped on the isolated island of Kili.[60] Ten years later, Ri Majol residents of the city attached to the U.S. testing facility on Kwajalein conducted a series of sits-ins and "sail-ins" to disrupt and protest missile tests.[61] And as previously mentioned, 350 Rongelapese people abandoned their contaminated home island for the island of Mejatto without permission or aid from the U.S. government in 1985.[62]

Ri Majol resistance entered a new phase in the late 1980s, not only due to the Compact of Free Association but also due to the 1986 founding of Jodrikdrik nan Jodrikdrik ilo Ejmour (Youth to Youth in Health, or YTYIH). While a government-sponsored peer education and health promotion program may not fit the expectations U.S. observers have of a political protest, recognizing that demilitarizing sexuality in general and reproduction in particular is a central concern for Marshallese people requires adjusting our lens. YTYIH recruited Ri Majol youth to promote reproductive health and general wellness in a culturally relevant way that within its first few years "rekindled pride in their culture among the group and sparked a sense of urgency about the need to improve health conditions in the islands."[63] The organization challenged stigma around discussions of sexual health, working with co-ed groups of youths as young as eight in both urban and rural areas and developing music and performance steeped in Marshallese traditions that addresses consent, pregnancy, sexually transmitted infections, and more. A 1994 study of the organization conducted by Darlene Keju-Johnson, whose words opened this chapter, found that YTYIH, which had become an independent NGO by that time, elicited highly positive perceptions from local focus groups despite its lack of resources. Parents quoted in the study indicated a wide range of benefits emerging from young women's increased access to knowledge of reproductive technologies, with one saying, "Even my granddaughter sings about condoms, pills, IUD, and Norplant."[64] YTYIH remains active in addressing the reproductive and other health impacts of colonization, nuclear testing, and the COFA even as, in recent years, the climate-change-driven threats to their future have precipitously increased.[65]

Another significant Ri Majol organization born in the post–Cold War pull back of U.S. sovereignty is Kokajoor im Koonmaanlok Kora (literally "Empowerment and Advancement of Women," but known in English as Women United Together Marshall Islands or WUTMI). Formed a year after YTYIH, WUTMI works to demilitarize reproduction by improving health outcomes, empowering women, and advancing a gendered analysis in addressing the impacts of military occupation, climate change, and other social conflicts. Rather than seeing gender equity as another foreign import with dangerous consequences, WUTMI frames women's advancement in Ri Majol society as an embrace of their traditional roles as "givers and sustainers of life."[66] They take on the customary responsibility of the "perpetuation of Marshallese culture" but refuse to be confined to customary and colonial roles that would limit their bodily autonomy, participation in public politics, or economic self-sufficiency.[67] According to WUTMI, domestic violence, the trafficking of Marshallese women for sex work with foreign customers, and the adoption of Ri Majol children to foreign parents all simultaneously strike at women's autonomy as individuals and the reproduction of the nation, but they remain committed to correcting these consequences of militarization.[68] Hilda Heine, a founding member of WUTMI who was born in Majuro the same month the United States created the world's first thermonuclear burn during the Operation Greenhouse tests on Enewetak, rose through the ranks of the Nitijela (RMI parliament) to become the first female president of a Pacific Island country in 2016. She is but one of the powerful Marshallese women making waves on an international stage.

Marshallese poet Kathy Jetñil-Kijiner opened the 2014 UN Climate Summit with an ode to her daughter, Matafele Peinam. The poem begins with Jetñil-Kijiner's praising her daughter's cuteness and enthusiasm for walks around "that lucid, sleepy lagoon lounging against the sunrise" before turning suddenly to how the sea will soon "devour," "gnaw," "chew," and "gulp down" their "island's shattered bones." She indicates that unnamed men have declared future generations of Marshallese girls "will wander rootless / with only a passport to call home." This is the fate scripted for the Ri Majol people by the COFA, which obliges them to suffer a nuclear threat to their future for the defense of the United States but does not obligate the United States to act in a way that would prevent the existential threat to the Marshallese from climate change, and which makes leaving the islands to work as noncitizens in the United States their best and only option.

But Jetñil-Kijiner, like many Ri Majol women before her, refuses to submit to the will of the giants that seek to remove her from her homeland. She urges her daughter not to weep, assuring her that "no blindfolded bureaucracies gonna push this mother ocean over the edge."[69] She expresses the will of the Marshallese to defy the expectations of transnational capital and international governments by saving their islands for the benefit of their descendants. Her naming of the ocean as mother also echoes the words of Tongan and Fijian scholar Epeli Hau'ofa, who in refusing the outside perception that Oceania consists of tiny specks of land surrounded by hostile waters said, "We are the sea, we are the ocean, we must wake up to this ancient truth and together use it to overturn all hegemonic views that aim ultimately to confine us."[70] The poem pushes back against the militarization of reproduction in the Marshall Islands by asserting that the human security of the next generation of Ri Majol people should take precedence over the national security of the United States.

It is important to distinguish between Marshallese attempts to demilitarize reproduction over recent decades and the militarized reproductive futurity increasingly embraced in defense of U.S. state violence over the same period. While Lee Edelman's rallying call of "no future" provides a useful critique of U.S. militarized heterosexuality, as Andrea Smith has argued, "An indigenous critique must question the value of 'no future' in the context of genocide, where Native peoples have already been determined by settler colonialism to have no future."[71] In contrast to the futurity embraced by the U.S. state, in which some children become the justification for inflicting massive violence upon other children, the Ri Majol people have embraced a version of what Unangan scholar Eve Tuck and her collaborator K. Wayne Yang have called "Indigenous futurity."[72] This form of futurity focuses on preserving the life of future generations of indigenous people through protecting the natural environment, decolonization as a concrete practice of facilitating life rather than an abstract metaphor.

Such a viewpoint can be seen elsewhere in the work of Jetñil-Kijiner, who continues to bear witness to the contemporary suffering of many Marshallese people while remaining focused on securing the future for the next generation. Her poem "For the Dakota Water Protectors" asks, "When we are attacked today does / our unborn children / feel it?" and, "When we raise our fist / is a song written /

by our great grandson?" to invoke the intergenerational impacts of both violence and resistance.[73] Emerging research in epigenetics is beginning to discover what women like Jetñil-Kijiner have known all along: militarized violence can change the very fabric of our bodies, but the work of demilitarizing can also be woven into future generations.[74]

Taking up the topic of COFA-driven migration in "Island Dropped from a Basket," Jetñil-Kijiner speaks to Native Hawaiians who now host many Ri Majol people in their islands, warning them, "The thieves / were once in our land too. / They sucked the marrow from our reef / cracked open our sun . . . / And, like you, we bled out our own children" while also assuring them that "all we wanted / was seedlings / to take back home."[75] Here, Jetñil-Kijiner references the ecological, nuclear, and reproductive destruction wrought by U.S. imperialism as well as the intentions of many Marshallese to return home as soon as circumstances allow. The metaphor of a basket referenced in the title, representing a woman's body as a container for culture, wealth, and the future, is woven throughout Jetñil-Kijiner's work.[76] The line "bled out our own children" indicates both the hemorrhaging that often accompanies a miscarriage as well as the trickling out of the life force of many indigenous communities through high rates of youth outmigration. The mention of trafficking in seedlings also invokes the historical connections between Micronesian and Polynesian navigators, who transplanted dozens of "canoe plants" like taro and breadfruit from the western Pacific to Hawai'i.[77]

Just as the histories of Ri Majol people are linked to their Pacific neighbors, so are their futures. The Republic of Kiribati shares with the Marshall Islands a history of nuclear testing, perpetrated by the British, and is equally imperiled by sea level rise. To the south, a portion of Samoa remains under U.S. jurisdiction with more than fifty thousand Samoans neither full citizens of the United States nor citizens of any independent country. To the west, the Chamorro people of Guahan and the Marianas, beset by the same status within U.S. empire but outside of the U.S. polity, struggle against the ecological impacts of militarism as well as the possibility that U.S. empire will draw their islands into a nuclear conflagration. And to the east,

Kanaka Maoli people grapple daily with the consequences of having the hub of U.S. empire in the Pacific on their Native land.[78] Sexual exploitation, the commodification of certain bodies, harm to reproductive health, the interruption of cultural transmission, and intergenerational trauma all proceed from the history of European encounters with the Pacific to the contemporary U.S. military presence there. These factors combined amount to a substantial militarization of sexuality but can provide fertile ground on which to cultivate transpacific resistance as well.

The demilitarized future envisioned by many Marshallese people is best exemplified by Jetñil-Kijiner's poem "Utilomar," which again draws upon Ri Majol tradition to identify historic and ongoing travesties before shifting toward generative imaginings of alternative possibilities. She first acknowledges her nightmares of salinized aquifers and dying sea creatures, linking them to a global climate catastrophe in which both flood and drought have become regular occurrences. She then indicates that she would rather focus on her dreams, in which the "next generation" connects with the natural environment through "voices," "chants," and "songs" while they "leap . . . into the water / before blossoming / to fly."[79]

A future in which Marshallese children can soar in the islands of their ancestors, as opposed to having those islands in the flight path of U.S. missile tests, requires demilitarizing reproduction and prioritizing generations to come over obtaining more precise instruments for eradicating human life. A future in which these children can imagine the next generation playing in unpolluted land and water, enacting the traditions of their ancestors, is a future we must all struggle to bring into being.

Conclusion

THE LONG WAR

The preceding chapters establish the multiple, persistent connections made between sexuality and militarism, as well as the processes through which the rhetoric espoused by government officials and media militarized sexuality during the 1990s. Cultural conceptions of sexual violence, heterosexuality, homosexuality, and reproduction changed over this period in ways that linked proper sexuality to support for militarized violence and offered improper sexuality as a justification or apologia for militarized violence. This was not the accomplishment of a unitary conspiracy hatched by government, business, or ideologues. Rather, the militarization of sexuality in the post–Cold War United States resulted from the confluence of the persistence of militarism with the rapidly changing conditions of both geopolitics and sexual politics in the 1990s.

Militarism, an ideology advocating the advance of military values and control into formerly nonmilitary aspects of life, may be an inevitable product of standing professional militaries; however, that ideology's success is never guaranteed. The drawdown of the Cold War in the late 1980s produced an unprecedented threat to militarists in government, military, business, and the cultural sphere who had experienced unparalleled success since World War II in orchestrating the collusion Eisenhower referred to as the military-industrial complex. As events obsoleted the anti-communist ideology under-girding decades of the United States' militarized violence, similarly vast historical forces rendered many once-hegemonic ideas about sexuality equally obsolete. Generational change, the HIV/AIDS crisis, emerging reproductive technology, and the digitization of everyday life each put cultural understandings of sexuality into flux, prompt-ing a series of culture war conflicts that intimately relate to armed conflict and militarism. The post–Cold War period was a moment of opportunity to redefine relationships between military and civilian life in ways that could just as easily produce sustainable peace as they could produce perpetual war.

Militarists seized this opportunity and, with the validating sup-port of government officials and the distribution networks of mass media, established new meanings. These new meanings were the terrain on which the next decades' struggles would be fought. Many observers of the United States have become so accustomed to this country's penchant for war that it seems to warrant no examination; others have been so captivated by the framing of militarism that they deeply believe in the benevolence and redemptive potential of U.S. militarism. Both sentiments condemn us to a continuation of the conditions of perpetual war that have persisted since 2001 and, as a result, are unacceptable paths forward. The task then becomes, first, to understand how militarism inserts itself into our ideas, culture, and lives; second, we must look toward grassroots movements that are already doing the work of demilitarization to find that path forward.

In this conclusion, I survey the struggles over sexuality and milita-rism characterizing the first decade of the ongoing "War on Terror." The parallels and continuities between these two decades have mostly gone unexamined in academia, and their preponderance demon-strates the significance of this relationship. Unfortunately, the War on Terror is not confined to a single decade, and its continued evolu-tion complicates analyzing it fully through the frame of documented events. I long for the day when this conflict can be studied in truly historical perspective and leave it to future studies to engage it more comprehensively. Unlike the previous chapters, which focused on the successes of militarization, this chapter only begins with those who seek to instrumentalize sexuality for militarism and ends with hopeful gestures toward those people currently working to ensure that we are not doomed to repeat the mistakes of recent history.

The continuity of and parallels between militarized sexuality in the 1990s and the first decade of the 2000s are almost too numerous to elucidate. As the opening scenes of the introduction attest, politicians and social movements, left and right, focused intensively on sexuality and sexual metaphors in their immediate responses to the events of September 11, 2001. Here, I make explicit some of the connections between the events described in the body of this work and three particular nodes of the War on Terror: the interventions abroad in Afghanistan and Iraq, the domestic security measures enacted in the wake of September 11, and the regulation of sexuality by the U.S. military. Each node points toward ways in which post-2001 militarism depended upon 1990s transitions in policy, practice, and ideology that helped reinvent U.S. militarism for a post–Cold War world.

Although U.S. leadership pointed to the events of September 11 as proximate justification for waging war against Afghanistan beginning in October 2001 and against Iraq beginning in March 2003, both interventions reprised a style pioneered in the 1990s. The wars in Afghanistan and Iraq were sold to the U.S. public as necessary measures to protect children from the threats of terrorism and weapons of mass destruction.[1] In the case of Afghanistan, the tropes of rescuing helpless women from a repressive sexual order allowed for the war's advocates to incorporate feminist critiques of the Taliban government into their militaristic case.[2] To support the war against Iraq, arguments and representations focused more heavily on the aggressive and threatening masculinity modeled by perennial boogeyman Saddam Hussein than on the innocence of Iraqi women.[3] Perhaps unsurprisingly, the New York Times played a major role in manufacturing public support for the war through the publication of information the editors later conceded to be patently false.[4]

Once the wars began, the gendered politics of the U.S. militarism also produced predictable results. Women like Aafia Siddiqui, a Pakistani neuroscientist, learned that the U.S. mission of liberating women in Afghanistan only applied to those who were politically compliant after she was hunted by the FBI, captured and shot by the U.S. military in Afghanistan, extradited to the United States to face trial, and sentenced despite almost no physical evidence to eighty-six years of imprisonment.[5] As had occurred during the 1990s interventions conducted with humanitarian justifications, militarized violence exacerbated existing gendered conflicts and promoted humanitarian disasters that fell heaviest upon women, especially on those from marginalized groups. As Iraqi-born scholar Yasmin Husein Al-Jawaheri wrote five years after the invasion, "Since March 2003, Iraqi women's daily lives seem different from anything they ever experienced previously. . . . The majority of Iraqi women are simply trying to survive from day to day in deteriorating circumstances."[6]

Despite a steady stream of editorials celebrating women's participation in creating these circumstances as members of the U.S. military, neither more women fighting for the United States nor the end of the combat exclusion policy indicates feminist progress.[7] This policy, revised in 1994 to include only units "whose primary mission is to engage in direct combat on the ground," underwent multiple revisions before being fully lifted in 2013, but several key units remain gender segregated as of 2018, and many women were using and receiving extreme violence in the War on Terror before the policy change.[8] Some servicemembers learned that their increased inclusion in combat operations came with their leaders' expectations about their ability to violate the assumed norms of Muslim men through sexualized interrogation tactics.[9] Others found themselves organized into "female engagement teams" that relied on an imagined sisterhood between women of occupied and occupying nations as well as an essentialist conception of women as more skilled at relational work to capitalize on the new tactical possibilities brought about by deploying more women in combat zones.[10]

As was clear in past interventions, the United States betrayed its true priorities by collaborating with male leaders uninterested in or downright hostile toward increasing women's sociopolitical power. As Afghan Parliament member Malalai Joya explained, "Some took

Laura Bush at her word when she said that purpose of the American invasion was to restore women's rights," but "it was obvious from the very first days that the United States had compromised the rights of Afghan women by supporting some of the worst enemies of women that our country had ever seen."[11] Unable to stage an appropriately cinematic rescue drama with Iraqi women, the U.S. military settled for infantilizing one of its own through the highly televised "rescue" of Private Jessica Lynch by heavily armed, all-male special forces from the Iraqi civilian hospital that had capably treated her injuries.[12] Later, the U.S. military's structural indifference to the culture of sexual violence in its ranks, apparent since Tailhook, became a global scandal following the publication of images of U.S. soldiers sexually assaulting and torturing Iraqi captives at the Abu Ghraib prison.[13]

While images of the torture of male Iraqi captives circulated widely, images attesting to the exploitation of and violence against Iraqi women at Abu Ghraib received significantly less attention. Furthermore, no images emerged publicly from many other sites of torture conducted by the United States in the opening years of the War on Terror, in part due to the destruction of evidence ordered by current CIA director Gina Haspel.[14] Other brutalities committed by U.S. soldiers underlined the emptiness of the rhetoric of rescue, notably the November 2005 killing of twenty-four unarmed civilians by U.S. marines in Haditha, Iraq, and the murder of sixteen civilians by an army sergeant in Panjwayi, Afghanistan, in March 2012.[15] However, no event revealed the hypocrisy of this rhetoric more clearly than the March 2006 Mahmudiyah killings. On March 12 of that year, a group of U.S. soldiers entered an Iraqi home, killed two adults and one of their children, then raped fourteen-year-old Abeer Qassim Hamza al-Janabi before murdering her and setting the corpse on fire.[16] Echoing events from Kosovo, U.S. soldiers both committed depredations against civilians and attempted to cover up their brutalities, paralleling the state's delivery of violence and simultaneous claim of benevolence.

In addition to sexual violence, the War on Terror has also continued the legacy of reproductive violence produced by U.S. militarism. In Iraq and Afghanistan, clusters of birth defects chillingly similar to those seen in the Marshall Islands have been reported and consistently linked to the military's extensive use of radioactive "depleted uranium" ordnance.[17] Maternal mortality and infant mortality worsened in both countries as a result of war, and risky amateur abortions have multiplied as increasingly empowered religious conservatives have constrained access to professional reproductive healthcare.[18] Recent wars have also had a tremendous impact on the reproductive capabilities of U.S. service members, who now suffer from issues ranging from genital damage to traumatic brain injuries that compel changes in their sexual lives to more indirect impacts through mental health traumas and chemical exposures that have yet to fully reveal their effects.[19] The increased activity and wide-ranging deployments of the U.S. military have also driven its already astounding fossil fuel consumption to new highs, exacerbating climate change and adding to the vulnerability of people across the globe living in low-lying or arid areas.[20] Once again, the actions of the state threaten those it claims to protect.

The trigger-happy style of global intervention adopted by the United States during the War on Terror drew directly from the murky concept of Responsibility to Protect established ex post facto the 1990s NATO interventions in the former Yugoslavia. The doctrine, not international law but an international norm embraced by many world and NGO leaders, suggests that governments have a responsibility to protect their citizens from harm and that, if they fail to do so, the "international community" has a responsibility to intervene.[21] In Neda Atanasoski's words, this reframing of transnational state violence as benevolent misrepresents the United States as "the first moral empire founded on the belief in the sacredness of human diversity rather than on territorial or economic exploitative ambitions."[22] That this doctrine made intervention in Libya necessary in 2011 but not in Syria soon after revealed that it is applied unevenly and more pragmatically case by case than by universal ethic. That the Russian government cited it in defending military assaults in support of irredentist movements in Georgia and Ukraine demonstrates that the doctrine is quite flexible indeed.

The short-lived Kony 2012 campaign exemplifies the civilian adoption of the militarized doctrine of Responsibility to Protect. Young, mostly white people from the Global North engaged in a campaign to make the northern Ugandan warlord Joseph Kony a household name in order to marshal opposition to his crimes against children. Conveniently, this campaign swept the internet only weeks after the United States began deploying "advisors" to Uganda and other countries in central Africa in order to complete ill-defined missions vaguely related to the War on Terror.[23] The United States appeared to be replaying the fantasy represented in the original seal of the Massachusetts Bay Colony, designed by a seventeenth-century white settler before his departure from England, which depicts an imagined Algonquin man with the text "Come over and help us."[24] Such self-aggrandizing justifications for invasion remain common throughout U.S. history but increasingly require appeals to proper sexuality and attacks grounded in sexual shame because of the growing illegitimacy of historical justifications for foreign intervention based in notions of white supremacy or the threat of communism.

This highly transnational and technological war retained other traces of some of the oldest battles fought on what the United States claims as its soil. While I have focused on the distinctive characteristics of post–Cold War militarism, much continuity exists. Reflecting on the connections between the genre of captivity literature in which white settlers narrated their experiences of being prisoners in wars against indigenous people, Susan Faludi writes, "After September 11, our recovery passed through a series of phases that uncannily recapitulated the metamorphosis of captivity literature into the comforting myth of American impregnability."[25] The U.S. military not only took comfort in nostalgia about past wars but also seemed eager to replay them. For example, during a ten-year manhunt utilizing a global digital surveillance apparatus and clandestine DNA sweeps masquerading as vaccinations for children, the government code-named Osama Bin Laden Geronimo after the famed Apache leader who the U.S. military hunted for decades in the late nineteenth century.[26]

As was the case in the nineties, sanitized histories of settler colonialism had material and cultural impacts on contemporary Native communities. Lori Piestewa (Hopi), who perished in the same raid in which Jessica Lynch was captured but received almost no comparable media attention, was the first Native woman to die in combat while enlisted in the U.S. military.[27] One Iraq war veteran, Eli PaintedCrow (Apache and Yaqui), told an interviewer, "My biggest enemy was my own company. I would hear officers who gave briefings referring to enemy territory as Indian country. . . . I wondered what side I should be on if this is Indian country."[28] On the Diné, or Navajo, reservation, according to Jennifer Denetdale (Diné), "Navajos responded to the atmosphere of fear and rallied around the American flag," creating a "militarized Navajo cultural landscape" that "re-inscribe[d] patriarchy" and resulted in the antigay Diné Marriage Act of 2005.[29] Despite the negative impacts of the War on Terror, indigenous nations remain key to resisting U.S. militarism and provide clear alternatives to the coercive systems of government and identity brought to this continent by settler colonialism.

Although the amorphous battlefields of the War on Terror extended transnationally beyond the full-scale wars against Iraq and Afghanistan to countries such as the Philippines, Pakistan, Yemen, Libya, Mali, Niger, and several other African nation-states, as the previous chapters show, foreign wars always have a domestic front. The efforts to harden the borders between the domestic and foreign through intensified airport security, immigration law, and border controls marked the first step in the post–September 11 process of domestic militarism. Each new security procedure and technology uniquely impacted individuals who present as Arab, Muslim, or Middle Eastern in U.S. society, regardless of their actual religion or ethnicity.[30] Panic about the imagined threat migrants pose to citizens and increasingly militarized institutional responses to this panic have also had unique and disproportionate impacts on Latino communities, gender-nonconforming people, and indigenous nations living along the borders of the United States.[31]

None of these measures, of course, have done anything to address the latest wave of angry white men shooting their way across the country, often in eerie parallel to the patriot militia movement of the early 1990s. From massacres targeting religious groups like the Oak Creek Sikh *gurdwara* in August 2012, the Overland Park Jewish Community Center in April 2014, the Charleston Emanuel African

Methodist Episcopal Church in June 2015, and the Sutherland Springs First Baptist Church in November 2017 to other mass killings such as the July 2012 Aurora movie theater shooting, the December 2012 Sandy Hook Elementary School shooting, and the October 2017 Las Vegas music festival shooting, in this new domestic security regime, government officials fail to notice the potential for white male violence until it explodes.[32]

The visibility of white nationalism receded substantially after the 1995 Oklahoma City bombing and remained quiet in the early years of the War on Terror but reemerged for a new chapter in 2009 through the Tea Party movement and its numerous offshoots. Groups such as the Oath Keepers, Minuteman Project, and Three Percenters captured even more interest with a national reinvigoration of white supremacist movements culminating in the August 2017 Unite the Right rally in Charlottesville. The participants responded to a perceived demographic crisis of whiteness and the patriarchal heterosexuality underlying it (their slogan: "you will not replace us") by organizing into paramilitaries, militias, and mobs that sought to restore an imagined orderly past ("make America great again") through the redemptive power of violence.[33] They demonstrated their ability to control urban space without inciting the violent responses often visited upon peaceful protestors of color, and in many ways their rally would have been considered a major success had it not ended with a vehicular homicide apparently committed by a far-right man who had spent four months in the U.S. Army.

That the U.S. military trained the perpetrators of the Oak Creek, Overland Park, and Sutherland Springs shootings—as well as many other acts of domestic terrorism such as the shootings in November 2009 and April 2014 at Fort Hood and in September 2013 at the Washington Navy Yard—should come as no surprise.[34] The conditions of contemporary warfare combined with official negligence have created a military mental health crisis that reflects a depraved indifference for the well-being of those in the military.[35] In a parallel failing, the U.S. military continued to regulate sexuality in a confused and oppressive fashion during the War on Terror, actively pursuing certain consensual sexual practices as misconduct while an epidemic of sexual assault went mostly unaddressed. Discharges of service members suspected of being lesbian, gay, or bisexual slowed but certainly did not stop as the military's need for certain bodies and talents increased over the course of the wars.[36] Meanwhile, one in eight women who graduated from the U.S. Air Force Academy in 2003 reported surviving rape or attempted rape, and across all branches during the War on Terror, a woman service member was more likely to be raped by a fellow service member than killed by an enemy.[37]

The U.S. military has become increasingly image-conscious in the era of the all-volunteer military and has faced many challenges in meeting recruiting goals. Unlike the major conflicts during and before the Cold War, the United States has no conscripted troops with which to fight; instead it must rely upon economic pressures and the ideological appeal of soldiering. Whereas the military once leaned almost exclusively upon hegemonic masculinity and selective service as levers for recruitment, the post–Cold War military continue to develop new strategies appealing to more diverse audiences and offer more individual benefits suited to a neoliberal economy. The visibility of the suffering of those who have served during the War on Terror deflated the post–September 11 boom in recruitment. Awareness of the military's Eurocentric culture of aggressive masculinity poses a particular challenge to the military's need for an increasingly pluralistic crop of recruits to fulfill its numerical and skill-specific goals. Consequently, the armed forces sought to address some of the more egregious abuses of the erotic within the military by forming the Sexual Assault Prevention and Response Office in 2005 and ending the antigay Don't Ask, Don't Tell policy in 2011.[38]

These changes, even as they begin to address some of the urgent needs of those currently in the military, are not demilitarizing sexuality and probably impede demilitarization more than they assist it. The military clearly still conceptualizes sexual autonomy and equity as subordinate to the conduct of war. As demonstrated by the military's reaction to the scandals at Tailhook and Aberdeen and to President Clinton's attempt to follow through on his promise to rescind the gay ban, military officials have been reluctant to cooperate with civilian rule. Not only did the government block attempts to remove authority in sexual assault investigations from the chain of command as recently as 2014, but the repeal of Don't Ask, Don't Tell also left in place discrimination against transgender service members, people with HIV, and those who were previously discharged under bans on gay service members, as well as continued criminalization of non-normative sexuality in the Uniform Code of Military Justice.[39] Even if the military was serious about treating women, LGBTQ people, and other marginalized people with respect, such cosmetic changes just disguise the underlying pathologies of militarism. To envision the potential for demilitarization, we need to look outside the state's reforms to those social movements doing the work of demilitarization and pushing for true postconflict transformation in the United States.

TOWARD A DEMILITARIZED FUTURE

In this final section, I shift from a highly critical analysis focused on the activities and language of militarists to a more expository analysis of the activities and language of antimilitarists. *Abuses of the Erotic* turns the gaze of an intersectional analytic developed by women of color toward hegemonic identities and institutions while placing the United States in a postconflict framework often reserved for analyzing societies emerging from conflict in the Global South. As an academic, I made the conscious decision to "study up" a critique of the powerful rather than "studying down" to create representations of those on the margins. At the same time, I decided to study the history of the country in which I was born to create a better future. The four main chapters of this book attest to the resistance that may not have carried the day in the 1990s but met militarism at every turn. By way of conclusion, I offer these pieces of ongoing resistance that I truly believe will win over war.

As has often been the case historically and across the globe, women have been at the forefront of movements to demilitarize the United States culturally and politically during the War on Terror. No one garnered greater attention for her antiwar activity during the most recent bout of U.S. interventions abroad than Cindy Sheehan. The mother of killed-in-action soldier Casey Sheehan became a household name when in August 2005 she began camping outside of President

George W. Bush's Crawford, Texas, ranch after he refused to grant her an audience to discuss her son's death. After a month at "Camp Casey," Sheehan became a fixture of the national antiwar movement, accumulating multiple arrests for civil disobedience at the White House and appearing across global media platforms, which called her the "Peace Mom."[40]

Feminists have long been skeptical of the transformative potential of women's activism grounded in motherhood, but Sheehan's work is better understood as a strategic position against the militarization of motherhood than an endorsement of an essentialist ethic of feminine care. Militarized motherhood, embodied by the "mama grizzly" character conjured by Alaska governor Sarah Palin in 2010, dictates that good mothers protect their children by endorsing militaristic policies. This stands in stark contrast to the discourse of essentially protective, antiwar femininity used by many women antiwar advocates since at least the beginning of the twentieth century. Despite their opposition, these constructions share a deep investment in whiteness in that, for centuries, mothers of color have had to confront institutional and cultural assumptions of incompetence or pathology in their mothering.[41] What these contradictory mobilizations of conventional femininity reveal is the ambivalent power of these conventions. The meaning of motherhood is always contested, and its power can be leveraged to militarize or demilitarize.

Code Pink also strategically deployed the discourses and tropes of femininity to their advantage in antimilitarist and antiwar efforts. Code Pink, founded in November 2002, describes itself as "a women-initiated grassroots peace and social justice movement working to end U.S. funded wars and occupations, to challenge militarism globally, and to redirect our resources into . . . life-affirming activities." The organization drew wide attention by bringing an unmistakable palate of bright pink clothes and banners to confront militaristic politicians, military recruiters, and war profiteers.[42] No other antiwar organization mobilizing against the War on Terror has embraced femininity and a feminist critique to the degree Code Pink has, and that has contributed to its endurance while other organizations have not been able to outlast the wars they formed to oppose. Code Pink confronts state violence both inside and outside the borders claimed by the United States and works in coalition to strategically raise up the voices of those most impacted by state violence.

Code Pink appropriated the government's Homeland Security Advisory System, maintaining the urgent language of *code* while mocking the practice of indexing the threat of terrorism by color and repurposing a color often associated with feminine frivolity for geopolitical critique. The organization turned a government attempt to instill atomizing fear about the threat terrorism posed to civilians into a wry call for civilians to come together against the particular brand of terror their state was busy producing abroad. Although Code Pink's rhetorical use of the youngest victims of war may at times fall into the heteronormative tropes of reproductive futurism, there is a significant difference between using children's suffering as rationale for ending (state) violence and using it as rationale for promoting (state) violence. Code Pink is demilitarizing sexuality by defining "life-affirming endeavors" through nonviolent, community-centered principles as opposed to the reactionary, nuclear-family-centered principles of militarized heteronormativity.

Of course, women in those countries most impacted by U.S. militarism also lead the way in building opposition and alternatives. Organizations like Okinawa Women Act against Military Violence, formed in the wake of the 1995 rape case discussed in chapter 1, have carried on the struggle against U.S.-backed Cold War militarization in their countries well into the era of the War on Terror. They are joined by other women-led peace initiatives across countries in East Asia scarred by U.S. militarism including GABRIELA in the Philippines and Women Cross DMZ in Korea. These organizations have a long history of drawing connections that remain highly relevant during the War on Terror between U.S. militarism, sexual violence by U.S. soldiers abroad against local women, political repression in their countries, and patriarchal values among local men.[43]

The Revolutionary Association of the Women of Afghanistan, which was founded in 1977 and has outlived multiple Afghan regimes, continues to draw attention to the pervasiveness of domestic, sexual, and structural violence against women in the post–U.S. invasion period.[44] Similarly, the Organization of Women's Freedom in Iraq (OWFI) is working to counter Iraqi women's losses in the most recent war, manifest in increased honor killings and incidences of domestic violence that seek to restrict women's sexualities as well as systemic changes in the constitution and public employment.[45] These organizations demilitarize sexuality by making public the sexual violence that characterizes recent U.S. wars abroad and demanding that the ethical imperative to address this injustice is not subsumed in favor of the military's interests.

Much like the feminists in the former Yugoslavia who formed alliances across the lines of hostility drawn by their governments, the women of OWFI formed a coalition with organizations in the United States with great potential for affecting demilitarization. Along with the pro-peace veterans' service organization Swords to Plowshares, OWFI created the transnational advocacy group Right to Heal to demand "that the human rights impacts of the war in Iraq be assessed and that concrete action be taken toward rehabilitation and reparations for those impacted by the lasting effects of the war."[46] This coalition engaged in transformational work by linking the sexual abuse suffered by both Iraqi civilians and U.S. soldiers in Iraq to environmental degradation, displacement, and interruption of kinship networks caused in both countries by the war. Although the campaign wound down in 2016, a number of its organizers and concerns have reemerged through the organization About Face: Veterans against the War, which seeks not just reforms but "to tackle the root causes of war by transforming ourselves, our values, and American society."[47]

Furthermore, across the Global North, LGBTQ activists are debating how to best succeed in the struggles for justice around gender and sexuality without collaborating with the injustices visited upon people in the Global South through predatory militarism and capitalism. Jasbir Puar lucidly explains how, during the War on Terror, the United States would "temporarily suspend its heteronormative imagined community to consolidate national sentiment and consensus through the recognition and incorporation of some, though not all or most, homosexual subjects," but some "homosexual subjects" actively refuse to be recognized or incorporated.[48] Organizations like Against Equality, Queers Undermining Israeli Terrorism, and Queers for Economic Justice have maintained through this latest bout of wars the historical tradition of oppositional queer activism that found its name in the early 1990s. They have been particularly effective at critiquing the "pinkwashing" of militarism that seeks to distract from the violence of military occupation with the ruse of LGBTQ inclusion. As Mattilda Bernstein Sycamore writes in the introduction to Against Equality's collection *Don't Ask to Fight Their Wars*, "Nothing could be more hypocritical than a movement centering around the right to go abroad to kill people and get away with it. If that is a 'civil rights' struggle, as we are led to believe, there is a problem with civil rights."[49] In the post–Cold War United States, that problem is militarism, and the consequences are deadly.

Finally, consciously intersectional organizations led by women of color are at work addressing the connections between state and sexual violence in ways that show great promise for demilitarizing sexuality. Organizations like INCITE! Women of Color against Violence, the Sylvia Rivera Law Project, and the Native Youth Sexual Health Network advocate for sexual-gender autonomy and equity by building community power rather than asking the state to provide it. They organize marginalized people into powerful communities through projects focusing on transformative and restorative justice, ending state and state-sanctioned violence against oppressed people, and educating each other through nonhierarchal pedagogies.[50] Rather than engaging the heteropatriarchal, white supremacist, and militaristic settler state on its own terms, these organizations create alternative, demilitarized sexualities that provide an attractive alternative to the bleak dystopia of hypermilitarized sexuality and perpetual war.

Furthermore, while movements focused explicitly on war and militarism have been limited in their organizing and mobilizations since the reopening of hostilities in Iraq in the spring of 2003, growing movements against state violence emerging from the most impacted communities have demonstrated how to reject the false promise of respectable sexuality and raise up the often-silenced perspectives emerging from the margins. The prison abolition movement, a diverse coalition of forces working toward a world without incarceration, has highlighted how we cannot simply rely on applying a greater amount of the state's coercive power as a corrective if we seek to address violence and domination. Abolitionism encourages us not to take state violence for granted, recognizing that human effort can undo the maladaptive complexes created through past efforts.[51] Due to the criminalization of LGBTQ people and the rigid gender ideology of the carceral system, prison abolition is a profoundly queer movement that helps illuminate the contemporary intertwining of sexuality and state violence.

The movements of undocumented people, especially those under the banners of Undocuqueer and Undocublack, have increasingly shifted away from a narrative of "deserving" immigrants that collaborates with inequities of sexuality, class, and race toward a narrative of "no one is illegal" that fundamentally challenges the settler state's power to regulate belonging. Their call to end immigrant detention dovetails with abolitionism, their call to dismantle Immigrations and Customs Enforcement pushes back against the expanding paramilitary forces of the Department of Homeland Security, and their call to demilitarize U.S.-claimed borders simultaneously addresses both domestic and transnational militarism.[52] Finally, the Movement for Black Lives, the Black Youth Project, and other associated groups highlight the power and potential of following the lead of queer women of color when attempting to undo the matrix of state violence, racism, misogyny, queerphobia, and other intersecting oppressions.[53] These movements have made significant progress in defanging domestic militarism through their efforts to demilitarize the police. While the post–Cold War era has been one of consistent military conflicts initiated by the U.S. government, it has also been one of continuous resistance by many in the United States who refuse to allow state violence to be committed in our names.

In early 2006, the Bush administration began to move away from the language of the "War on Terror" to speak of a more amorphous concept, "The Long War."[54] Rather than commit to a particular geographic context, ideological opponent, or time frame, the U.S. government sought public consent for an endless transnational armed conflict against a totally undefined enemy. Although the language of "Long War" was eventually dropped in favor of other enigmatic constructions like "Overseas Contingency Operations" and "Countering Violent Extremism," there remains no clear opponent, spatial boundary, or temporal deadline in sight.[55] As of 2018 the Authorization for Use of Military Force against Terrorists sanctioning the War on Terror has been used to conduct seventeen years of military operations across six continents with well over a million casualties and trillions of dollars in costs. Neither the overthrow of the Taliban government, "Mission Accomplished" in Iraq, the killing of Osama Bin Laden, or the growing list of countries in which terrorists supposedly operate have stirred mass action from the public or effective checks from within the government. Sexuality continues to be exploited for militarism, and sexual violence remains a major component of state violence, both reducing the erotic to what Audre Lorde dismissed as "the confused, the trivial . . . plasticized sensation."

But just as the erotic is subject to the sort of abuses documented throughout much of this project, "the erotic offers a well of replenishing and provocative force," too. The power of the erotic manifests in the many organizations and individuals utilizing the erotic power that "rises from our deepest and nonrational knowledge" to overcome those oppressions anchored in and making use of sexuality.[56] *Abuses of the Erotic* testifies to the danger of assuming that the final chapter of one war cannot be a prelude to the next one; at the same time, it points toward how we can resist militarization by taking sexuality seriously. Just as militarization defined sexuality during the 1990s, demilitarization could be the defining characteristic of the next generation's sexualities. I see enormous hope in how many young people today reject binary gender, hegemonic masculinity, the allure of gun violence, and other values that easily concur with militarization. This project on the *post–Cold War* militarization of sexuality should contribute to identifying how sexuality might be used in order to create a world that is simply *postwar*.

ACKNOWLEDGMENTS

I formed the first ideas underlying this project on the traditional and unceded territories of the Penacook people, occupied since Metacomet's War in the 1670s. Following that, I spent a considerable amount of time on the lands inhabited, long before my ancestors arrived from Europe, by the Pequot people, Quitirrisi Huetar people, Potawatomi, and other indigenous nations before I moved to a piece of Haudenosaunee territory from which many Seneca people were forcibly removed by the United States in the first few decades of the country's existence. I completed my manuscript near the shores of the Salish Sea, home to the Lummi and Nooksack people since time immemorial and to non-Native settlers attempting to expropriate their land since the 1850s. I begin by thanking the land that sustained me and its original protectors, as well as by acknowledging the many contradictions that underlie my confronting American empire from the inside as one of its primary beneficiaries.

This project took shape as a monograph after an encouraging meeting with Alicia Christensen at the National Women's Studies Association Conference in Milwaukee. I thank her and everyone else at the University of Nebraska Press who played a part in putting this together. Ariana Vigil has been particularly supportive of this project and generous in her feedback throughout the process. Nora Tykelar, Adrienne Hill, Chelsea Jones, and Carolyn Stirling were a crack team of proofreaders who worked quickly and do impressive work of their own. Cristy Road was gracious in allowing her artwork to adorn the cover.

I forged the tools to craft this project in the Global Gender Studies program at SUNY University at Buffalo under the supervision of Theresa Runstedtler along with Carine Mardorossian and Cindy Wu. I couldn't have asked for a better team of advisors but had additional help and support from Alexis De Veaux and Theresa McCarthy anyways. Theresa also graciously introduced me to the incredible community of Haudenosaunee intellectuals in the area, all of whom taught me a great deal, especially Jodi Maracle. I relished the company of my fellow graduate students at UB, particularly Fernanda Glaser, Drew Friedfertig, Cayden Mak, Adam Drury, Steve Demchak, Kritika Agarwal, Jessi Lee Jackson, and Adrianna Hernandez. Deborah Pierce-Tate did a lot of hard work that made my life easier. Buffalo was a great place to strive for justice, and I thank everyone from the Buffalo Prison Abolition Reading Group, UB CLEAR, Defend Our Education Coalition, and Burning Books for their dedication to a better future. Buffalo also lived up to its reputation as the "City of Good Neighbors" and gave me lifelong friends like Erin Sharkey, Zoe Holloman, Harold Dumke, and Robin Jordan.

Upon leaving Buffalo, I began working at Western Washington University and prepared articles for special issues of *Gender and History* and *Radical History Review* that eventually evolved into chapters of this book. I thank the editors and reviewers I worked with on both of those pieces as well as everyone who participated in the Gender and Global Warfare in the Twentieth Century symposium at the University of Minnesota for their contributions to those evolutions. At WWU, I am fortunate to have great colleagues in both the History Department and Women, Gender, and Sexuality Studies as well as across the university, especially Vicki Hsueh, Simon McGuire, Lysa Rivera, Tiana Kahakauwila, Sarah Zimmerman, Ricardo Lopez, Steven Garfinkle, Johann Neem, Jennie Huber, Bill Lyne, Ruth Steele, Rich Brown, and Travis Tennessen. Kristin Mahoney, Kaveh Askari, and Kevin Leonard are no longer at Western but are dearly missed.

The folks who participated in my wgss Works In Progress session; the Research and Sponsored Programs Office, which provided a summer research grant, a minigrant, and a manuscript completion grant to support this project; and the students who continually remind me to break it down clearly all deserve thanks as well. Special thanks to Kaitlyn Sullivan and Vaughn Shubert for laboring alongside me as teaching assistants. AB Brown read and provided wise comments on several parts of this manuscript, and they are also a fantastic friend.

The Pacific Northwest has been a fertile location to continue struggling with groups like Imagine No Kages and Red Line Salish Sea. I consider it an enormous privilege to work alongside people like Junga Subedar, Michelle Vendiola, Michael Vendiola, Maru Mora-Villapando, Neah Monteiro, Tina McKim, Liz Darrow, and others. The pnw also provided an opportunity to become friends with Elissa Washuta, Kendall Dodd, Donnell Williams, Anna Booker, Zoe Redwoman, and Doug Lutz. Additionally, I've had the chance to maintain and cultivate ties to other friends near and far including Nick Bazin, Sean Khalepari, Mariella Cruzado, and T. J. Tallie. Solidarity forever with the suny Graduate Student Employees Union, United Faculty of Western Washington, and organized labor everywhere.

Long before I had heard of Bellingham, Washington, or queer theory, I became an astute (and prolific) critic of the culture that produced me through diy punk, and I am forever grateful toward the friends I made through that: Rick Stec, Matt McCarthy, Adam and Risa Caires, Jarrod and Danielle Delong, Jenna Lemieux, Pat Smith, and many others helped this happen. I had some excellent teachers and professors along the way: thank you to Frank Davis, Joan Hedrick, Elli Findly, Raymond Baker, Rob Corber, and Anouk Guiné. I also started off with the enormous unearned advantage of a family that encouraged and supported my education at many key points. Diane Cerretti taught me the importance of taking care of people, Jim Cerretti taught me the importance of building a solid structure, and Jamie Cerretti taught me everything that really matters. I am also fortunate enough to be one of the seven Cerretti cousins; thanks to Joey, Jared, Lauren, Kayla, and Aaron for being more like siblings.

As the years have gone on, Tate Williams and several of the Warbur-tons have also become my family, and I like it that way.

Theresa Warburton has put more labor into what you're holding in your hands than anyone except me, and some days it feels like even that is debatable. My life is made much richer by her intellectual prowess.

Finally, I dedicate this work to three people who are not here to see it. Christopher "Dubs" Dalphond was a dear friend who we lost far too young, and Fred Pfeil taught me so much about how to be an activist-scholar in the three short years I knew him. My grandmother—whose first name was either Margaret or Margot, who at different times carried the last names Bradley, Johnson, and Chaput, and who to most was simply known as "Peggy"—nurtured the way of seeing that eventually and unpredictably blossomed into what you are reading today as we sat in her living room by Lake Mascuppic watching soap operas and the news for hours.

NOTES

INTRODUCTION

1. See Gustav Niebuhr, "After the Attacks: Finding Fault; U.S. 'Secular' Groups Set Tone for Terror Attacks, Falwell Says," *New York Times*, September 14, 2001; Laurie Goodstein, "Falwell's Finger-Pointing Inappropriate, Bush Says," *New York Times*, September 15, 2001; and Gustav Niebuhr, "A Nation Challenged: Placing Blame; Falwell Apologizes for Saying an Angry God Allowed Attacks," *New York Times*, September 18, 2001. Falwell presumably was referring to the burning of Washington DC or other events during the War of 1812 without realizing that most of those events occurred between 1813 and 1815.
2. George W. Bush, "Address to a Joint Session of Congress and the Nation," September 20, 2001.
3. Charles Schumer, "Democratic Radio Response," September 15, 2001, accessed February 2, 2014, www.c-span.org/video/?166073-1 /democratic-radio-response.
4. Alex Kuczynski, "The New Feminist Mystique; Variety of Brash Magazines Upset the Old Stereotypes," *New York Times*, September 10, 2001.
5. Eleanor Smeal, "Special Message from the Feminist Majority on the Taliban, Osama Bin Laden, and Afghan Women," Feminist Majority Foundation Press Release, September 18, 2001.
6. Servicemembers Legal Defense Network, *Conduct Unbecoming*.
7. Lorde, *Sister Outsider*, 53.
8. I have found the metaphor of constellations to be particularly useful for describing the components of sexuality in that, in both cases, we see

patterns between the independent features that have great explanatory significance to us but no actual bearing on the components in question.

9. Cameron and Kulick, *Language and Sexuality*, 62.
10. For more on the social and historical construction of sexualities, see Allyn, *Make Love, Not War*; Bland and Doan, *Sexology Uncensored*; Butler, *Bodies That Matter*; D'Emilio and Freedman, *Intimate Matters*; Duberman, Vicinus, and Chauncey, *Hidden from History*; Fausto-Sterling, *Sexing the Body*; Kessler, *Lessons from the Intersexed*; Meyerowitz, *How Sex Changed*; and Weeks, *Against Nature*.
11. Combahee River Collective, *Combahee River Collective Statement*.
12. See Califia, *Speaking Sex to Power*, 76–77.
13. A growing body of historically informed work thankfully addresses this gap, including but by no means limited to Nyong'o, *The Amalgamation Waltz*; Freedman, *Redefining Rape*; and Brier, Downs, and Morgan, *Connexions*.
14. hooks, *Black Looks*, 22.
15. See Stoler, *Carnal Knowledge and Imperial Power*.
16. See Somerville, *Queering the Color Line*; Carter, *The Heart of Whiteness*.
17. Collins, *Black Feminist Thought*, 128.
18. Foucault, *The History of Sexuality*, 1:103. My emphasis.
19. Jones, "End to the Neglect"; Davis, "Reflections"; Rich, "Compulsory Heterosexuality and Lesbian Existence"; and MacKinnon, *Sexual Harassment of Working Women*.
20. Enloe, *Maneuvers*, 3.
21. Three definitions of militarism from Eide and Thee, *Problems of Contemporary Militarism*: "Militarism represents a system of thought and attitudes that places military institutions above civilian institutions and introduces the military mentality into civilian decision-making" (Ernie Regehr, "What Is Militarism?," 129); "the tendency of a nation's *military apparatus* . . . to assume *ever-increasing control* over the lives and behaviour of its citizens; and for *military goals* . . . and *military values* . . . increasingly to dominate national culture, education, the media, religion, politics and the economy at the expense of civilian institutions" (Michael Klare, "Militarism: The Issues Today," 36); and "such symptoms as a rush to armaments, the growing role of the military (understood as the military establishment) in national and international affairs, the use of force as an instrument of supremacy and political power, and the increasing influence of the military in civilian affairs" (Marek Thee, "Militarism and Militarization in Contemporary International Relations," 15).
22. See Berghahn, *Militarism*.

23. Dwight Eisenhower, "Farewell Address by President Dwight D. Eisenhower," January 17, 1961.
24. See, for example, Mike Davis, "Hell Factory in the Field: A *Prison Industrial Complex*," *Nation*, February 20, 1995; Davis, *The Prison-Industrial Complex*; INCITE!, *The Revolution*; and Yee, *Feminism for Real*.
25. Wallensteen, Galtung, and Portales, *Global Militarization*, xi.
26. Gibson, *Warrior Dreams*, 9, 11. Emphasis removed from "dream."
27. Andrew Rosenthal, "The Malta Summit; Bush and Gorbachev Proclaim a New Era for U.S.-Soviet Ties; Agree on Arms and Trade Aims," *New York Times*, December 4, 1989. For more on the significance of the Malta Summit in perspective, see Gates, *From the Shadows*.
28. Regan, *Organizing Societies for War*, 1.
29. Greider, *Fortress America*, viii.
30. For some examples, see Alsunltany, *Arabs and Muslims in the Media*; Beverley, *Latinamericanism after 9/11*; Hafetz, *Habeas Corpus after 9/11*; Herman, *Taking Liberties*; Puar, *Terrorist Assemblages*; and Welch, *Scapegoats of September 11th*.
31. For examples, see Chomsky, *Hegemony or Survival*; Faludi, *The Terror Dream*; Goodman, *National Insecurity*; Ivie, *Democracy and America's War*; Johnson, *The Sorrows of Empire*; and Westad, *The Global Cold War*.
32. Enloe, *The Morning After*, 3.
33. For more on the "new left" of the 1990s, see Baer, *Reinventing Democrats*; and Selfa, *The Democrats*. For more on the "new right" of the 1990s, see Martin, *With God on Our Side*; and Capps, *The New Religious Right*.
34. Fukuyama, *The End of History*; Huntington, *The Clash of Civilizations*.
35. Masco, *The Theater of Operations*, 202.
36. I am not aware of any other full-length scholarly work purporting to do this. Two Clinton administration national security officials did publish a nonacademic policy book explicitly using a similar framing of era but with significantly different approaches and conclusions. See Chollet and Goldgeier, *America between the Wars*.
37. Grimmett, "Instances of Use of United States Armed Forces Abroad."
38. See Staff of the *Los Angeles Times*, *Understanding the Riots*; Walter, *Every Knee Shall Bow*; Reavis, *The Ashes of Waco*; and Balko, *Rise of the Warrior Cop*.
39. Bacevich, *The New American Militarism*, 55–56.
40. Bacevich, *The New American Militarism*, 3.
41. For some recent works on Cold War sexualities, see Corber, *Cold War Femme*; Johnson, *The Lavender Scare*; Lewis, *Prescription for Heterosexuality*; and Schmidt, *Desegregating Desire*. For work on sexuality in the War on Terror, see Puar, *Terrorist Assemblages*; Faludi, *Terror Dream*;

Bhattacharyya, *Dangerous Brown Men*; Fusco, *Field Guide for Female Interrogators*; and Lugo-Lugo and Bloodsworth-Lugo, *New Kind of Containment*. The only full-length work of which I am aware that attempts to locate the historically and culturally specific features of 1990s U.S. sexualities is Duggan, *The Twilight of Equality?*.

42. While I offer this taxonomy as a linear list, these modalities of militarization may appear alone or in combination in any sequence.

43. James, *Resisting State Violence*; Alexander, *Pedagogies of Crossing*. Also see Mohanty, Pratt, and Riley, *Feminism and War*.

44. Enloe, *Maneuvers*; Enloe, *Morning After*; Enloe, *Does Khaki Become You?*; Enloe, *Bananas, Beaches, and Bases*; Enloe, *Globalization and Militarism*; Enloe, *Nimo's War, Emma's War*; Pettman, *Worlding Women*; Cockburn, *Antimilitarism*. Also see Sjoberg, *Gendering Global Conflict*; Alexander and Hawkesworth, *War and Terror*; and Nokov, Sutton, and Morgen, *Security Disarmed*.

45. Belkin, *Bring Me Men*; Berube, *Coming Out under Fire*; Canaday, *The Straight State*.

46. Puar, *Terrorist Assemblages*; Duggan, *Twilight of Equality*; Berlant, *The Queen of America*.

47. Communications Management Incorporated, "Sixty Years of Daily Newspaper Circulation Trends: Canada, United States, United Kingdom," May 6, 2011, accessed March 10, 2014, http://media-cmi.com /downloads/Sixty_Years_Daily_Newspaper_Circulation_Trends _050611.pdf.

48. Gonzalez and Torres, *News for All the People*, 347.

49. Schwarz, *Endtimes*, 3.

50. Kauanui, "'A Structure, Not an Event.'"

51. Newcomb, *Pagans in the Promised Land*, 132.

52. Said, *Representations of the Intellectual*, 98.

53. Lorde, *Sister Outsider*, 56.

1. NO POLITICIAN CAN AFFORD

1. George H. W. Bush, "Address to Nation on Panama Invasion," December 20, 1989.

2. Scott, *G.I. Jane*.

3. See Kelly, "Everyday/Everynightness of Rape," 114–23; and Ticktin, "Gendered Human of Humanitarianism," 250–65.

4. Grewal and Kaplan, *Scattered Hegemonies*, 17.

5. Richie, *Arrested Justice*; Deer, *Beginning and End of Rape*.

6. See Hoganson, *Fighting for American Manhood*; Jensen, *Mobilizing Minerva*, 29–35.

7. U.S. Department of Defense, *Population Representation in the Military Services: Fiscal Year 2010*.
8. United Nations Security Council Resolution 1325, October 31, 2000, available at un.org/womenwatch/osagi/wps/.
9. See Duggan, *Twilight of Equality*; Atanasoski, *Humanitarian Violence*.
10. George H. W. Bush, "Address to Nation."
11. The story of the navy lieutenant and his wife was first told at a Defense Department press conference on Sunday, December 17, and first appeared in print as "Excerpts From U.S. Account of Officer's Death in Panama," *New York Times*, December 18, 1989, alongside Thomas Friedman, "Panama Shooting Condemned by U.S.," *New York Times*, December 18, 1989, and William Branigin, "U.S. Assails Panama in Killing of GI; Account of Shooting Denounced as False," *Washington Post*, December 18, 1989. Using the *New York Times* and *Washington Post* as their sources, the story was repeated as "Panama Killing Outrages U.S.," *St. Petersburg Times*, December 18, 1989; "U.S. Forces Mobilize in Panama," *St. Louis Post-Dispatch*, December 18, 1989, and elsewhere. The story of the lieutenant and his wife is referred to as "previously unreported" in Tom Kenworthy and Patrick Tyler, "U.S. Condemns Violence in Panama; 2 Incidents Involving Officers Portrayed as Product of Noriega's Rule," *Washington Post*, December 18, 1989. Reports referring to the officers' confrontation at the roadblock without any mention of the navy lieutenant and his wife include "U.S. Serviceman Is Killed by Panamanian Crowd, Soldiers," *St. Louis Post-Dispatch*, December 17, 1989; "Panama Starts War with U.S., Soldier Killed," *Sunday Mail* (Australia), December 18, 1989; Mary Brasier, "U.S. Troops on Alert after Panama Clash: Killing of American Marine Sparks New Noriega Crisis," *Guardian* (UK), December 18, 1989; Marc Champion, "U.S. Plays Down Soldier's Death," *Independent* (UK), December 18, 1989; and Andrew Rosenthal, "President Calls Panama Slaying a Great Outrage," *New York Times*, December 19, 1989.
12. Yates, *U.S. Military Intervention in Panama*, 275.
13. McConnell, *Just Cause*, 19–20.
14. Buckley, *Panama*, 226–27.
15. Gemma and Gutiérrez, Introduction, 1.
16. Gemma and Gutiérrez, Introduction, 2.
17. Edilma Icaza, "I Want to Relive the Invasion"; Dixon, "The People."
18. For the debate over the number of casualties, see Larry Rohter, "Panama and U.S. Strive to Settle on Death Toll," *New York Times*, April 1, 1990. For more specific details about the impact of the war on Panamanian civilians, see Trent, *The Panama Deception*; and the 1990

lawsuit *Salas v. United States* initiated by the Center for Constitutional Rights and adjudicated at the Inter-American Court for Human Rights, accessed January 18, 2014, www1.umn.edu/humanrts/cases/31 %5E93us.pdf.

19. James, *Resisting State Violence*, 82.
20. Mejía, "A Crime against Humanity," 65.
21. Mejía, "A Crime against Humanity," 65.
22. Hearing of the Subcommittee on Western Hemisphere Affairs of the House Foreign Affairs Committee, "Current Situation in Panama," July 30, 1991, accessed September 2, 2017, www.c-span.org/video/?19895-1 /current-situation-panama.
23. Simons, *Vietnam Syndrome*, 20; and George H. W. Bush, "Remarks to the American Legislative Exchange Council," March 1, 1991.
24. Robert McFadden, "A Few More Refugees Reach the Saudi Border," *New York Times*, August 11, 1990; "Kuwaitis Resist Iraqis by Work Boycott and Armed Raids, 'Eyewitness' Articles Say," *New York Times*, August 23, 1990; Barbara Crossette, "Shocks From Kuwait Hit the Third World," *New York Times*, September 9, 1990; and William Safire, "The Phony War," *New York Times*, October 1, 1990. The early *New York Times* coverage (and most U.S. newspaper coverage that week) relied exclusively upon Caryle Murphy, "In Eye of Storm, Kuwaitis and Foreigners Dodge Iraqis," *Washington Post*, August 22, 1990. Her story of being "the only American newspaper reporter in Kuwait" appeared later as "'A Front-Row Seat . . . Witnessing a Small Nation Being Crushed,'" *Washington Post*, August 29, 1990.
25. See Sideris, "Rape in War and Peace."
26. Thomas Friedman, "Bush and Baker Explicit in Threat to Use Force," *New York Times*, October 30, 1990.
27. See Peter Gemma, "This Summit Repeats the Soviets' Old Tricks," *USA Today*, September 7, 1990; George Melloan, "The Shifting Sands of Soviet Policy," *Wall Street Journal*, September 10, 1990; Neal Gertz, "Only in America," *Chicago Tribune*, September 26, 1990; "Oil's Role in Persian Gulf Crisis," *Los Angeles Times*, September 29, 1990; and "The Peace Dividend, Unredeemed," *New York Times*, November 17, 1990. For examples of increased frequency in early 1991, see William Safire, "The Letter," *New York Times*, January 7, 1991; Richard Ullman, "Flunking World Order 101," *New York Times*, January 12, 1991; "The Message, Stronger," *New York Times*, January 13, 1991; "The Stakes in the Gulf," *New York Times*, January 15, 1991; and Safire, "Don't Throw Away Victory," *New York Times*, January 31, 1991.
28. Sasson, *The Rape of Kuwait*, 75–92.

29. Sasson, *The Rape of Kuwait*, 139–52.
30. Gary Lee and John Lancaster, "'Rape of Kuwait' Book, Ad Campaign Try to Make Case for Military Force," *Washington Post*, January 17, 1991; "Paperback Best Sellers," *New York Times*, March 3, 1991; "Paperback Best Sellers," *New York Times*, March 17, 1991.
31. James Cox, "Author Defends Her Tale of Kuwait," *USA Today*, April 4, 1991.
32. Judith Miller, "Atrocities by Iraqis in Kuwait, Numbers Hard to Verify," *New York Times*, December 16, 1990.
33. Miller, "Atrocities by Iraqis in Kuwait."
34. Ramsey Campbell, "Lake Woman Co-authors Story behind 'God Bless the U.S.A.,'" *Orlando Sentinel*, May 23, 1993.
35. Greenwood and McLin, *God Bless the U.S.A.* Also see "God Bless the U.S.A. Persian Gulf War Tribute," youtube.com/watch?v=DSOgEC7HvDg.
36. Meintjes, Pillay, and Turshen, "There Is No Aftermath," 3, 12.
37. See Al-Ali and Pratt, *What Kind of Liberation?*.
38. Zangana, *City of Widows*, 74.
39. Associated Press, "Crimes in Gulf Cited," *New York Times*, July 18, 1992.
40. Eric Schmitt, "Navy Says Dozens of Women Were Harassed at Pilots Convention," *New York Times*, May 1, 1992; Eric Schmitt, "Wall of Silence Impedes Inquiry into a Rowdy Navy Convention," *New York Times*, June 14, 1992. Other early original reporting on the scandal included Gregory Vistica, "Navy Brass Accused of Ignoring Molestation Reports," *San Diego Union-Tribune*, April 28, 1992; "Navy Officers Reportedly 'Stonewalled' Investigation into Sex Abuse," *Los Angeles Times*, April 29, 1992; and Susanne Schaefer, "Navy Probe of Harassment at Tailhook Meeting Finds Conduct Unacceptable," *Sun* (Baltimore), April 29, 1992.
41. U.S. Department of Defense Inspector General, *Tailhook 91—Part 2, Events of the 35th Annual Tailhook Convention*, February 1993, Sections 5, 6, and 7.
42. Eric Schmitt, "Military Court Assails Navy in Ruling on Tailhook," *New York Times*, January 12, 1994.
43. Schmitt, "Navy Says Dozens of Women Were Harassed."
44. Eric Schmitt, "Navy Investigations, a Raft of Failures," *New York Times*, June 28, 1992.
45. John Lancaster, "Statement Puts Navy Secretary in Suite at Convention Being Probed for Abuse," *Washington Post*, June 17, 1992; Susanne Schaefer, "Secretary of Navy Resigns, Takes Blame for Assaults," *Buffalo News*, June 27, 1992; Eric Schmitt, "Navy Chief Admits to Being Close By during Lewd Party," *New York Times*, June 17, 1992.

46. Schmitt, "Navy Investigations, a Raft of Failures."

47. Eric Schmitt, "Officials Say Navy Tried to Soften Report," *New York Times*, July 8, 1992.

48. "Navy Investigator Removed from Inquiry on Assaults," *New York Times*, July 9, 1992.

49. James Webb, "Witch Hunt in the Navy," *New York Times*, October 6, 1992.

50. Eric Schmitt, "Two out of Three Women in Military Study Report Harassment," *New York Times*, September 12, 1990; Linda Harrington, "Military Cool to Women in Combat," *Chicago Tribune*, June 19, 1991; Eric Schmitt, "Navy Plans Training to Fight Sexual Harassment," *New York Times*, June 6, 1992, "Admiral Predicts Dismissal of Officers in Harassment Case," *Boston Globe*, June 29, 1992; John Cushman Jr., "Top Admiral Backs Full Combat Roles for Women in Navy," *New York Times*, April 5, 1993.

51. Associated Press, "Admiral Testifies in Tailhook Case," *New York Times*, November 30, 1993; Associated Press, "Admiral Contradicted on Tailhook Meeting," *New York Times*, December 3, 1993; Eric Schmitt, "Judge Dismisses Tailhook Cases, Saying Admiral Tainted Inquiry," *New York Times*, February 9, 1994; Associated Press, "Excerpts from Ruling Dismissing Case against Three Officers," *New York Times*, February 9, 1994.

52. Eric Schmitt, "In Tailhook Deal, Top Admiral Says He'll Retire Early," *New York Times*, February 16, 1994; "The Tailhook Fiasco," *New York Times*, February 17, 1994; Associated Press, "Kelso to Retire with 4 Stars Intact, Female Senators Denounce Decision," *Daily Press* (Newport News), April 20, 1994.

53. Warren Bates "Navy Liability Rejected in Tailhook Lawsuits," *Las Vegas Journal*, April 20, 1992; Associated Press, "Most Tailhook Suits by 5 Dismissed," *Boston Globe*, April 21, 1994; Associated Press, "Tailhook File Is Shut, No Cases Being Tried," *New York Times*, June 8, 1994.

54. Zimmerman, *Tailspin*, 280.

55. Zimmerman, *Tailspin*, 280.

56. See Girard, *Haiti*; Renda, *Taking Haiti*.

57. Amy Wilentz, "Haiti's Death Mask," *New York Times*, March 24, 1994.

58. Pamela Constable, "Ire, Fear at Burial in Slums of Haiti," *Boston Globe*, June 2, 1994.

59. Anna Hamilton Phelan, "The Latest Political Weapon in Haiti: Military Rapes of Women and Girls," *Los Angeles Times*, June 5, 1994.

60. Howard French, "Haitian Dissident Tells of Rape By Police Agents," *New York Times*, June 26, 1994.

61. Garry Pierre-Pierre, "Drownings of Haitians Rise as Exodus Continues," *New York Times*, July 6, 1994.

62. Pierre-Pierre, "Drownings of Haitians Rise"; Garry Pierre-Pierre, "Hundreds of Refugees Held," *New York Times*, June 26, 1994.
63. See Mike Kelly, "Amid Tension and Despair, Haitians Wait," *Record* (Bergen County NJ), September 3, 1994; Carol Morello, "Patience Fades in Guantanamo Refugee Camps," *Philadelphia Inquirer*, September 11, 1994.
64. Elaine Sciolino, "Invasion of Haiti Would Be Limited, Clinton Aides Say," *New York Times*, September 13, 1994.
65. Sciolino, "Invasion of Haiti."
66. Bill Clinton, "Address to the Nation on Haiti," September 15, 1994.
67. Clinton, "Address to the Nation on Haiti."
68. Steven Greenhouse, "Amnesty Plan for the Military Angers Aristide," *New York Times*, September 20, 1994.
69. R. W. Apple, "Mission to Haiti, In Perspective: The GIs Are in Haiti, Now for the Hard Part," *New York Times*, September 20, 1994.
70. Apple, "Mission to Haiti."
71. Merlet, "Haiti," 133–36.
72. Carol Williams, "UN Confronts Another Sex Scandal," *Los Angeles Times*, December 15, 2007; Steve Stecklow and Joe Lauria, "UN Peacekeepers Dodge Discipline," *Wall Street Journal*, March 22, 2010; Neil MacFarquhar, "Peacekeepers' Sex Scandals Linger, On Screen and Off," *New York Times*, September 8, 2011; "Two UN Peacekeepers Convicted of Sexually Assaulting Haitian Boy," *Caribbean News Corporation*, March 14, 2012.
73. Andrew Pollack, "Marines Seek Peace with Okinawa in Rape Case," *New York Times*, October 8, 1995; Teresa Watanabe, "Out to Buy Sex, They Decided 'on Rape,'" *Houston Chronicle*, October 29, 1995.
74. Nicholas Kristof, "Okinawans Look Back and Call War Futile," *New York Times*, June 22, 1995.
75. "Rape Case in Japan Turns Harsh Light on U.S. Military," *New York Times*, September 20, 1995; Eric Talmadge, "As U.S. Servicemen Reflect, Anger over Okinawa Rape Simmers," *San Francisco Chronicle*, October 5, 1995; Pollack, "Okinawa Governor Takes on Both Japan and U.S.," *New York Times*, October 5, 1995.
76. Interview with Tatsuko Yamada in Keyso, *Women of Okinawa*, 71–72.
77. Reuters, "Schoolgirl's Rape Spurs Review of Japan Treaty," *New York Times*, September 22, 1995; Sheryl WuDunn, "Rage Grows in Okinawa over U.S. Military Bases," *New York Times*, November 4, 1995.
78. Interview with Nobuko Karimata in Keyso, *Women of Okinawa*, 87.
79. "List of Main Crimes Committed and Incidents Concerning the U.S. Military on Okinawa," *Okinawa Times*, October 12, 1995.

80. Thomas Shapley, "Child's Rape Echoes Rape of Okinawa Itself," *Seattle Post-Intelligencer*, November 26, 1995; Antonia Levi, "Okinawa: Thousand-Year Rape of an Entire People," *Seattle Times*, November 9, 1995.

81. Johnson, "Okinawa," 115.

82. Eric Talmadge, "U.S. Bases Told to Get Out," *Record* (Bergen County NJ), October 22, 1995; "In Okinawa, Protest Against U.S. Military Following Rape Case," *New York Times*, October 22, 1995; Nicholas Kristof, "U.S. to Turn over Troops Accused of Murder or Rape to Japan," *New York Times*, October 26, 1995.

83. David Holley, "GI Pleads Guilty to Rape of Japanese Schoolgirl," *Los Angeles Times*, November 7, 1995; Pollack, "One Pleads Guilty to Okinawa Rape, 2 Others Admit Role," *New York Times*, November 8, 1995.

84. Ronald Smothers, "Accused Marines' Kin Incredulous," *New York Times*, November 6, 1995. For more on rape and race in U.S. history, see Davis, "Rape, Racism."

85. Graham Bradley and John Harris, "Rape Case Comments Sink Admiral," *Washington Post*, November 18, 1995; Irvin Molotsky, "Admiral Has to Quit over His Comments on Okinawa Rape," *New York Times*, November 18 1995.

86. Laura King, "Uproar over Admiral Greets Gore in Japan," *Buffalo News*, November, 19, 1995; Eric Schmitt, "Admiral's Gaffe Pushes Navy to New Scrutiny of Attitudes," *New York Times*, November 19, 1995.

87. Angst, "Sacrifice of a Schoolgirl," 152.

88. Reuters, "Accused U.S. Sailor Turned over to Japanese," *New York Times*, July 21, 1996; Reuters, "Marine Is Accused of Attempted Rape Near Okinawa Base," *New York Times*, January 16, 2000; Associated Press, "Japan Charges U.S. Serviceman with Rape," *New York Times*, July 19, 2001.

89. William McMichael, "TRADOC Reports Rapes at MD School," *Daily Press* (Newport News), November 8, 1996; Sonja Barisic, "Female Recruits Raped, Army Says," *Chicago Sun-Times*, November 8, 1996; Jay Apperson, Tom Bowman, and Lisa Respers, "2 Aberdeen Army Trainers Charged in Rape of Recruits," *Sun* (Baltimore), November 8, 1996.

90. Matthew Wald, "2 Are Charged with Rapes at an Army Training Center," *New York Times*, November 8, 1996.

91. Associated Press, "Rape Charges Prompt Army to Reinforce Buddy System," *New York Times*, November 9, 1996; Wald, "2 Are Charged."

92. Associated Press, "15 Suspended in Harassment Case at Army Base," *New York Times*, November 10, 1996; Associated Press, "Sex Complaints Flood Phones Set Up by Army," *New York Times*, November 12, 1996; Tim Weiner, "One Sergeant Pleads Guilty as Army Widens Sex

Inquiry," *New York Times*, November 13, 1996; Tom Bowman and Gilbert Lewthwaite, "Victims List Grows to 34 at Aberdeen," *Sun* (Baltimore), November 23, 1996.

93. Associated Press, "More Rape Charges Filed," *New York Times*, December 21, 1996; Eric Schmitt, "Army Investigators Press Search for Sex Offenders," *New York Times*, December 26, 1996; Eric Schmitt, "Sex Scandal Poses a Hurdle in Recruiting Army Women," *New York Times*, December 7, 1996; Eric Schmitt, "Role of Women in the Military Is Again Bringing Debate," *New York Times*, December 29, 1996.

94. Steven Myers, "Pentagon Is Urged to Separate Sexes," *New York Times*, December 16, 1997.

95. Steven Myers, "Defense Chief Rejects Advice to Separate Sexes in Training," *New York Times*, March 17, 1998.

96. Associated Press, "Trials Over, Army Faces Issues of Sex," *New York Times*, November 9, 1997; "Captain Enters Guilty Plea in Sexual Abuse of Private," *New York Times*, March 21, 1997; Associated Press, "Sergeant Gets 25-Years Term for 18 Rapes of Recruits," *New York Times*, May 7, 1997; Jackie Spinner, "Last Pending Rape Charged Dropped at Aberdeen," *Washington Post*, May 28, 1997; and Francis Clines, "Drill Sergeant Gets 6 Months for Sex Abuse at Army Post," *New York Times*, May 31, 1997.

97. Dana Priest and Jackie Spinner, "Close Look at Army Cases Urged," *Washington Post*, March 13, 1997.

98. Ian Fischer, "Black Soldiers Wrestle with Tangled Notions of Race and Justice in the Military," *New York Times*, June 17, 1997.

99. Tim Weiner, "One Sergeant Pleads Guilty as Army Widens Sex Inquiry," *New York Times*, November 13, 1996.

100. Frank Bruni, "Military Jury Acquits Cadet in Rape Case," *New York Times*, January 25, 1997; Reuters, "Army Sergeant Is Convicted of Sex Assaults," *New York Times*, June 13, 1997; Eric Schmitt, "General Removed over Relationship," *New York Times*, May 30, 1997; David Stout, "New Investigations of Harassment in Military," *New York Times*, May 31, 1997; Philip Shenon, "Commander at Aberdeen to Retire over Affair," *New York Times*, June 3, 1997; Associated Press, "Two Marines Are Indicted in Attack at Campsite," *New York Times*, June 28, 1997; Associated Press, "Sergeant in Sex Case Dishonorably Discharged," *New York Times*, September 1, 1997; Associated Press, "Ex-Drill Sergeant Convicted in Sex Case," *New York Times*, November 28, 1997; Philip Shenon, "Army's Leadership Blamed in Report on Sexual Abuses," *New York Times*, September 12, 1997.

101. See Benson, *Yugoslavia*.

102. See Klip and Sluiter, *International Criminal Tribunal*.

103. John Burns, "Bosnian Survivors Recount Brutality and Mass Slayings," *New York Times*, June 21, 1992.

104. See John Burns, "150 Muslims Say Serbs Raped Them in Bosnia," *New York Times*, October 3, 1992; Alan Riding, "European Inquiry Says Serbs' Forces Have Raped 20,000," *New York Times*, January 9, 1993; Marlise Simons, "Bosnian Rapes Go Untried by the UN," *New York Times*, December 7, 1994; Chuck Sudetic, "In Sarajevo, War Also Means Battle of the Sexes," *New York Times*, June 6, 1993.

105. See Buckley, *Kosovo*; Zirojević, "Kosovo."

106. "Clinton Voices Anger and Compassion at Serbian Intransigence Over Kosovo," *New York Times*, March 20, 1999.

107. Craig Whitney with Eric Schmitt, "NATO Had Signs Its Strategy Would Fail Kosovars," *New York Times*, April 1, 1999; John Kifner, "The Refugee Drama; Refugees Tell of Methodical Emptying of Pristina," *New York Times*, April 2, 1999; Carlotta Gall, "Rebel Officer Tells of Massacres Despite NATO Bombing," *New York Times*, April 4, 1999; Roger Cohen, "Tribunal Is Said to Cite Milosevic for War Crimes," *New York Times*, May 27, 1999; Celestine Bohlen, "Moscow, Seeing Obstacle, Sends Envoy to Belgrade," *New York Times*, May 28 1999.

108. Mladjenovic, "Caring at the Same Time," 183.

109. Mladjenovic, "Caring at the Same Time," 186–87.

110. See King and Mason, *Peace at Any Price*.

111. Associated Press, "US Sergeant in Kosovo Accused of Killing Girl," *New York Times*, January 10, 2000; Melissa Eddy, "US Peacekeepers Charged with Killing Girl," *Chicago Tribune*, January 17, 2000; Carlotta Gall, "G.I.'s in Kosovo Face Barrage of Complaints," *New York Times*, January 29, 2000; Steven Erlanger, "The Ugliest American," *New York Times Magazine*, April 2, 2000, 52; Roger Cohen, "US Sergeant Gets Life in Murder of Kosovo Girl, 11," *New York Times*, August 2, 2000; Steven Lee Myers, "Inquiry into Abuse by G.I.'s in Kosovo Faults Training," *New York Times*, September 19, 2000.

112. Critical Resistance and INCITE! Women of Color Against Violence, "Gender Violence," 223.

2. CONFRONTING AN ENEMY ABROAD

1. For more on violence, heteronormativity, and "home," see Mohanty and Martin, "What's Home Got to Do with It?"; and "At Home with Sex" in Johnston and Longhurst, *Space, Place, and Sex*. For an examination of the dual meaning of *domestic* in U.S. history, see "Manifest Domesticity" in Kaplan, *The Anarchy of Empire*.

2. Reddy, *Freedom with Violence*; Puar, *Terrorist Assemblages*; Morgensen, *Spaces between Us*.

3. Duggan, *Twilight of Equality*.
4. Vigil, *War Echoes*, 50; Vigil, "Heterosexualization and the State," 86–109.
5. Katz, *The Invention of Heterosexuality*, 14.
6. Canaday, *Straight State*, 4.
7. See Berlant and Warner, "Sex in Public," 547–66.
8. See Butler, *Frames of War*.
9. See Said, *Covering Islam*; Salaita, *Holy Land in Transit*; Trask, "The Color of Violence."
10. Michael Gordon, "Iraq Army Invades Capital of Kuwait in Fierce Fighting," *New York Times*, August 2, 1990. Also see Haj, *Making of Iraq, 1900–1963*; Hourani, *History of the Arab People*.
11. Steven Holmes, "Congress Backs Curbs against Iraq," *New York Times*, July 28, 1990.
12. "U.S., Soviets to Cut Chemical Weapons," 709–11.
13. See Limber and Wilcox, "Application of the UN Convention," 1246–50.
14. Joseph Treaster, "171 Americans Arrive in Jordan from Kuwait," *New York Times*, September 8, 1990.
15. Enloe, *Morning After*, 166.
16. Walter Goodman, "The Iraq Conflict on American TV," *New York Times*, September 17, 1990.
17. See "Bush to Meet Lawmakers as Anti-war Stand Grows," *Houston Chronicle*, December 29, 1990; Jonathan Kaufman, "European Public May Lag in US-led War," *Boston Globe*, January 13, 1991; Jane Gross, "Berkeley; Coffee Is Strong, Opinion Is Split," *New York Times*, January 14, 1991; Bob Keeler, "War United Feuding Peace Groups," *Newsday*, January 18, 1991.
18. See Glenn Frankel, "Iraq, Kuwait Waging an Old-Fashioned War of Propaganda," *Washington Post*, September 10, 1990; Lisa Leff, "Weary, Wary Evacuees Bring Tales of Horror," *Washington Post*, September 11, 1990; Maureen Dowd, "World Summit for Children: Bush Is in New York for the U.N. Conference," *New York Times*, September 30, 1990; and Johanna Neuman, "Kuwaiti's 'Shell of a Society,'" *USA Today*, October 1, 1990.
19. "Nayirah Kuwaiti girl testimony," June 15, 2010, accessed October 23, 2018, youtube.com/watch?v=LmfVs3WaE9Y.
20. "Excerpts from Speech by Bush at Marine Post," *New York Times*, November 23, 1990.
21. "Amnesty Report Says Iraqis Tortured and Killed Hundreds," *New York Times*, December 20, 1990; George H. W. Bush, "Address to the Nation on the Invasion of Iraq," January 16, 1991.
22. Walton, *Appeal to Pity*.
23. "Deception on Capitol Hill," *New York Times*, January 15, 1992.

24. Edelman, *No Future*; Peacock, *Innocent Weapons*; Stockton, *The Queer Child*.

25. Ken Fireman, "Victory in the Gulf: Iraqis Accept Peace Terms," *Washington Post*, March 4, 1991.

26. "Excerpts from Letter to U.N.," *New York Times*, April 8, 1991.

27. Zangana, *City of Widows*, 73.

28. Al-Ali and Pratt, *What Kind of Liberation?*, 46.

29. George H. W. Bush, "State of the Union Address," January 28, 1992.

30. George H. W. Bush, "Address to a Joint Session of Congress," September 11, 1990.

31. Tracy Wood and Faye Fiore, "No Charges Filed against Suspect Beaten by Police," *Los Angeles Times*, March 7, 1991.

32. Jason DeParle, "General and Troops Have Domestic Mission," *New York Times*, May 3, 1992; Charles Mohr, "To Modernize, the Army Is Bringing Back Light Infantry," *New York Times*, November 25, 1984. For a fuller history, see "Headquarters, 7th Infantry Division, 'Bayonets,'" GlobalSecurity.org, accessed September 2, 2017, www.globalsecurity.org/military/agency/army/7id.htm.

33. Gilmore, "Terror Austerity," 29–30.

34. Gonzalez, *Securing Paradise*, 149.

35. See Staff of the *Los Angeles Times*, *Understanding the Riots*.

36. Tom Matthews, "The Siege of L.A.," *Newsweek*, May 11, 1992.

37. Seth Mydans, "23 Dead after 2nd Day of Los Angeles Riots," *New York Times*, May 1, 1992.

38. Andrew Rosenthal, "Quayle Says Riots Sprang from Lack of Family Values," *New York Times*, May 20, 1992.

39. Midge Decter, "How the Rioters Won," *Commentary*, July 1, 1992.

40. "Excerpts from Speech by Bush in Los Angeles," *New York Times*, May 9, 1992.

41. Ferguson, *Aberrations in Black*, 89.

42. "Strange Juice (or the Murder of Latasha Harlins)" in Sapphire, *American Dreams*, 156–57.

43. "April 29th, 1992 (Miami)" in Sublime, *Sublime*.

44. See Balko, *Rise of the Warrior Cop*.

45. David Matustik, "Waco Davidian Sects Take Separate Paths," *Austin American-Statesman*, March 4, 1993; "Sect Arose from Split with Adventists," *New York Times*, March 1, 1993.

46. Various, sometimes slightly contradictory, lists of the national origins and demographics of the Branch Davidians can be found at "Total List of Texas Branch Davidians," Waco Cult, wacocult.tripod.com/neveragain/total.bd.html; "Branch Davidian Victims," Carol Moore's Waco Pages, carolmoore.net/waco/waco-victims.html; and

"Clive Doyle's Complete List of Mt. Carmel Deaths," Waco Holocaust Electronic Museum, February 28, 2001, web-ak.com/waco/death/map /d_list03.html. All sites accessed October 23, 2018.

47. Mark England and Darlene McCormick, "Violent Cult Had Faith in Twisted Leader," *San Francisco Chronicle*, March 1, 1993; Michael Kennedy and Cathleen Decker, "4 Federal Agents Killed in Shootout with Cult in Texas Violence," *Los Angeles Times*, March 1, 1993; Sam Howe Verhovek, "4 US Agents Killed in Texas Shootout with Cult," *New York Times*, March 2, 1993; Sam Howe Verhovek, "400 Law Agents Are in Standoff with Texas Cult," *New York Times*, March 2, 1993.

48. Sam Howe Verhovek, "Hardly Mentioned at Cultists' Trial: Their Leader," *New York Times*, February 26, 1994; Peter Applebome, "Bloody Sunday's Roots in Deep Religious Soil," *New York Times*, March 2, 1993; Sam Howe Verhovek, "'Messiah' Fond of Bible, Rock, and Women," *New York Times*, March 3, 1993; William Falk, "As Boy, Cult Chief Took Refuge in Revelation," *Newsday*, March 7, 1993; Walter Goodman, "As Television, Waco Drama Had a Grim Inevitability," *New York Times*, April 20, 1993.

49. "Apocalypse in Waco," *New York Times*, April 20, 1993; Verhovek, "'Messiah' Fond of Bible, Rock, and Women."

50. Verhovek, "4 US Agents Killed."

51. Verhovek, "400 Law Agents."

52. Adam Nossiter, "Warning of Violence Was Unheeded after Cult Leader's Gun Battle in '87," *New York Times*, March 10, 1993.

53. "The Waco Whitewash," *New York Times*, October 12, 1993; Verhovek, "Hardly Mentioned at Cultists' Trial."

54. Stephen Labaton with Sam Howe Verhovek, "Missteps in Waco: A Raid Re-Examined," *New York Times*, March 28, 1993. See also Sue Pressley and Mary Jordan, "20 'Mighty Men' Served Koresh as Loyal Warriors," *San Francisco Chronicle*, April 23, 1993; Stephen Labaton, "Agent's Advice: Attack on a Sunday," *New York Times*, March 3, 1993.

55. U.S. House of Representatives, *Military Involvement in the Government Operations at Waco.*

56. Sam Howe Verhovek, "Texas Cult Fortress Is Becoming Prison behind Barbed Wire," *New York Times*, April 13, 1993.

57. Stephen Labaton, "Reno Sees Error in Move on Cult," *New York Times*, April 20, 1993.

58. Stephen Labaton, "Confusion Abounds in the Capital on Rationale for Assault on Cult," *New York Times*, April 21, 1993; Sam Howe Verhovek, "Death in Waco: The Overview," *New York Times*, April, 20, 1993.

59. Robert Kessler and Timothy Phelps, "The FBI and Reno: Why They Ordered the Raid," *Newsday*, April 22, 1993.

60. Labaton, "Confusion Abounds in the Capital."
61. "Excerpts from Clinton News Conference," *New York Times*, April 21, 1993; Labaton, "Confusion Abounds in the Capital."
62. U.S. Department of Justice, *Report to the Deputy Attorney General on the Events at Waco, Texas, February 28 to April 19, 1993*, Section VII-A-2. See also "Sex Abuse Ruled Out at Koresh Compound," *Chicago Tribune*, May 5, 1993.
63. Verhovek, "In Shadow of Texas Siege, Uncertainty for Innocents," *New York Times*, March 8, 1993.
64. Labaton, "Confusion Abounds in the Capital."
65. U.S. Department of Justice, *Report to the Deputy Attorney General on the Events at Waco, Texas, February 28 to April 19, 1993*, Sections VII-B-4 and VII-A-1.
66. "Waco Whitewash"; William Safire, "Waco, Reno, Iraqgate," *New York Times*, October 14, 1993.
67. David Johnston, "US Saw Waco Assault as Best Option," *New York Times*, April 25, 1993.
68. Dick Reavis, "Remembering Waco, and Stealing It," *New York Times*, May 13, 1995.
69. See Pfeil, *White Guys*.
70. Reavis, "Remembering Waco."
71. Rick Bragg, "In Shock, Loathing, Denial: 'This Doesn't Happen Here,'" *New York Times*, April 20, 1995.
72. "Savagery in Oklahoma City," *New York Times*, April 20, 1995; Thomas Friedman, "Beirut, Okla.," *New York Times*, April 23, 1995; Bragg, "In Shock, Loathing, Denial"; John Kifner, "At Least 31 Are Dead," *New York Times*, April 20, 1995.
73. Serge Schmemann, "New Images of Terror," *New York Times*, April 24, 1995.
74. Dirk Johnson, "The Care Center," *New York Times*, April 20, 1995; Bragg, "In Shock, Loathing, Denial"; Kifner, "At Least 31 Are Dead."
75. Mohanty and Martin, "What's Home Got to Do with It?," 90.
76. Melinda Henneberger, "Oklahoma City; Where Nothing Ever Happens, Terrorism Did," *New York Times*, April 21, 1995.
77. Gerald Seib and John Harwood, "Oklahoma City Terror Bombing May Intensify Hard-Line Views on Crime and Immigration," *Wall Street Journal*, April 21, 1995.
78. A. M. Rosenthal, "Ending Forgiveness," *New York Times*, April 21, 1995.
79. Goodman, "Although Unrestrained in a Crisis, Television Is a Tie That Binds," *New York Times*, April 28, 1995.
80. Bragg, "In Shock, Loathing, Denial."
81. "A Twisted Rage," *New York Times*, April 24, 1995.

82. "Tiny Victim Shown in Dramatic Photo," *New York Times*, April 21, 1995; "Child in Photo Was 1-Year-Old Girl," *New York Times*, April 22, 1995.

83. Rick Bragg, "Tender Memories of Day-Care Center Are All That Remain after the Bomb," *New York Times*, April 20, 1995; "Statements by the President and Attorney General," *New York Times*, April 20, 1995.

84. "A Twisted Rage." Almon's gender was unconfirmed at first, producing pronoun confusion.

85. Todd Purdum, "Undertones of Relevance," *New York Times*, April 20, 1995; Linda Greenhouse, "Exposed—Again, Bombs in the Land of the Free," *New York Times*, April 23, 1995.

86. Todd Purdum, "Clinton and First Lady Offer Solace to the Young," *New York Times*, April 23, 1995.

87. "A Twisted Rage"; Peter Applebome, "The Pariah as Client," *New York Times*, April 28, 1995; Bragg, "Tender Memories"; Rick Bragg, "Blast Toll Is No Longer in Deaths, but Shattered Lives," *New York Times*, April 19, 1996; James Brooke, "All-American Defendant?," *New York Times*, June 2, 1996; Jim Yardley, "Execution on TV Brings Little Solace," *New York Times*, June 12, 2001; "History and Timothy McVeigh," *New York Times*, June 11, 2001; Jo Thomas, "McVeigh Guilty on All Counts in the Oklahoma City Bombing," *New York Times*, June 3, 1997.

88. John Kifner, "Authorities Hold a Man of 'Extreme Right-Wing Views," *New York Times*, April 22, 1995.

89. Sam Howe Verhovek, "Many Theories about Choice of the Target," *New York Times*, April 26, 1995; David Johnston, "Oklahoma Bombing Plotted for Months," *New York Times*, April 25, 1995.

90. Robert McFadden, "A Life of Solitude and Obsession," *New York Times*, May 4, 1995; Jo Thomas, "Nichols Convicted of Plot and Manslaughter Counts but Not of Actual Bombing," *New York Times*, December 24, 1997; "History and Timothy McVeigh."

91. McFadden, "A Life of Solitude."

92. Michel and Herbeck, *American Terrorist*, 106–7, 285.

93. Bragg, "On the Eve of His Execution, McVeigh's Legacy Remains Death and Pain," *New York Times*, June 10, 2001. Full text of the letter available at "McVeigh's Apr. 26 Letter to Fox News," Fox News, April 26, 2001, foxnews.com/story/0,2933,17500,00.html.

94. Pam Belluck, "McVeigh Said to Play Role in Seeking Holes in Government's Case," *New York Times*, May 11, 1995. My emphasis.

95. Antiterrorism and Effective Death Penalty Act of 1996, S.735, 104th Congress, 1996, Title I and Title II, Sec. 233(c); Title III, Sec. 324 (1); Neil Lewis, "Anti-Terrorism Bill: Blast Turns a Snail into a Race Horse," *New York Times*, April 21, 1995.

96. Antiterrorism and Effective Death Penalty Act of 1996, Title III, Sec. 301; Title II, Sec. 221; Title IV, Sec. 401; and Title IV, Sec. 421.

97. Illegal Immigration Reform and Immigrant Responsibility Act of 1996, H.R.3610, 104th Congress, 1996; Welch, *Detained*.

98. Illegal Immigration Reform and Immigrant Responsibility Act of 1996, Title V.

99. Personal Responsibility and Work Opportunity Reconciliation Act, H.R.3734, 104th Congress, 1996, Sec. 101.

100. Defense of Marriage Act, H.R.3396, 104th Congress, 1996, Sec. 3.

101. Roberts, *Killing the Black Body*, 217, 202.

102. U.S. Department of Health and Human Services, *Indicators of Welfare Dependence, Annual Report to Congress, 2008*, Table TANF 1. Also see U.S. Department of the Census, *Poverty Status of People, by Age, Race, and Hispanic Origin, 1959–2011*, accessed October 20, 2012, http://www.census.gov/hhes/www/poverty/data/historical/hstpov3.xls.

103. Teller-Elsberg et al., *Field Guide to the U.S. Economy*, 98–99.

104. Roberts, "Feminism, Race, and Adoption Policy," 44.

3. INTENT TO ENGAGE IN HOMOSEXUAL ACTS

1. Tracey Cooper-Harris, "Letter to President Barack H. Obama," *America Blog*, May 10, 2010, americablog.com/2010/05/a-letter-about-dadt-to-obama-from-former-sgt-tracey-l-cooper-harris.html.

2. Throughout this chapter, I deploy the commonly interchanged terms *gay, lesbian, homosexual*, and a number of acronyms with the greatest precision that linguistic conventions allow. I use the acronym LGBTQ to refer broadly to the heterogeneous and loosely coalitional community of lesbian, gay, bisexual, transgender, and queer people with the recognition that many more identities compose this collectivity, including intersex, pansexual, asexual, and genderqueer people, as well as many others. These letters are not omitted because the identities and people are unimportant but because the possible permutations of this acronym are endless; consequently, each individual must find the subjective point at which they see inclusiveness and clarity as most balanced. When I omit the B, T, or Q from the acronym here, it is intentional. I use *homosexuality* in reference to an abstract identity, never referring to any individual as "a homosexual," due to its medicalized and offensive tenor, though such phrasing was common during the 1990s. Whenever possible, I use both *lesbian* and *gay* together to address the frequent erasure of lesbianism from accounts of same-sex eroticism and LGBTQ movements, but again I am at times compelled to adopt the language used in my archive and use only *gay* when *gay and lesbian*

would be more accurate. I use *queer* in its more specific senses of an anti-assimilationist LGBT identity and an intellectual movement toward deconstructing normativities rather than its common contemporary usage as an umbrella term for LGBTQ communities and people. While I have prioritized precision and stipulated some limitations, I also understand that each of these terms is power-laden, and their misuse, even with the best intentions, can trigger both outrage as well as feelings of marginalization or erasure. I remain open to any and all critiques of my diction in this work as such concerns are by no means insignificant.

3. Hammond, "Interview with Audre Lorde," 19.

4. Larry Kramer, "Where Are We Now?," draft of *Gay Men's Health Crisis Newsletter*, Fall 1982, Box 1, Folder 7, Larry Kramer Papers, Beinecke Library, Yale University.

5. Halperin, *How to Be Gay*, 12–13.

6. Cohen, "Contested Membership," 362–64.

7. *Time*, September 8, 1975. A significant body of literature was produced in the 1990s both for and against the full integration of lesbian and gay soldiers. For work in favor of integration, see Halley, *Don't*; Shawyer, *And the Flag Was Still There*; Humphrey, *My Country, My Right*; Zeeland, *Barrack Buddies and Soldier Lovers*; and Shilts, *Conduct Unbecoming*. For some work against integration, see Ray, *Gays*; and Wells-Petry, *Exclusion*.

8. According to Emily Hobson, "Money for AIDS, not war" was used in San Francisco as early as 1983 during campaigns against the homophobic Proposition N and U.S. involvement in El Salvador. It would spread throughout the decade, especially in moments of increased military activity, gaining more attention after ACT UP New York member Adam Ralston created a stamp designed to mark U.S. bills with "Money for AIDS or war" (see ACT UP *Weekly Report*, October 2, 1989, Box 5, Folder 13, Larry Kramer Papers).

9. Ghaziani, *The Dividends of Dissent*; "Official MMOW Platform Ballot," *Advocate*, September 14, 1999, 57; Lou Chibbaro Jr., "Our History of Marching in Washington," *Between the Lines News*, June 11, 2017.

10. Neal Riley, "Bradley [*sic*] Manning Won't Get Pride Honors," *San Francisco Chronicle*, June 8, 2013. The event eventually included both a military recruiting tent and a community contingent marching in honor of Manning with Vietnam-era whistleblower Daniel Ellsberg accepting the honor while she remained incarcerated. See Caitlin Carmody, "San Francisco Pride, Chelsea Manning, and Queer Assimilation," *Found SF*, www.foundsf.org/index.php?title=San_Francisco_Pride,_Chelsea _Manning,_and_Queer_Assimilation.

11. Hobson, *Lavender and Red*; Hanhardt, *Safe Space*; Gould, *Moving Politics*. For more on the history of LGBTQ radicalism, see Stryker, *Transgender History*; Mecca, *Smash the Church*; and Power, *No Bath*.
12. Gould, *Moving Politics*, 122–75.
13. Larry Kramer, transcript of speech delivered at the New York Civil Liberties Union Constitution Day Celebration, September 17, 1987, Box 5, Folder 7, Larry Kramer Papers.
14. S. Thomas Corbett to Larry Kramer, March 13, 1988, Box 4, Folder 19, Larry Kramer Papers; "Marty" to Larry Kramer, April 2, 1987, Box 3, Folder 18, Larry Kramer Papers.
15. Lorde, *A Burst of Light*, 30.
16. "War on AIDS" had appeared occasionally in print before then, but its use grew precipitously during this time. For example, see Randy Shilts, "Koop Urges Reagan to Take the Lead in 'War' on AIDS," *San Francisco Chronicle*, March 5, 1987; Frances McMorris, "Gays Protest Lack of Drugs to Wage War against AIDS," *New York Daily News*, March 25, 1987; Judith Cummings, "Doctors, Fighting the War on AIDS, Find They Are among the Casualties," *New York Times*, April 11, 1987; Ronald Kotulak and Jon Van, "A Glimmer of Hope in the War on AIDS," *Chicago Tribune*, June 7, 1987; Robert Greskovic, "12 Troupes Join 'Dancing for Life' War on AIDS," *Los Angeles Times*, October 7, 1987; Lynne Duke, "Black Women's Group Declares War on AIDS," *Washington Post*, November 11, 1987.
17. "Gay Rights Leaders Gather in Virginia," *United Press International*, February 27, 1988, www.upi.com/Archives/1988/02/27/Gay-rights-leaders-gather-in-Virginia/5403572936400/; "Living in Wartime" in Callen, *Purple Heart*; Vito Russo, "Why We Fight," YouTube video, 11:45, posted by "Dr. Atmos," July 21, 2012, youtube.com/watch?v=e4ctXqdoVwk.
18. Larry Kramer, draft of "1,112 and Counting," article for the *New York Native*, Box 1, Folder 7, Larry Kramer Papers. In 1983 Larry Kramer wrote in multiple letters and article drafts with statements like, "I am not joking when I tell you that I am ready to plant bombs and organize an Irgun (the Israeli underground terrorist organization)." No such statement appeared in the final version. Ten years later the anonymous broadside *Wake Up Queers or We're All Through* declared, "Red ribbons remind me not of the dead, but of the rest of us . . . A red armband would be more like it. Or a red grenade, slung off the side of your belt," but again, statements with potential militarized sentiment like this were apparently never backed with militarized action.
19. Jason DeParle, "Rude, Rash, Effective, Act-Up Shifts AIDS Policy," *New York Times*, January 3, 1990. For a fuller history of

ACT UP, see France, *How to Survive a Plague*; Hubbard, *United in Anger*; and ACT UP NY's digital Capsule History, available at www.actupny.org/documents/capsule-home.html.

20. Hobson, *Lavender and Red*, 155–86.

21. Highleyman, "Peace Activism"; Esther Kaplan, "The Mighty ACT UP Has Fallen: The Philadelphia Story," *POZ Magazine*, November 2001; Jason Schafer, "'Fuck the Draft': The Amazing Story of Kiyoshi Kuromiya, Creator of the Iconic Protest Poster," *Dangerous Minds*, February 9, 2015, dangerousminds.net/comments/fuck_the_draft_the_amazing _story_of_kiyoshi_kuromiya_creator_of_the_iconic.

22. Thomas Shultz, Neal Broome, and Robert Price to Larry Kramer, July 25, 1988, Box 5, Folder 7, Larry Kramer Papers.

23. Jane Hall, "AIDS Activists Barge in on CBS, 'MacNeil/Lehrer' Show," *Los Angeles Times*, January 23, 1991; "Protesters Disrupt CBS Evening News with Dan Rather 1991," YouTube video, 0:34, posted by "Old Tape Archive," January 1, 2010, youtube.com/watch?v=Im_VektDXqM; "News Zaps," ACT UP NY, accessed January 22, 2017, www.actupny.org /diva/CBnews.html.

24. "Rush-Hour Protest Calls Attention to AIDS," *New York Times*, January 24, 1991; "Day of Desperation Synopsis," ACT UP NY, accessed January 23, 2017, www.actupny.org/diva/synDesperation.html.

25. Anonymous Queers, *Queers Read This*, 1990, Box 6, Folder 14, Larry Kramer Papers; *Wake Up Queers or We're All Through*, Box 7, Folder 4, Larry Kramer Papers.

26. Randy Shilts, "Politics Confused with Therapy," *San Francisco Chronicle*, June 26, 1989.

27. Crimp, *Melancholia and Moralism*, 228.

28. Duggan's term *homonormativity* was first extended by Puar's *homonationalism* and has subsequently been further extended into *settler homonationalism* and into *homomilitarism*. See Morgensen, "Settler Homonationalism," 105–31; Camacho, "Homomilitarism," 144–75.

29. Frank, *Gays in Foreign Militaries*; Eric Schmitt, "Military's Anti-Gay Rule Is Costly, a Report Says," *New York Times*, June 20, 1992.

30. For the uses of social science by the military during World War II, see Berube, *Coming Out Under Fire*. For Roosevelt's "gay witch hunt" in Rhode Island, see Chauncey, "Christian Brotherhood or Sexual Perversion?," 294–317.

31. Tamar Lewin, "Gay Groups Suggest Marines Selectively Prosecute Women," *New York Times*, December 4, 1988.

32. Lewin, "Gay Groups."

33. Cooper-Harris, "Letter to President Barack H. Obama."

34. "Marines Are Said to Suspend Alleged Lesbians," *New York Times*, February 23, 1988.
35. Lewin, "Gay Groups."
36. Williams Institute, "Discharges Under the Don't Ask/Don't Tell Policy: Women and Racial/Ethnic Minorities," accessed December 4, 2016, williamsinstitute.law.ucla.edu/wp-content/uploads/Gates -Discharges2009-Military-Sept-2010.pdf.
37. Williams Institute, "Discharges."
38. Charles Bogino and AJ Plunkett, "Navy Looks at Suicide Theory in *Iowa* Blast," *Newport (VA) Daily Press*, May 25, 1989.
39. Jeffrey Schmalz, "Sailor Says He Had No Role in Blast," *New York Times*, May 29, 1989; Richard Halloran, "Suicide Theory Pursued in *Iowa* Blast," *New York Times*, June 3, 1989; David Johnston, "Navy's Evidence Suggests Sailor Set Off Ship Blast to Kill Himself," *New York Times*, July 19, 1989.
40. Robert Zelnick and Mark Brender, "Did Leaks from USS *Iowa* Probe Smear Sailor?," *Daily News*, July 8, 1989; Richard Halloran, "*Iowa* Captain Doubts Sailor Named by Inquiry Set Blast," *New York Times*, December 12, 1989; Richard Halloran, "2 Survivors of *Iowa* Blast Deny Shipmate Set It Off," *New York Times*, December 14, 1989; Stephen Engelberg, "Navy Finding on *Iowa* Blast Is Drawing Criticism," *New York Times*, November 5, 1989; Ken Ringle, "The Gunner's Mate, Firing Back," *Washington Post*, December 12, 1989; Richard Halloran, "Navy Account of *Iowa* Explosion Is Criticized," *New York Times*, December 13, 1989.
41. Jeffrey Schmalz, "Gay Politics Goes Mainstream," *New York Times Magazine*, October 11, 1992.
42. See Alessandra Stanley, "Republicans in Houston: The Religious Rights; Many Delegates See an Immoral and Scary America," *New York Times*, August 20, 1992. James Davidson Hunter's *Culture Wars* can be credited with sparking some interest in the term, which has been endlessly recycled since, but a cursory Google search reveals that Buchanan's speech still appears to be the primary referent. Full text of Buchanan's speech is available on his official website under "1992 Republican National Convention Speech," http://buchanan.org/blog/1992 -republican-national-convention-speech-148; and on YouTube under "Pat Buchanan culture war."
43. Jeffrey Schmalz, "A Delicate Balance: The Gay Vote; Gay Rights and AIDS Emerging as Divisive Issues in Campaign," *New York Times*, August 20, 1992.
44. Eric Schmitt, "The 1992 Campaign: Clinton and Bush Agree on Trimming Armed Forces, but Their Paths Vary," *New York Times*, October 21, 1992.

45. Duggan, *Twilight of Equality*, 15.
46. Jeffrey Schmalz, "The 1992 Elections: The States—The Gay Issues; Gay Areas Are Jubilant Over Clinton," *New York Times*, November 5, 1992.
47. Thomas Friedman, "Clinton to Open Military's Ranks to Homosexuals," *New York Times*, November 12, 1992; Thomas Friedman, "New Tune for Clinton: Sounds of Compromise," *New York Times*, November 22, 1992; Richard Whittle, "A Hot Potato for Clinton, Homosexuals in the Military: Will It Burn Clinton?," *Salt Lake Tribune*, November 29, 1992.
48. Adam Clymer, "Lawmakers Revolt on Lifting Gay Ban in Military Service," *New York Times*, January 27, 1993; Art Pine, "Issue Explodes into an All-Out Lobbying War," *Los Angeles Times*, January 28, 1993; Gwen Ifill, "The Gay Troop Issue; Clinton Accepts Delay in Lifting Military Gay Ban," *New York Times*, January 30, 1993.
49. Melissa Healy, "Nunn's Offer on Military Gays: Don't Ask, Don't Tell," *Los Angeles Times*, March 30, 1993.
50. In addition to his rabid support for the gay ban, Nunn admitted to firing two aides in separate occasions during the 1980s because of their homosexuality. See Jeffrey Schmalz, "The Transition; Nunn under Fire from Gay Groups," *New York Times*, December 6, 1992. For more on Moskos, see Nathaniel Frank, "The Real Story of Military Sociology and 'Don't Ask, Don't Tell,'" *Lingua Franca*, October 2000, 71–81.
51. Michael Finkel, "Complications," *New York Times*, May 27, 2001; "Don't Ask, Don't Tell," *New York Times*, February 1, 1998; David Kocieniewski, "On Politics; Unbought and Unbossed, or 'Don't Ask, Don't Tell'?," *New York Times*, October 29, 2000; Timothy Ferris, "Quantum Leaps; Weirdness Makes Sense," *New York Times*, September 29, 1996.
52. Policy Concerning Homosexuality in the Armed Forces, Title 10, U.S. Code, Section 654, 2.
53. Policy Concerning Homosexuality.
54. Clinton signed Executive Order 12968, which says, "The United States Government does not discriminate on the basis of race, color, religion, sex, national origin, disability, *or sexual orientation* in granting access to classified information," in August 1995 (my emphasis). In May 1998 he signed Executive Order 13087, which prohibited discrimination based on sexual orientation in the federal government's civilian workforce.
55. See U.S. Constitution, Article 1, Section 8, Clause 14, "The Congress shall have Power to . . . make Rules for the Government and Regulation of the land and naval Forces."
56. "Homosexuals in the Military Part 2," C-SPAN video, 2:29:18, at minute 99, www.c-span.org/video/?40574-1/homosexuals-military-part-2.

57. Sedgwick, *Epistemology of the Closet*; Signorile, *Queer in America*; Cheryl Lavin, "A Who's Who of the Outed," *Chicago Tribune*, June 8, 1993.
58. See Callen, *Surviving AIDS*, 168; Liebman, *Coming Out Conservative*; Redmont, *Generous Lives*, 81; and Stratton, *Coming Out Jewish*.
59. Snorton, *Nobody*.
60. Joan Biskupic, "Hawaii Ruling May Allow Gay Marriages," *San Francisco Chronicle*, May 7, 1993.
61. Defense of Marriage Act, H.R.3396, 104th Congress, 1996, Sec. 3. Massachusetts began offering marriage licenses to same-sex couples in May of 2004. Later that year eleven states passed constitutional amendments defining marriage as "the union of one man and one woman," but these would be some of the last victories against same-sex marriages. DOMA was ruled unconstitutional in *United States v. Windsor* in June 2013, and Hawai'i issued its first same-sex marriage licenses later that year.
62. Elisabeth Bumiller, "Out and Proud to Serve," *New York Times*, September 20, 2011.
63. Frank Rich, "Summer of Matthew Shepard," *New York Times*, July 3, 1999; Philip Shenon, "Revised Military Guidelines Fail to Quell Gay Concerns," *New York Times*, August 14, 1999; Associated Press, "Soldier Convicted of Killing Army Private with Bat," *Record* (Bergen County NJ), December 9, 1999. It is particularly telling how many newspapers' editorial boards came out against the policy in direct response to the conviction of Winchell's killers. For examples, see "Proof of the Failure of 'Don't Ask, Don't Tell,'" *San Francisco Chronicle*, December 10, 1999; "Policy Has Wrong Effect, No More 'Don't Ask, Don't Tell,'" *Syracuse Herald Journal*, December 13, 1999; "'Don't Ask, Doesn't Work' Policy Doesn't Protect Gays in the Military," *Record*, December 16, 1999; and "'Don't Ask, Don't Tell': A Failure from the Start," *USA Today*, December 16, 1999.
64. Philip Shenon, "Pentagon Moving to End Abuses of 'Don't Ask, Don't Tell' Policy," *New York Times*, August 13, 1999.
65. Robert Pear, "President Admits 'Don't Ask' Policy Has Been Failure," *New York Times*, December 12, 1999.
66. Burrelli, "'Don't Ask, Don't Tell,'" Table I.
67. The first quote is by SLDN cofounder C. Dixon Osburn and the second by Rear Admiral (ret.) Alan Steinman; Bailey, *The Strange History of Don't Ask Don't Tell*.
68. Anjani Trivedi, "Lesbian Army Veteran Should Get Benefits, Federal Judge Rules," *Time*, August 30, 2013.
69. See Autumn Sandeen, "The Policies Keeping Trans People from Military Service," *Advocate*, March 17, 2014.

70. Chris Geidner, "Meet the Trans Scholar Fighting against the Campaign for Out Trans Military Service," *Buzzfeed News*, September 9, 2013, buzzfeed.com/chrisgeidner/meet-the-trans-scholar-fighting-against-the-campaign-for-out.

71. Tom Brook, "Mattis Freezes Transgender Policy," *USA Today*, August 29, 2017.

4. A MUTUALLY BENEFICIAL RELATIONSHIP

1. Darlene Keju, "Speech to World Council of Churches, Vancouver 1983," accessed October 18, 2016, youtube.com/watch?v=1hxCGlA5oJQ.

2. For a history of Micronesian origin and arrival, see Kirch, *On the Road*, 165–206; and Matsuda, *Pacific Worlds*, 9–29. For a critique of the Euro-American division of Micronesian, Polynesian, and Melanesian, see Arvin, "Possessions of Whiteness."

3. For contemporaneous examples of these, see Susan Rasky, "Senate Upholds Ban of Abortions," *New York Times*, August 4, 1990; and both the Report of the International Criminal Tribunal for Rwanda and the Report of the International Criminal Tribunal for the former Yugoslavia.

4. For example, Joseph Masco's influential work *Nuclear Borderlands* focuses almost exclusively on the U.S. Southwest. James Yamazaki's *Children of the Atom Bomb* only mentions the Marshall Islands on a few pages (108–12) despite being a useful study of the intergenerational consequences of radiation. More recently, while not predominantly about sexuality, Parsons and Zaballa, *Bombing the Marshall Islands* has placed these events in the broader Cold War context and addresses human reproduction in an appendix.

5. See Price, "What Is Reproductive Justice?," 42–65.

6. For an overview of indigenous feminisms, see Green, *Making Space for Indigenous Feminism*. This chapter owes a particular debt to the indigenous feminism developed by Muscogee Creek legal scholar and activist Sarah Deer.

7. Here I use Gerald Vizenor's term, a portmanteau of *survival* with either *resistance* or *endurance* representing a state of active survival, first described in *Manifest Manners*.

8. Compact of Free Association Agreement between the United States of America and the Marshall Islands, Amending the Agreement of June 25, 1983, Concerning the Compact of Free Association, as Amended, Signed at Majuro April 30, 2003, 1.

9. Lyons, *American Pacificism*, 27.

10. For an extensive history of U.S. involvement in the Pacific, see Crocombe, *The Pacific Islands*. For the role of commercial enterprises specifically, see Rigby, "Origins of American Expansion," 221–37.

11. Lyons, *American Pacificism*, 139.
12. See Chappell, *Double Ghosts*, 19; and O'Brien, *The Pacific Muse*, 116–21.
13. Hezel, *First Taint of Civilization*, 200.
14. See Bensimon, *The Bikini Book*.
15. Teaiwa, "Bikinis and Other S/pacific N/oceans." Originally presented at the Pacific History Association Conference, Christchurch, New Zealand, December 1992.
16. Teaiwa, "Bikinis and Other S/pacific N/oceans," 23.
17. For an account of the U.S. World War II campaigns in Micronesia, see Crowl and Love, *United States Army*.
18. United Nations Security Council Resolution 21, Articles 3, 6, and 7.
19. Stone, *Radio Bikini*.
20. See LaDuke, *Militarization of Indian Country*.
21. John Anjain, quoted in Dibblin, *Day of Two Suns*, 25.
22. The most complete account of the impacts of the U.S. nuclear program on the Marshallese is Smith-Norris, *Domination and Resistance*.
23. Quoted in Smith-Norris, *Domination and Resistance*, 135.
24. Jeton Anjain, "Statement of Senator Jeton Anjain, Rongelap Atoll, Republic of the Marshall Islands, Trust Territory of the Pacific Islands, Before the Fourth Committee of the United Nations," October 30, 1985.
25. The People of Rongelap, "Is Rongelap Atoll Safe?," statement at "Resettlement of Rongelap Atoll, Republic of the Marshall Islands," hearing before the Committee on Energy and Natural Resources, United States Senate, 102nd Congress, September 19, 1991, 14.
26. Jeton Anjain, statement at "Resettlement of Rongelap Atoll, Republic of the Marshall Islands," hearing before the Committee on Energy and Natural Resources, United States Senate, 102nd Congress, September 19, 1991, 10.
27. Ogilvy-Stuart and Shalet, "Effect of Radiation," 109–16.
28. See Barzelatto, "Understanding Sexual and Reproductive Violence," 13–18; and "Politics of Reproductive Violence," 583–91.
29. See Hickel, *Who Owns America?*, 208.
30. See Lawrence, "The Indian Health Service," 400–419.
31. "In 1983 dose rates calculated for cesium-137 in young females (59 mrem/y) were nearly twice those calculated for adult males and females (32 mrem/y). Adolescent females had cesium-137 body burdens exceeding those of both adult males and adult females during the measurements years 1981–1984 and 1989" (National Research Council's Committee on Radiological Safety in the Marshall Islands Board on Radiation Effects Research, *Radiological Assessments*, 56–57).

32. Lemeyo Abon, "Health and Resettlement in the Marshall Islands," presentation, 8th Plenary Meeting, 21st Regular Session of the UN Human Rights Council, Geneva, September 13, 2012.

33. Kathy Jetñil-Kijiner, "History Project," from Jetñil-Kijiner, *Iep Jaltok*, 20.

34. Yamazaki, *Children of the Atom Bomb*, 112 and 117.

35. Barclay, *Melal*, 20–21, quote on 82.

36. Numbers on maternal mortality from United Nations Children's Fund, *State of the World's Children 2015 Country Statistical Tables*. For examples, the 2015 maternal mortality rate was 215 in Papua New Guinea, 124 in Tonga, 100 in the Federal States of Micronesia, 78 in Vanuatu, 30 in Fiji, and 14 in the United States. Because of the Marshall Islands' circumstances, their maternal mortality data is based on the 2008–12 average rather than the most updated data (see "Marshall Islands Statistics," UNICEF, December 27, 2013, www.unicef.org/infobycountry /marshallislands_statistics.html).

37. "GBD Profile: Marshall Islands," 1.

38. Abacca Anjain-Maddison, "Statement of the President, Iju in Ean club (Rongelapese Women Club)," presentation, 8th Plenary Meeting, 21st Regular Session of the UN Human Rights Council, Geneva, September 14, 2012.

39. See Robinson and Hamilton, "Radiation Doses for Marshall Islands," 1–11.

40. Ms. Dribo and Ms. Lorennij's Fifth-Grade Class at Ebeye Public Elementary School, *Life in the Marshall Islands*, 8.

41. United Nations Food and Agriculture Organization, *Marshall Islands and FAO Partnering to Improve Food Security and Income-Earning Opportunities*, 2015, accessed August 4, 2017, www.fao.org/3/a-av262e.pdf.

42. See Smith-Norris, *Domination and Resistance*, 125–51; Currie, *Kwajalein Atoll*, 118–53.

43. Compact of Free Association, 1.

44. Compact of Free Association, Section 111, 2.

45. Compact of Free Association, Sections 311 and 313, 29–30.

46. Compact of Free Association Section 321 guarantees the continuation of access to Kwajalein, and Section 212 details the financial compensation paid to the RMI for it. Section 161 also ensures that U.S. activity at Kwajalein Atoll is exempt from any U.S. environmental policy or regulation. Pp. 29, 20, 9.

47. Compact of Free Association, Section 174, 13.

48. See Smith-Norris, *Domination and Resistance*, 156–57.

49. See Hamilton, *Report: A Visual Description*.

50. Compact of Free Association, Sections 141–43, 4–8.

51. See Economic Policy, Planning, and Statistics Office, *RMI 2011 Census*; and Michael Duke, "Marshall Islanders: Migration Patterns and Health

Care Challenges," *Migration Information Source*, May 22, 2014, accessed August 2, 2017, www.migrationpolicy.org/article/marshall-islanders -migration-patterns-and-health-care-challenges.

52. Deer, *Beginning and End of Rape*, 72.

53. U.S. Department of State, *Trafficking in Persons Report*, June 2016.

54. Julianne Walsh, "Adoption and Agency: American Adoptions of Marshallese Children," presentation at Out of Oceania: Diaspora, Community, and Identity conference, University of Hawaii at Manoa, October 22, 1999, accessed April 4, 2017, adoptionbirthmothers.com/adoption -and-agency-american-adoptions-of-marshallese-children/.

55. Personal Responsibility and Work Opportunity Reconciliation Act of 1996, Sections 401 and 431.

56. Personal Responsibility and Work Opportunity Reconciliation Act of 1996, Section 400.

57. Compact of Free Association, Section 141; Williams and Hampton, "Barriers to Health Services," 317–26.

58. Secretariat of the Pacific Regional Environmental Program, *Report of the SPC/UNEP/ASPEI Intergovernmental Meeting*.

59. See Hezel, *Strangers in Their Own Land*.

60. Smith-Norris, *Domination and Resistance*, 26–27 and 57–61.

61. Smith-Norris, *Domination and Resistance*, 118–20.

62. Smith-Norris, *Domination and Resistance*, 99.

63. Johnson, "Youth Lead Youth in Marshall Islands," 35.

64. Braun and Keju-Johnson, "Community Perceptions of *Youth to Youth in Health*," 54.

65. The ongoing work of YTYIH can be seen on their Facebook page at facebook.com/Jodrikdrik/ as well as through their ongoing U.S. Health and Human Services Department grant for the RMI Urban Teenage Pregnancy Prevention Project at www.hhs.gov/ash/oah/grant -programs/teen-pregnancy-prevention-program-tpp/current-grantees /youth-to-youth-in-health/index.html.

66. Lieom-Loeak and Maddison, "Women's Organizations," 82.

67. Lieom-Loeak and Maddison, "Women's Organizations," 83.

68. See Lieom-Loeak and Maddison, "Women's Organizations," 84– 90; and Birchall, *"Someone to Save Me from Him."*

69. Kathy Jetñil-Kijiner, "Dear Matafele Peinem," September 23, 2014, accessed April 9, 2017, youtube.com/watch?v=DJuRjy9k7GA. Also in Jetñil-Kijiner, *Iep Jaltok*, 70–73.

70. Hau'ofa, "Our Sea of Islands," 16.

71. Smith, "Queer Theory and Native Studies," 48.

72. Tuck and Yang, "Decolonization Is Not a Metaphor."

73. Kathy Jetñil-Kijiner, "For the Dakota Water Protectors," September 5, 2016, accessed August 15, 2017, kathyjetnilkijiner.com/nodapl/.

74. See, for example, Mulligan, "Early Environments," 233. For a specifically indigenous context, see Bombay, Matheson, and Anisman, "Intergenerational Effects of Indian Residential Schools," 320–38.

75. Kathy Jetñil-Kijiner, "Islands Dropped from a Basket," March 8, 2017, accessed August 9, 2017, kathyjetnilkijiner.com/islands-dropped-from-a-basket/.

76. Jetñil-Kijiner's book title *Iep Jaltok*, according to an epigraph, translates as "'a basket whose opening is facing the speaker.' Said of female children. She represents a basket whose contents are made available to her relatives. Also refers to matrilineal society of the Marshallese" (2). The book contains two concrete poems shaped like baskets as well.

77. St. John and Jendrusch, "Plants Introduced to Hawai'i."

78. See Kauanui, "Native Hawaiian Decolonization," 281–87; McIntosh, "Polynesian Voyaging and Pacific Self-Determination," 6; McIntyre, "Partition of the Gilbert and Ellice Islands," 135–46; Na'puti, "Speaking the Language of Peace," 301–13; Poblete-Cross, "Bridging Indigenous and Immigrant Struggles," 501–22; and Veran, "Oceania Rising," 12–13.

79. Kathy Jetñil-Kijiner, "Utilomar," December 8, 2016, accessed August 8, 2017, kathyjetnilkijiner.com/utilomar/.

CONCLUSION

1. For examples of those claiming war on Afghanistan would protect U.S. civilians, see Serge Schmemann, "War Zone; What Would 'Victory' Mean?," *New York Times*, September 16, 2001; Elisabeth Bumiller, "Bush Pledges Attack on Afghanistan Unless It Surrenders Bin Laden Now; He Creates Cabinet Post for Security," *New York Times*, September 21, 2001; and Patrick Tyler, "Jets Pound Taliban Sites for a Second Night; FBI Agents Shift Antiterror Tactics," *New York Times*, October 9, 2001. For examples of those claiming war on Iraq would protect U.S. civilians, see George W. Bush and Tony Blair, "Facing 'Common Enemy,' Terrorism and Weapons of Mass Destruction," *New York Times*, February 1, 2003; Colin Powell, "Powell's Address, Presenting 'Deeply Troubling' Evidence on Iraq," *New York Times*, February 6, 2003; Max Boot, "A War for Oil? Not This Time," *New York Times*, February 13, 2003; Tom Zeller, "How Americans Link Iraq and Sept. 11," *New York Times*, March 2, 2003; George W. Bush, "Excerpts from Bush's News Conference on Iraq and Likelihood of War," *New York Times*, March 7, 2003; John McCain, "The Right War for the Right Reasons," *New York Times*, March 12, 2003.

2. For some examples, see Barry Bearak, "The Taliban; Once Vigilantes, Now Strict Rulers," *New York Times*, September 19, 2001; George W. Bush, "President Bush's Address on Terrorism before a Joint Meeting of Congress," *New York Times*, September 21, 2001; David Rohde, "Rebel Region; Education Offers Women in Northern Afghanistan a Ray of Hope," *New York Times*, October 3, 2001; Thomas Friedman, "Yes, but What?," *New York Times*, October 5, 2001; Neil MacFarquhar, "Teachings; Bin Laden and His Followers Adhere to an Austere, Stringent Form of Islam," *New York Times*, October 7, 2001; and Hillary Clinton, "Clinton at Yale: Optimistic on Crisis, but Work Is Ahead," *New York Times*, October 14, 2001. For some critiques of this repurposing of feminism, see Chew, "What's Left?"; and Hunt, "'Embedded Feminism.'"

3. For examples of articles characterizing Hussein as pathologically hypermasculine, see Kenneth Pollack, "A Last Chance to Stop Iraq," *New York Times*, February 21, 2003; Colin Powell, "Saddam Hussein Remains Guilty," *New York Times*, March 6, 2003; Roger Morris, "A Tyrant 40 Years in the Making," *New York Times*, March 14, 2003; Ibrahim al-Marashi, "Just Following (Saddam Hussein's) Orders," *New York Times*, March 25, 2003; Amatzia Baram, "Loyalty at the Point of a Gun," *New York Times*, March 28, 2003.

4. *New York Times* reporter Judith Miller was at the center of two related controversies in the early years of the War on Terror, the false-reporting controversy and a controversy around the "outing" of Valerie Plame as a CIA operative that resulted in Miller's imprisonment for refusing to reveal anonymous government sources. Two of her most egregiously misleading publications were Michael Gordon and Judith Miller, "U.S. Says Hussein Intensifies Quest for A-Bomb Parts," *New York Times*, September 8, 2002; and Judith Miller, "Illicit Arms Kept Till Eve of War, an Iraqi Scientist Is Said to Assert," *New York Times*, April 21, 2003. After the start of the war, the *New York Times* published a number of pieces conceding that there were "a number of instances of coverage that was not as rigorous as it should have been," including "The Times and Iraq," *New York Times*, May 26, 2004; Don Van Natta Jr., Adam Liptak, and Clifford Levy, "'The Miller Case': A Notebook, a Cause, a Jail Cell, and a Deal," *New York Times*, October 16, 2005; and Byron Calame, "The Miller Mess: Lingering Issues among the Answers," *New York Times*, October 23, 2005. For reporting on Miller's work from outside of the publication where she worked, see William Jackson Jr., "Miller's Star Fades (Slightly) at NY Times," *Editor and Publisher*, October 2, 2003; James Moore, "How Chalabi and the White House Held the Front Page," *Guardian*, May 28, 2004; Franklin Foer, "The Source of

the Trouble," *New York Magazine*, May 21, 2005; David Corn, "CIA Leak Scandal: Judy Miller and the Times Speak," *Nation*, October 16, 2005; and Massing, *Now They Tell Us*.

5. Like many events occurring at the blurry margins of the War on Terror, Siddiqui's story is murky and marked with great uncertainty. That story is headline news in Pakistan and goes barely noticed in the United States. The U.S. government publicly identified Siddiqui as an Al-Qaeda operative in May 2004 after Khalid Sheikh Mohammed allegedly named her during one of his 183 waterboardings by CIA operatives. Siddiqui was not seen or heard from in transnational media until a lawyer submitted a petition for habeas corpus in Pakistan in July 2008, alleging the United States had been holding her for four years. That same month, she is alleged to have shot multiple U.S. army personnel and FBI agents with an M4 carbine stolen from one of the army officers during an interrogation. Siddiqui nearly died in the subsequent gunfight but survived to be flown to the United States in August and indicted in New York in September for assault with attempt to kill. See John Broder, "American Being Sought by the FBI Found His Place in Islam, Relatives Say," *New York Times*, May 28, 2004; "IHC Moved against Dr. Aafia Siddiqui Detention under Habeas Corpus in Afghanistan," *Frontier Star* (Pakistan), July 29, 2008; Eric Schmitt, "Pakistani Suspected of Qaeda Ties Is Held," *New York Times*, August 5, 2008; Benjamin Weiser and Eric Schmitt, "Scientist Tied to Al Qaeda Is Ordered Held without Bail," *New York Times*, August 6, 2008; Alex Rodriguez, "Is She a Victim of the U.S. or Is She 'Terror Mom,'" *Los Angeles Times*, February 3, 2010; CJ Hughes, "Pakistani Scientist Found Guilty of Firing at Americans," *New York Times*, February 4, 2010; and *United States v. Aafia Siddiqui*, Southern District of New York, July 31, 2008.

6. Al-Jawaheri, *Women in Iraq*, 141–43.

7. See, for example, Robin Gerber, "Don't Send Military Women to the Back of the Troop Train," *USA Today*, September 23, 2002; Cynthia Tucker, "Warrior Women Fit to Conquer Whatever Awaits," *Atlanta Journal-Constitution*, March 23, 2003; Ann McFeatters, "U.S. Prohibition on Women in Combat Is Outmoded," *Deseret News*, April 20, 2003; and David Zucchino, "Equal Right to Fight," *Los Angeles Times*, April 10, 2004.

8. See Elisabeth Bumiller, "Pentagon Allows Women Closer to Combat, but Not Close Enough," *New York Times*, February 9, 2012; Craig Whitlock, "4 Women Sue Over Pentagon's Combat-Exclusion Policy," *Washington Post*, November 28, 2012; Harris, *Living Legends and Full Agency*; and Shawn Snow, "Where Are the Female Marines?," *Marine Corps Times*, March 5, 2018.

9. See Fusco, *A Guide for Female Interrogators*; and McKelvey, *One of the Guys*.

10. See Paula Broadwell, "Women Soldiers Crucial to US Mission," *Boston Globe*, August 26, 2009; for the military's self-description, Sgt. Christopher McCullough, "Female Engagement Teams: Who They Are and Why They Do It," accessed March 15, 2018, army.mil/article/88366/female _engagement_teams_who_they_are_and_why_they_do_it; and, for a critical perspective, Dyvik, "Women as 'Practitioners' and 'Targets.'"

11. Joya, *A Woman among Warlords*, 185.

12. For more on Jessica Lynch, see Jim Yardley, "TV Images Confirm Fears of Prisoners' Kin," *New York Times*, March 25, 2003; John Broder, "Commandos Rescue Soldier; She Was Held Since Ambush," *New York Times*, April 2, 2003; Alessandra Stanley, "In Hoopla Over a P.O.W., a Mirror of U.S. Society," *New York Times*, April 18, 2003; David Kirkpatrick, "Jessica Lynch Criticizes U.S. Accounts of Her Ordeal," *New York Times*, November 7, 2003; and Frank Rich, "Pfc. Jessica Lynch Isn't Rambo Anymore," *New York Times*, November 9, 2003. Also see Brittain, "Benevolent Invaders, Heroic Victims"; and "Precious Little Jessi" in Faludi, *Terror Dream*.

13. For more on Abu Ghraib, see Thom Shanker, "6 G.I.'s in Iraq Are Charged with Abuse of Prisoners," *New York Times*, March 21, 2004; James Risen, "G.I.'s Are Accused of Abusing Iraqi Captives," *New York Times*, April 29, 2004; Douglas Jehl and Eric Schmitt, "In Abuse, a Portrayal of Ill-Prepared, Overwhelmed G.I.'s," *New York Times*, May 9, 2004; and Eric Schmitt, "Iraq Abuse Trial Is Again Limited to Lower Ranks," *New York Times*, March 23, 2006. Also see "Wielding Masculinity inside Abu Ghraib and Guantanamo" in Enloe, *Globalization and Militarism*; Nusair, "Gendered, Racialized, and Sexualized Torture."

14. See Mark Mazzetti, "New Head of C.I.A.'s Clandestine Service Is Picked, as Acting Chief Is Passed Over," *New York Times*, May 7, 2013; Chris Megerian, "CIA Agent's Past Casts a Shadow," *Los Angeles Times*, April 1, 2018; and John Kiriakou, "I Went to Prison for Exposing Torture. Gina Haspel Covered It Up," *Washington Post*, March 18, 2018.

15. For more on the Haditha massacre, see the highly misleading first mention ("15 Iraqi civilians and a marine were killed Saturday when a roadside bomb exploded in Haditha") in Edward Wong, "Road Bomb Aimed at Convoy Kills 15 Civilians and a Marine in Restive Iraqi Province," *New York Times*, November 21, 2005; and the more accurate Tim McGirk, "Collateral Damage or Civilian Massacre in Haditha?," *Time*, March 19, 2006; Ellen Knickmeyer, "In Haditha, Memories of a Massacre," *Washington Post*, May 27, 2006; Michael Schmidt, "Junkyard Gives Up Secret Accounts of Massacre in Iraq," *New York Times*, December 14, 2011; and

Charlie Savage and Elisabeth Bumiller, "An Iraqi Massacre, a Light Sentence, and a Question of Military Justice," *New York Times*, January 27, 2012. For more on the Panjwai massacre, see Taimoor Shah and Graham Bowley, "G.I. Kills Afghan Villagers; Children among 16 Dead," *New York Times*, March 12, 2012; Taimoor Shah and Graham Bowley, "For an Afghan, Coming Home to a Massacre," *New York Times*, March 13, 2012; Kirk Johnson, "Hearing Starts for Soldier Accused of Killing 16 Afghan Civilians," *New York Times*, November 5, 2012; and Jack Healy, "In 2 Cases of Mass Murder, Military Juries Render Heavy Judgments: Life Without Parole for Killing 16 Afghans," *New York Times*, August 24, 2013.

16. For more on Mahmudiyah, see Edward Wong, "G.I.'s Investigated in Slayings of Four and Rape in Iraq," *New York Times*, July 1, 2006; David Cloud and Kirk Semple, "Former G.I. Held in Rape and Four Slayings in Iraq," *New York Times*, July 4, 2006; Reuters, "Three More U.S. Soldiers Charged with Rape and Murder," *New York Times*, July 9, 2006; Campbell Robertson and Atheer Kakan, "Ex-G.I. Guilty of Rape and Killings in Iraq," *New York Times*, May 9, 2009; James Dao, "Ex-Soldier Gets Life for Killings in Iraq," *New York Times*, May 22, 2009; and David Zucchino, "Soldier Convicted in Rape, Murder of Iraqi Girl Is Found Hanged," *Los Angeles Times*, February 18, 2014.

17. Fathi et al., "Environmental Pollution," 7–25. For more reports, see Sarah Morrison, "Iraq Records Huge Rise in Birth Defects," *Independent*, October 13, 2012; "Iraq: War's Legacy of Cancer," *Al Jazeera English*, March 15, 2013; Nafeez Ahmed, "How the World Health Organisation Covered Up Iraq's Nuclear Nightmare," *Guardian*, October 13, 2013; Frederick Reese, "Depleted Uranium and the Iraq War's Legacy of Cancer," *Mint Press News*, July 2, 2014; and Barbara Koeppel, "How the U.S. Made Dropping Radioactive Bombs Routine," *Washington Spectator*, March 30, 2016.

18. Sune Engel Rasmussen and Fatima Faizi, "'I Am a Criminal, What Is My Crime?': The Human Toll of Abortion in Afghanistan," *Guardian*, April 26, 2017.

19. Cohen et al., "Reproductive and Other Health Outcomes"; Patricia Kime, "Wounded Troops Battle Obstacles to Sex and Intimacy," *Military Times*, December 29, 2014; Denise Grady, "Study Maps 'Uniquely Devastating' Genital Injuries among Troops," *New York Times*, January 13, 2017.

20. See Office of the Under Secretary of Defense for Acquisition, Technology, and Logistics, *Fiscal Year 2016 Operational Energy Annual Report*; and, for a critique, John Lawrence, "The US Military Is a Major Contributor to Global Warming," *San Diego Free Press*, June 2014.

21. For more on Responsibility to Protect, see Warren Hoge, "Report Urges Big Changes for the U.N.," *New York Times*, December 1, 2004; James

Traub, "The Un-U.N.," *New York Times*, September 11, 2005; David Rieff, "A Nation of Pre-emptors?," *New York Times*, January 15, 2006; Hoge, "Intervention, Hailed as a Concept, Is Shunned in Practice," *New York Times*, January 20, 2008; Scott Malcomson, "When to Intervene," *New York Times*, December 14, 2008; Neil MacFarquhar, "When to Step In to Step War Crimes Causes Fissures," *New York Times*, July 23, 2009; and Mark Landler, "U.S. Urged to Adopt Policy Justifying Intervention," *New York Times*, July 24, 2013. Responsibility to Protect has also been the subject of several recent book-length projects, including Bellamy, *Responsibility to Protect*; Glanville, *Sovereignty and the Responsibility to Protect*; and Hehir, *The Responsibility to Protect*. Also see the International Coalition for the Responsibility to Protect website at responsibilitytoprotect.org.

22. Atanasoski, *Humanitarian Violence*, 23.

23. For more on U.S. intervention in central Africa and Kony 2012, see Thom Shanker and Rick Gladstone, "Armed U.S. Advisers to Help Fight African Renegade Group," *New York Times*, October 15, 2011; Noam Cohen, "A Video Campaign and the Power of Simplicity," *New York Times*, March 12, 2012; Brain Stelter, "From Flash to Fizzle," *New York Times*, April 15, 2012; and Jeffrey Gettleman, "In Vast Jungle, U.S. Is Aiding Hunt for Kony," *New York Times*, April 30, 2012.

24. See "The History of the Arms and Great Seal of the Commonwealth of Massachusetts," Secretary of the Commonwealth of Massachusetts, accessed January 14, 2014, https://www.sec.state.ma.us/pre/presea /sealhis.htm. The connection between "Come over and help us" and Responsibility to Protect was also made by Noam Chomsky in his July 2009 address at the UN General Assembly, "'Come Over and Help Us': A History of R2P," *Monthly Review*, accessed January 14, 2014, http:// mrzine.monthlyreview.org/2009/chomsky 030809.html.

25. Faludi, *Terror Dream*, 215.

26. For more on the hunt for Osama Bin Laden, see Mark Mazzetti and Helene Cooper, "Detective Work on Courtier Led to Breakthrough on Bin Laden," *New York Times*, May 2, 2011; Mark Mazzetti, Helene Cooper, and Peter Baker, "Behind the Hunt for Bin Laden," *New York Times*, May 3, 2011; Thomas Friedman, "Farewell to Geronimo," *New York Times*, May 4, 2011; and Mark Mazzetti, "Vaccination Ruse Used in Pursuit of Bin Laden," *New York Times*, July 12, 2011.

27. As a crude measure of media attention, Piestewa was mentioned in 8 *New York Times* articles between March 2003 and 2004, whereas Jessica Lynch was mentioned in 115. Shoshana Johnson, a Black woman captured alongside Lynch, received mention in 10 arti-

cles during this period. For more on Piestewa, see Patti Jo King, "Remembering Lori Ann Piestewa: Hopi Woman Warrior," *Indian Country Today Media Network*, April 13, 2011, accessed March 4, 2014, indiancountrytodaymedianetwork.com/2011/04/13/remembering-lori -ann-piestewa-hopi-woman-warrior-27896.

28. Shigematsu, Bhagwati, and PaintedCrow, "Women-of-Color Veterans," 101.
29. Denetdale, "Securing Navajo National Boundaries," 133–34.
30. For more on the profiling of Arabs, Muslims, and others assumed to be Arab or Muslim, see Sharma, "White Nationalism, Illegality and Imperialism"; Murray, "Profiled"; and Cainkar, *Homeland Insecurity*.
31. For impacts on Latinos, see Borderlands Autonomist Collective, "Resisting the Security-Industrial Complex"; Diaz-Cotto, "Latinas"; Falcón, "'National Security'"; and Gordillo, "The Bracero." For impacts on gender-non-conforming people, see Bassichis, Lee, and Spade, "Building an Abolitionist Trans and Queer Movement." For impacts on Native nations, see Tamez, "The Texas-Mexico Border Wall."
32. See Marc Lacey and David Herszenhorn, "Congresswoman Is Shot in Rampage Near Tucson," *New York Times*, January 9, 2011; Dan Frosch and Kirk Johnson, "Gunman Kills 12 at Colorado Theater; Scores Are Wounded, Reviving Debate," *New York Times*, July 21, 2012; Steven Yaccino, Michael Schwirtz, and Marc Santora, "Gunman Kills 6 at Sikh Temple near Milwaukee," *New York Times*, August 6, 2012; Peter Applebome and Michael Wilson, "'Who Would Do This to Our Poor Little Babies,'" *New York Times*, December 15, 2012. For some analysis of these events, see Paul Farhi, "Adam Lanza, and Others Who Committed Mass Shootings, Were White Males," *Washington Post*, December 20, 2012; and David Leonard, "The Unbearable Invisibility of White Masculinity: Innocence in the Age of White Male Mass Shootings," *Gawker*, January 12, 2013, accessed March 3, 2014, http://gawker.com /5973485/the-unbearable-invisibility-of-white-masculinity-innocence -in-the-age-of-white-male-mass-shootings.
33. See Joe Heim, "Recounting a Day of Rage, Hate, Violence and Death," *Washington Post*, August 14, 2017.
34. Robert McFadden, "12 Killed, 31 Wounded in Rampage at Army Post; Officer Is Suspect," *New York Times*, November 6, 2009; Michael Shear and Michael Schmidt, "12 Shot to Death by Lone Gunman at a Naval Base," *New York Times*, September 17, 2013; and Dave Montgomery, Manny Fernandez, and Ashley Southall, "Iraq Veteran at Fort Hood Kills 3 and Himself," *New York Times*, April 3, 2014.
35. For more on the military mental health crisis, see Morrison, *The Inside Battle*.

36. Discharges under DADT peaked at 1,227 in 2001 (about 85 separations per 100,000 service members, just below the 1983 peak in homosexuality-related discharges of 97 per 100,000), dropping in all but two of the next eight years to 428 in 2009. See Williams Institute, "Discharges."

37. For more on the Air Force Academy scandal, see Diana Schemo, "Rate of Rape at Academy Is Put at 12% in Survey," *New York Times*, August 29, 2003; Diana Schemo, "Air Force Ignored Academy Abuse," *New York Times*, September 23, 2003; and Thom Shanker, "Commanders Are Faulted on Assaults at Academy," *New York Times*, December 8, 2004. For the relative likelihood of sexual assault and combat death for women in the military, see Jane Harman, "Rapists in the Ranks: Sexual Assaults Are Frequent, and Frequently Ignored, in the Armed Services," *Los Angeles Times*, March 31, 2008. For more on the military sexual assault crisis generally, see Benedict, *The Lonely Soldier*; Hunter, *Honor Betrayed*; and Nelson, *For Love of Country*.

38. Andrea Stone, "Mental Toll of War Hitting Female Servicemembers; On Front Lines, Women Face Trauma Like Never Before," *USA Today*, January 2, 2008; and Elisabeth Bumiller, "Obama Ends 'Don't Ask, Don't Tell' Policy," *New York Times*, July 22, 2011.

39. See Helene Cooper, "Senate Rejects Blocking Military Commanders from Sex Assault Cases," *New York Times*, March 7, 2014; and "Freedom to Serve: The Definitive Guide to LGBT Military Service," *Servicemembers Legal Defense Network*, July 27, 2011, 3.

40. For more on Cindy Sheehan, see Monica Davey, "G.I. Families United in Grief, but Split by the War," *New York Times*, January 2, 2005; Richard Stevenson, "Mother Takes Protest to Bush's Ranch," *New York Times*, August 7, 2005; Richard Stevenson, "Of Many Deaths in Iraq, One Mother's Loss Becomes a Protest," *New York Times*, August 8, 2005; Anne Kornblut, "Mother's Grief-Fueled Vigil Becomes Nexus for Antiwar Protesters," *New York Times*, August 13, 2005; Elisabeth Bumiller, "Protester Vows to Continue Her Vigil Near Bush Ranch," *New York Times*, August 17, 2005; Elisabeth Bumiller, "Turning Out to Support a Mother's Protest," *New York Times*, August 18, 2005; Marc Santora, "Mother Who Lost Son in Iraq Continues Fight Against War," *New York Times*, September 19, 2005; and Jennifer Steinhauer and Carolyn Marshall, "Sheehan Says She's Quitting as Face of Peace Movement," *New York Times*, May 30, 2007.

41. For more on militarized motherhood, see Lizette Alvarez, "Wartime Soldier, Conflicted Mom," *New York Times*, September 26, 2009; de Alwis, "Ambivalent Maternalisms"; and Haw, "Militarism and Motherhood." For more on "mama grizzlies," see Judith Warner, "The New

Momism," *New York Times*, October 31, 2010; and Gail Collins, "The Grizzly Manifesto," *New York Times*, November 6, 2010.

42. For more on Code Pink, see "With Passion and a Dash of Pink, Women Gather to Protest War," *New York Times*, March 9, 2003; Benjamin and Evans, *Stop the Next War Now*; and their website at codepink4peace.org.

43. For more on Okinawa Women Act Against Military Violence, see Harumi Ozawa and James Hardy, "Rape Exposes Darker Side of U.S. Military Presence," *Daily Yomiuri* (Tokyo), April 17, 2005; Eric Johnston, "Latest U.S. Troops Incident Mobilizes Activists," *Japan Times*, February 13, 2008; Justin McCurry, "Arrests of US Sailors in Okinawa Reignites Opposition to Bases," *Christian Science Monitor*, October 18, 2012; and their website at www.genuinesecurity.org/partners/okinawa.html. More on GABRI-ELA can be found at gabrielaph.com and Women Cross DMZ at www .womencrossdmz.org. For more on women's peace movements more generally, see Cockburn, *Antimilitarism*; Enloe, *Globalization and Militarism*.

44. For more on the Revolutionary Association of the Women of Afghanistan, see Brodsky, *With All Our Strength*; Chavis, *Meena, Heroine of Afghanistan*; and their website at rawa.org.

45. For more on the Organization of Women's Freedom in Iraq, see Lauren Sandler, "Veiled and Worried in Baghdad," *New York Times*, September 16, 2003; Medea Benjamin, "A Day for Marching," *Washington Post*, March 20, 2004; Sabrina Tavernise, "Shielding Women from a Renewal of Domestic Violence," *New York Times*, October 14, 2004; Houzan Mahmoud, "Why I Am Not Taking Part in These Phoney Elections; the Elections in Iraq," *Independent*, January 28, 2005; "Accidental Activist Fights for Freedom; Yanar Mohammed Started by Tackling Iraq's Emerging Flesh Market 10 Years Ago," *Toronto Star*, April 12, 2013; Fatimah Waseem, "Human Rights Groups Slams Iraq over Treatment of Women in Prison," *McClatchy-Tribune News Service*, February 7, 2014; and their website at owfi.info/EN.

46. See the Right to Heal website at righttoheal.org. For more on the group, see Common Dream, "Washington: #RightToHeal: 11 Years After U.S. Invasion, Bearing Witness to Iraq War's Lasting Harm," *U.S. Official News*, March 28, 2014; and Jada Smith, "'Environmental Poisoning' of Iraq Is Claimed," *New York Times*, March 27, 2014.

47. About Face, "Who We Are," accessed May 20, 2018, aboutfaceveterans .org/who-we-are/.

48. Puar, *Terrorist Assemblages*, 3–4.

49. Sycamore, Introduction. For more on Against Equality, Queers Undermining Israeli Terrorism, and Queers for Economic Justice, see their websites at againstequality.org, quitpalestine.org, and q4ej.org.

50. For more on INCITE, the Sylvia Rivera Law Project, and the Native Youth Sexual Health Network, see their websites at incite-national.org, srlp.org, and nativeyouthsexualhealth.com.

51. For more on prison abolition, visit the organization Critical Resistance at criticalresistance.org.

52. For more on Undocuqueer, see equalityarchive.com/issues /undocuqueer-movement; for Undocublack, see undocublack.org; and for a key group organizing around these principles, visit Mijente at mijente.net.

53. For more on these movements, visit the Movement for Black Lives at policy.m4bl.org and the Black Youth Project at byp100.org.

54. Bradley Graham and Josh White, "Abizaid Credited with Popularizing the Term 'Long War,'" *Washington Post*, February 3, 2006.

55. See Scott Wilson and Al Kamen, "'Global War on Terror' Is Given New Name," *Washington Post*, March 25, 2009; and the Department of Homeland Security's website on "Countering Violent Extremism," dhs .gov/topic/countering-violent-extremism.

56. Lorde, *Sister Outsider*, 53.

BIBLIOGRAPHY

ARCHIVAL SOURCES

Larry Kramer Papers. Beinecke Library, Yale University. New Haven CT.

PUBLISHED SOURCES

Abon, Lemeyo. "Health and Resettlement in the Marshall Islands." Presentation, 8th Plenary Meeting, 21st Regular Session of the UN Human Rights Council, Geneva, September 13, 2012.

Al-Ali, Nadje, and Nicola Pratt. *What Kind of Liberation? Women and the War on Iraq.* Berkeley: University of California Press, 2009.

Alexander, Karen, and Mary Hawkesworth, eds. *War and Terror: Feminist Perspectives* Chicago: University of Chicago Press, 2008.

Alexander, M. Jacqui. *Pedagogies of Crossing: Meditations on Feminism, Sexual Politics, Memory, and the Sacred.* Durham: Duke University Press, 2005.

Al-Jawaheri, Yasmin Husein. *Women in Iraq: The Gender Impact of International Sanctions.* Boulder CO: Lynne Rienner Publishers, 2008.

Allyn, David. *Make Love, Not War: The Sexual Revolution; An Unfettered History.* New York: Routledge, 2001.

Alsultany, Evelyn. *Arabs and Muslims in the Media: Race and Representation after 9/11.* New York: New York University Press, 2012.

Angst, Linda Isako. "The Sacrifice of a Schoolgirl: The 1995 Rape Case, Discourses of Power, and Women's Lives in Okinawa." In *Local Violence, Global Media: Feminist Analysis of Gendered Representations*, edited by Lisa Cuklanz and Sujata Moorti, 132–59. New York: Peter Lang Publishing, 2009.

Anjain, Jeton. Statement at "Resettlement of Rongelap Atoll, Republic of the Marshall Islands," hearing before the Committee on Energy and Natural Resources, United States Senate, 102nd Congress, September 19, 1991.

———. "Statement of Senator Jeton Anjain, Rongelap Atoll, Republic of the Marshall Islands, Trust Territory of the Pacific Islands, Before the Fourth Committee of the United Nations." October 30, 1985.

Anjain-Maddison, Abacca. "Statement of the President, Iju in Ean Club (Rongelapese Women Club)." Presentation, 8th Plenary Meeting, 21st Regular Session of the UN Human Rights Council, Geneva, September 14, 2012.

Antiterrorism and Effective Death Penalty Act of 1996, S.735, 104th Congress, 1996.

Arvin, Maile. "Possessions of Whiteness: Settler Colonialism and Anti-Blackness in the Pacific." *Decolonization: Indigeneity, Education and Society*, June 2, 2014.

Atanasoski, Neda. *Humanitarian Violence: The US Deployment of Diversity*. Minneapolis: University of Minnesota Press, 2013.

Bacevich, Andrew. *The New American Militarism: How Americans Are Seduced by War*. Oxford, UK: Oxford University Press, 2005.

Baer, Kenneth. *Reinventing Democrats: The Politics of Liberalism from Reagan to Clinton*. Lawrence: University Press of Kansas, 2000.

Bailey, Fenton, dir. *The Strange History of Don't Ask Don't Tell*. HBO Productions, 2010.

Balko, Radley. *The Rise of the Warrior Cop: The Militarization of America's Police Forces*. New York: PublicAffairs, 2013.

Barclay, Robert. *Melal: A Novel of the Pacific*. Honolulu: University of Hawaii Press, 2002.

Barzelatto, Jose. "Understanding Sexual and Reproductive Violence: An Overview." *International Journal of Gynecology and Obstetrics* 63, Suppl. 1 (December 1998): 13–18.

Bassichis, Morgan, Alexander Lee, and Dean Spade. "Building an Abolitionist Trans and Queer Movement with Everything We've Got." In *Captive Genders: Trans Embodiment and the Prison-Industrial Complex*, edited by Eric Stanley and Nat Smith. Oakland: AK Press, 2011.

Bayer, Ronald. *Homosexuality and American Psychiatry: The Politics of Diagnosis*. Princeton: Princeton University Press, 1987.

Belkin, Aaron. *Bring Me Men: Military Masculinity and the Benign Façade of American Empire, 1898–2001*. New York: Columbia University Press, 2012.

Bellamy, Alex. *Responsibility to Protect*. New York: Polity, 2009.

Benedict, Helen. *The Lonely Soldier: The Private War of Women Serving in Iraq*. Boston: Beacon Press, 2009.

Benjamin, Medea, and Jodi Evans, eds. *Stop the Next War Now: Effective Responses to Violence and Terrorism*. Honolulu: Inner Ocean Publishing, 2005.

Bensimon, Kelly. *The Bikini Book*. New York: Assouline, 2005.

Benson, Leslie. *Yugoslavia: A Concise History*. New York: Palgrave Macmillan, 2004.

Berghahn, V. R. *Militarism: The History of an International Debate, 1861–1979*. Cambridge, UK: Cambridge University Press, 1984.

Berlant, Lauren. *The Queen of America Goes to Washington City: Essays on Sex and Citizenship*. Durham: Duke University Press, 1997.

Berlant, Lauren, and Lisa Duggan, eds. *Our Monica, Ourselves: The Clinton Affair and the National Interest*. New York: New York University Press, 2001.

Berlant, Lauren, and Michael Warner. "Sex in Public." *Critical Inquiry* 24, no. 2 (Winter 1998): 547–66.

Berube, Allan. *Coming Out Under Fire: The History of Gay Men and Women in World War II*. New York: The Free Press, 1990.

Beverley, John. *Latinamericanism after 9/11*. Durham: Duke University Press, 2011.

Bhaskaran, Suparna. *Made in India: Decolonizations, Queer Sexualities, Trans/national Projects*. New York: Palgrave Macmillan, 2004.

Bhattacharyya, Gargi. *Dangerous Brown Men: Exploiting Sex, Violence and Feminism in the War on Terror*. London: Zed Books, 2008.

Birchall, Alison. *"Someone to Save Me from Him": Findings from the Community Engagement Study on the Design of the Violence against Women and Girls Support Service in the Republic of the Marshall Islands*. Majuro: Women United Together Marshall Islands, 2015.

Bland, Lucy, and Laura Doan, eds. *Sexology Uncensored: The Documents of Sexual Science*. Chicago: University of Chicago Press, 1998.

Bombay, Amy, Kimberly Matheson, and Hymie Anisman. "The Intergenerational Effects of Indian Residential Schools: Implications for the Concept of Historical Trauma." *Transcultural Psychology* 51, no. 3 (2014): 320–38.

Borderlands Autonomist Collective. "Resisting the Security-Industrial Complex: Operation Streamlines and the Militarization of the Arizona-Mexico Borderlands." In *Beyond Walls and Cages: Prisons, Borders, and Global Crisis*, edited by Jenna Loyd, Matt Mitchelson, and Andrew Burridge. Athens: University of Georgia Press, 2012.

Braun, Kathryn, and Darlene Keju-Johnson. "Community Perceptions of *Youth to Youth in Health*: A Peer Education Program for Primary Health Care, Marshall Islands." *Pacific Health Dialog* 4, no. 1 (1994).

Brier, Jennifer, Jim Downs, and Jennifer Morgan, eds. *Connexions: Histories of Race and Sex in North America*. Urbana-Champaign: University of Illinois Press, 2016.

Brigham, Robert. *Iraq, Vietnam, and the Limits of American Power*. New York: Perseus Books, 2006.

Brittain, Melisa. "Benevolent Invaders, Heroic Victims, and Depraved Villains: White Femininity in Media Coverage of the Invasion of Iraq." In *(En)gendering the War on Terror: War Stories and Camouflaged Politics*, edited by Krista Hunt and Kim Rygiel. London: Ashgate, 2006.

Brodsky, Anne. *With All Our Strength: The Revolutionary Association of the Women of Afghanistan*. New York: Routledge, 2003.

Browder, Laura. *Her Best Shot: Women and Guns in America*. Chapel Hill: University of North Carolina Press, 2006.

Buckley, Kevin. *Panama: The Whole Story*. New York: Simon and Schuster, 1991.

Buckley, William Joseph, ed. *Kosovo: Contending Voices on Balkan Interventions*. Grand Rapids: William Eerdmans, 2000.

Burrelli, David. "'Don't Ask, Don't Tell': The Law and Military Policy on Same-Sex Behavior." *Congressional Research Service*, October 14, 2010.

Bush, George H. W. "Address to a Joint Session of Congress," September 11, 1990.

———. "Address to Nation on Panama Invasion." December 20, 1989.

———. "Address to the Nation on the Invasion of Iraq." January 16, 1991.

———. "Remarks to the American Legislative Exchange Council." March 1, 1991.

———. "State of the Union Address." January 28, 1992.

Bush, George W. "Address to a Joint Session of Congress and the Nation." September 20, 2001.

Butler, Judith. *Bodies That Matter: On the Discursive Limits of Sex*. New York: Routledge, 1993.

———. *Frames of War: When Is Life Grievable?* London: Verso, 2009.

———. "Imitation and Gender Insubordination." In *The Lesbian and Gay Studies Reader*, edited by Henry Abelove, Michele Aina Barale, and David Halperin, 307–20. New York: Routledge, 1993.

Cainkar, Louise. *Homeland Insecurity: The Arab American and Muslim American Experience After 9/11*. New York: Russell Sage Foundation, 2009.

Califia, Patrick. *Speaking Sex to Power: The Politics of Queer Sex*. New York: Cleis Press, 2001.

Callen, Michael. *Purple Heart*. Tops and Bottoms Music, 1988.

———. *Surviving AIDS*. New York: HarperCollins, 1990.

Camacho, Keith. "Homomilitarism: The Same-Sex Erotics of the US Empire in Guam and Hawai'i." *Radical History Review* 123 (October 2015): 144–75.

Cameron, Deborah, and Don Kulick. *Language and Sexuality*. Cambridge, UK: Cambridge University Press, 2003.

Cammermeyer, Margarethe, with Chris Fisher. *Serving in Silence: Vietnam Nurse, Mother of Four, Highest-Ranking Officer to Challenge the Military's Antigay Policy*. New York: Viking Penguin, 1994.

Canaday, Margot. *The Straight State: Sexuality and Citizenship in Twentieth-Century America*. Princeton: Princeton University Press, 2009.

Capps, Walter. *The New Religious Right: Piety, Patriotism, and Politics*. Columbia: University of South Carolina Press, 1990.

Carter, Julian. *The Heart of Whiteness: Normal Sexuality and Race in America, 1880–1940*. Durham: Duke University Press, 2007.

Chappell, David. *Double Ghosts: Oceanian Voyagers on Euroamerican Ships*. London: M. E. Sharpe, 1997.

Chauncey, George, Jr. "Christian Brotherhood or Sexual Perversion? Homosexual Identities and the Construction of Sexual Boundaries in the World War I Era." In *Hidden from History: Reclaiming the Gay and Lesbian Past*, edited by Martin Duberman, Martha Vicinus, and George Chauncey Jr. New York: Meridian, 1989.

Chavis, Melody. *Meena, Heroine of Afghanistan: The Martyr Who Founded RAWA, the Revolutionary Association of the Women of Afghanistan*. New York: St. Martin's Griffin, 2004.

Chew, Huibin Amelia. "What's Left? After 'Imperial Feminist' Hijackings." In *Feminism and War*, edited by Chandra Talpade Mohanty, Minnie Bruce Pratt, and Robin Riley. London: Zed Books, 2008.

Chollet, Derek, and James Goldgeier. *America between the Wars, from 11/9 to 9/11: The Misunderstood Years between the Fall of the Berlin Wall and the Start of the War on Terror*. New York: Public Affairs, 2008.

Chomsky, Noam. *Hegemony or Survival: America's Quest for Global Dominance*. New York: Henry Holt, 2003.

Churchill, Robert. *To Shake Their Guns in the Tyrant's Face: Libertarian Political Violence and the Origins of the Militia Movement*. Ann Arbor: University of Michigan Press, 2011.

Clinton, Bill. "Address to the Nation on Haiti." September 15, 1994.

Cockburn, Cynthia. *Antimilitarism: Political and Gender Dynamics of Peace Movements*. New York: Palgrave Macmillan, 2012.

Cohen, Beth, Shira Maguen, Daniel Bertenthal, Ying Shi, Vanessa Jacoby, and Karen H Seal. "Reproductive and Other Health Outcomes in Iraq and Afghanistan Women Veterans Using VA Care." *Women's Health Issues* 22, no. 5 (2012).

Cohen, Cathy. "Contested Membership: Black Gay Identities and the Politics of AIDS." In *Queer Theory/Sociology*, edited by Steven Seidman, 362–94. Oxford, UK: Blackwell, 1996.

Combahee River Collective. *Combahee River Collective Statement*. Self-published, 1977.

Compact of Free Association Agreement between the United States of America and the Marshall Islands, Amending the Agreement of June 25,

1983, Concerning the Compact of Free Association, as Amended, Signed at Majuro April 30, 2003.

Conrad, Ryan, ed. *Don't Ask to Fight Their Wars*. San Francisco: Against Equality Press, 2011.

Corber, Robert. *Cold War Femme: Lesbianism, National Identity, and Hollywood Cinema*. Durham: Duke University Press, 2011.

Cranna, Michael, ed. *The True Cost of Conflict*. New York: New Press, 1994.

Crimp, Douglas. *Melancholia and Moralism: Essays on AIDS and Queer Politics*. Cambridge: MIT Press, 2002.

Critical Resistance and INCITE! Women of Color Against Violence. "Gender Violence and the Prison-Industrial Complex." In *The Color of Violence*, edited by INCITE! Women of Color Against Violence. Cambridge: South End, 2006.

Crocombe, Ron. *The Pacific Islands and the USA*. Honolulu: Institute of Pacific Studies, 1995.

Crowl, Philip, and Edmund Love. *United States Army in World War II: The War in the Pacific, Seizure of the Gilberts and Marshalls*. Washington DC: Office of the Chief of Military History, 1955.

Currie, Ruth Douglas. *Kwajalein Atoll, the Marshall Islands and American Policy in the Pacific*. Jefferson: McFarland, 2016.

Davis, Angela. *The Prison Industrial Complex [Audiobook]*. Oakland: AK Press, 1999.

———. "Rape, Racism, and the Myth of the Black Rapist." In *The Angela Y. Davis Reader*, edited by Joy James, 111–28. Oxford, UK: Blackwell, 1998.

———. "Reflections on the Black Woman's Role in the Community of Slaves." In *The Angela Y. Davis Reader*, edited by Joy James, 111–28. Oxford, UK: Blackwell, 1998.

———. *Women, Race, and Class*. New York: Random House, 1981.

de Alwis, Malahi. "Ambivalent Maternalisms: Cursing as Public Protest in Sri Lanka." In *The Aftermath: Women in Post-Conflict Transformation*, edited by Sheila Meintjes, Anu Pillay, and Meredeth Turshen. London: Zed Books, 2001.

Deer, Sarah. *The Beginning and End of Rape: Confronting Sexual Violence in Native America*. Minneapolis: University of Minnesota Press, 2015.

Defense of Marriage Act, H.R.3396, 104th Congress, 1996.

D'Emilio, John, and Estelle Freedman. *Intimate Matters: A History of Sexuality in America*. New York: Harper and Row, 1988.

Denetdale, Jennifer. "Securing Navajo National Boundaries: War, Patriotism, Tradition, and the Dine Marriage Act of 2005." *Wíčazo Ša Review* 24, no. 2 (Fall 2009): 131–48.

Diamond, Edwin. *Behind the Times: Inside the New New York Times*. New York: Villard, 1993.

Diaz-Cotto, Juanita. "Latinas and the War on Drugs in the United State, Latin America, and Europe." In *Global Lockdown: Race, Gender, and the Prison-Industrial Complex*, edited by Julia Sudbury, 137–54. New York: Routledge, 2005.

Dibblin, Jane. *Day of Two Suns: U.S. Nuclear Testing and the Pacific Islanders*. New York: New Amsterdam Books, 1988.

Dixon, Graciela. "The People Have Been Pushed into Concentration Camps." In *The U.S. Invasion of Panama: The Truth behind Operation "Just Cause,"* edited by Independent Commission of Inquiry on the U.S. Invasion of Panama. Cambridge: South End Press, 1991.

Duberman, Martin, Martha Vicinus, and George Chauncey Jr., eds. *Hidden from History: Reclaiming the Gay and Lesbian Past*. New York: Meridian, 1990.

Dubois, Laurent. *Haiti: The Aftershocks of History*. New York: Henry Holt, 2012.

Duggan, Lisa. *The Twilight of Equality? Neoliberalism, Cultural Politics, and the Attack on Democracy*. Boston: Beacon Press, 2004.

Duke, Michael. "Marshall Islanders: Migration Patterns and Health Care Challenges." *Migration Information Source*, May 22, 2014.

Dyal, Donald. *Historical Dictionary of the Spanish American War*. Westport CT: Greenwood Publishing Group, 1996.

Dyer, Richard. *White: Essays on Race and Culture*. New York: Routledge, 1997.

Dyvik, Synne Laastad. "Women as 'Practitioners' and 'Targets': Gender and Counterinsurgency in Afghanistan." *International Feminist Journal of Politics* 16, no. 3 (July 2014): 410–29.

Economic Policy, Planning, and Statistics Office. *RMI 2011 Census of Population and Housing*. Majuro: Office of the President, 2012.

Edelman, Lee. *No Future: Queer Theory and the Death Drive*. Durham: Duke University Press, 2004.

Eide, Asbjørn, and Marek Thee, eds. *Problems of Contemporary Militarism*. New York: St. Martin's Press, 1980.

Eisenhower, Dwight. "Farewell Address by President Dwight D. Eisenhower." January 17, 1961.

Enloe, Cynthia. *Bananas, Beaches, and Bases: Making Feminist Sense of International Politics*. Berkeley: University of California Press, 1989.

———. *Does Khaki Become You? The Militarisation of Women's Lives*. Cambridge: South End Press, 1983.

———. *Globalization and Militarism: Feminists Make the Link*. New York: Rowman and Littlefield, 2007.

———. *Maneuvers: The International Politics of Militarizing Women's Lives*. Berkeley: University of California Press, 2000.

———. *The Morning After: Sexual Politics at the End of the Cold War*. Berkeley: University of California Press: 1993.

———. *Nimo's War, Emma's War: Making Feminist Sense of the Iraq War*. Berkeley: University of California Press, 2010.

Falcón, Sylvanna. "'National Security' and the Violation of Women: Militarized Border Rape at the US-Mexico Border." In *The Color of Violence*, edited by INCITE! Women of Color Against Violence. Cambridge: South End, 2006.

Faludi, Susan. *The Terror Dream: Fear and Fantasy in Post-9/11 America*. New York: Metropolitan Books, 2007.

Fathi, Riyad Abdullah, Hana Said Al-Salih, Lilyan Yaqup Matti, and Douglas Godbold. "Environmental Pollution by Depleted Uranium in Iraq with Special Reference to Mosul and Possible Effects on Cancer and Birth Defect Rates." *Medicine, Conflict, and Survival* 29, no. 1 (2013): 7–25.

Fausto-Sterling, Anne. *Sexing the Body: Gender Politics and the Construction of Sexuality*. New York: Basic Books, 2000.

Ferguson, Roderick. *Aberrations in Black: Toward a Queer of Color Critique*. Minneapolis: University of Minnesota Press, 2004.

Firestone, Shulamith. *The Dialectic of Sex: The Case for Feminist Revolution*. New York: Farrar, Strauss, and Giroux, 2003.

Foucault, Michel. *The History of Sexuality*. Vol. 1, *An Introduction*. 1978. New York: Vintage Books, 1990.

France, David, dir. *How to Survive a Plague*. Public Square Films, 2012.

Frank, Nathaniel. *Gays in Foreign Militaries 2010: A Global Primer*. Santa Barbara: Palm Center, 2010.

———. "The Real Story of Military Sociology and 'Don't Ask, Don't Tell.'" *Lingua Franca*, October 2000: 71–81.

Freedman, Estelle. *Redefining Rape: Sexual Violence in the Era of Suffrage and Segregation*. Cambridge: Harvard University Press, 2013.

Fukuyama, Francis. *The End of History and the Last Man*. New York: Free Press, 1992.

Fusco, Coco. *A Field Guide for Female Interrogators*. New York: Seven Stories Press, 2008.

Gallaher, Carolyn. *On the Fault Line: Race, Class, and the American Patriot Movement*. New York: Rowman and Littlefield, 2002.

Gardner, Lloyd, and Marilyn Young, eds. *Iraq and the Lessons of Vietnam: Or, How Not to Learn from the Past*. New York: The New Press, 2008.

Gates, Robert. *From the Shadows: The Ultimate Insider's Story of Five Presidents and How They Won the Cold War*. New York: Simon and Schuster, 2007.

"GBD Profile: Marshall Islands." In *Global Burden of Diseases, Injuries, and Risk Factors Study 2010*, by Institute for Health Metrics and Evaluation. Seattle: Institute for Health Metrics and Evaluation, 2010.

Gemma, Gavrielle, and Teresa Gutiérrez. Introduction to *The U.S. Invasion of Panama: The Truth behind Operation "Just Cause,"* edited by Independent Commission of Inquiry on the U.S. Invasion of Panama. Cambridge: South End Press, 1991.

Ghaziani, Amin. *The Dividends of Dissent: How Conflict and Culture Work in Lesbian and Gay Marches on Washington*. Chicago: University of Chicago Press, 2008.

Gibson, James William. *Warrior Dreams: Paramilitary Culture in Post-Vietnam America*. New York: Hill and Wang, 1994.

Gilmore, Ruth Wilson. "Terror Austerity Race Gender Excess Theater." In *Reading Rodney King/Reading Urban Uprising*, edited by Robert Gooding-Williams, 23–37. New York: Routledge, 1993.

Girard, Philippe. *Haiti: The Tumultuous History, From Pearl of the Caribbean to Broken Nation*. New York: Palgrave Macmillan, 2010.

Glanville, Luke. *Sovereignty and the Responsibility to Protect: A New History*. Chicago: University of Chicago Press, 2013.

Gonzalez, Juan, and Joseph Torres. *News for All the People: The Epic Story of Race and the American Media*. London: Verso, 2011.

Gonzalez, Vernadette Vicuna. *Securing Paradise: Tourism and Militarism in Hawai'i and the Philippines*. Durham: Duke University Press, 2013.

Goodman, Melvin. *National Insecurity: The Cost of American Militarism*. San Francisco: City Lights, 2013.

Gordillo, Luz Maria. "The Bracero, the Wetback, and the Terrorist: Mexican Immigration, Legislation, and National Security." In *A New Kind of Containment: "The War on Terror," Race, and Sexuality*, edited by Carmen Lugo-Lugo and Mary Bloodsworth-Lugo. Amsterdam: Rodopi, 2009.

Gould, Deborah. *Moving Politics: Emotion and ACT UP's Fight against AIDS*. Chicago: University of Chicago Press, 2009.

Green, Joyce, ed. *Making Space for Indigenous Feminism*. London: Zed Books, 2008.

Greenwood, Lee, and Gwen McLin. *God Bless the U.S.A.: Biography of a Song*. Gretna: Pelican Publishing, 2001.

Greider, William. *Fortress America: The American Military and the Consequences of Peace*. New York: Public Affairs, 1998.

Grewal, Inderpal, and Caren Kaplan. *Scattered Hegemonies: Postmodernity and Transnational Feminist Practices*. Minneapolis: University of Minnesota Press, 1994.

Grimmett, Richard. "Instances of Use of United States Armed Forces Abroad, 1798–2004." *Congressional Research Service*, October 5, 2004.

Grubacic, Andrej. *Don't Mourn, Balkanize! Essays after Yugoslavia*. Oakland: PM Press, 2010.

Hafetz, Jonathan. *Habeas Corpus after 9/11: Confronting America's New Global Detention System*. New York: New York University Press, 2011.

Haj, Samira. *The Making of Iraq, 1900–1963.* Albany: SUNY Press, 1996.

Halley, Janet. *Don't: A Reader's Guide to the Military's Anti-Gay Policy.* Durham: Duke University Press, 1999.

Halperin, David. *How to Be Gay.* Cambridge: Harvard University Press, 2012.

Hamilton, Terry. *Report: A Visual Description of the Concrete Exterior of the Cactus Crater Containment Structure LLNL-TR-648143.* Livermore: Lawrence Livermore National Laboratories, 2010.

Hammond, Karla. "An Interview with Audre Lorde." *American Poetry Review* 9, no. 2 (March/April 1980): 18–21.

Hanhardt, Christina. *Safe Space: Gay Neighborhood History and the Politics of Violence.* Durham: Duke University Press, 2013.

Harris, G. L. A. *Living Legends and Full Agency: Implications of Repealing the Combat Exclusion Policy.* Boca Raton FL: CRC Press, 2015.

Hau'ofa, Epeli. "Our Sea of Islands." In *A New Oceania: Rediscovering Our Sea of Islands,* edited by Epeli Hau'ofa, Vijay Naidu, and Eric Waddell, 2–16. Suva: University of the South Pacific, 1993.

Haw, Farhat. "Militarism and Motherhood: The Women of the Lashkar-i-Tayyabia in Pakistan." In *War and Terror: Feminist Perspectives,* edited by Karen Alexander and Mary Hawkesworth. Chicago: University of Chicago Press, 2008.

Hehir, Aidan. *The Responsibility to Protect: Rhetoric, Reality, and the Future of Humanitarian Intervention.* New York: Palgrave Macmillan, 2012.

Herman, Susan. *Taking Liberties: The War on Terror and the Erosion of American Democracy.* Oxford: Oxford University Press, 2011.

Hezel, Francis. *The First Taint of Civilization: A History of the Caroline and Marshall Islands in the Pre-Colonial Days, 1521–1885.* Honolulu: University of Hawaii Press, 1983.

———. *Strangers in Their Own Land: A Century of Colonial Rule in the Caroline and Marshall Islands.* Honolulu: University of Hawaii Press, 1995.

Hickel, Walter. *Who Owns America?* New York: Prentice Hall, 1971.

Hobson, Emily. *Lavender and Red: Liberation and Solidarity in the Gay and Lesbian Left.* Berkeley: University of California Press, 2016.

Hoganson, Kristin. *Fighting for American Manhood: How Gender Politics Provoked the Spanish-American and Philippine-American Wars.* New Haven: Yale University Press, 1998.

hooks, bell. *Black Looks: Race and Representation.* Cambridge: South End Press, 1992.

———. *Talking Back: Thinking Feminist, Thinking Black.* Boston: South End Press, 1989.

Hourani, Albert. *A History of the Arab People.* Cambridge: Harvard University Press, 1991.

Hubbard, Jim, dir. *United in Anger: A History of ACT UP*. Jim Hubbard and Sarah Schulman, 2012.

Hull, Gloria, Patricia Bell Scott, and Barbara Smith, eds. *But Some of Us Are Brave: All the Women Are White, All the Blacks Are Men, Black Women's Studies*. New York: Feminist Press, 1982.

Humphrey, Mary Ann. *My Country, My Right to Serve: Experiences of Gay Men and Women in the Military, World War II to the Present*. New York: HarperCollins, 1990.

Hunt, Krista. "'Embedded Feminism' and the War on Terror." In *(En)gendering the War on Terror: War Stories and Camouflaged Politics*, edited by Krista Hunt and Kim Rygiel. London: Ashgate, 2006.

Hunt, Krista, and Kim Rygiel, eds. *(En)gendering the War on Terror: War Stories and Camouflaged Politics*. London: Ashgate, 2006.

Hunt, Swanee. *Worlds Apart: Bosnian Lessons for Global Security*. Durham: Duke University Press, 2011.

Hunter, James Davidson. *Culture Wars: The Struggle to Control the Family, Art, Education, Law, and Politics in America*. New York: Basic Books, 1991.

Hunter, Mic. *Honor Betrayed: Sexual Abuse in America's Military*. Fort Lee NJ: Barricade Books, 2007.

Huntington, Samuel. *The Clash of Civilizations and the Remaking of World Order*. New York: Simon and Schuster, 1996.

Icaza, Edilma. "I Want to Relive the Invasion with You." In *The U.S. Invasion of Panama: The Truth behind Operation "Just Cause,"* edited by Independent Commission of Inquiry on the U.S. Invasion of Panama. Cambridge: South End Press, 1991.

Illegal Immigration Reform and Immigrant Responsibility Act of 1996, H.R.3610, 104th Congress, 1996.

INCITE! Women of Color against Violence, eds. *Color of Violence*. Cambridge: South End Press, 2006.

———. *The Revolution Will Not Be Funded: Beyond the Non-Profit Industrial Complex*. Cambridge: South End Press, 2009.

Independent Commission of Inquiry on the U.S. Invasion of Panama, ed. *The U.S. Invasion of Panama: The Truth behind Operation "Just Cause."* Cambridge: South End Press, 1991.

Institute for Health Metrics and Evaluation. *Global Burden of Diseases, Injuries, and Risk Factors Study 2010*. Seattle: Institute for Health Metrics and Evaluation, 2010.

Ivie, Robert. *Democracy and America's War on Terror*. Tuscaloosa: University of Alabama Press, 2006.

James, Joy. *Resisting State Violence: Radicalism, Gender, and Race in U.S. Culture*. Minneapolis: University of Minnesota Press, 1996.

Jensen, Kimberly. *Mobilizing Minerva: American Women in the First World War.* Champaign: University of Illinois Press, 2008.

Jetñil-Kijiner, Kathy. *Iep Jaltok: Poems from a Marshallese Daughter.* Tucson: University of Arizona Press, 2017.

Johnson, Chalmers, ed. *Okinawa: Cold War Island.* Oakland: Japan Policy Research Institute, 1999.

———. "Okinawa: The Political and Military Setting." In *Okinawa: Cold War Island,* edited by Chalmers Johnson. Oakland: Japan Policy Research Institute, 1999.

———. *The Sorrows of Empire: Militarism, Secrecy, and the End of the Republic.* New York: Metropolitan Books, 2004.

Johnson, David. *The Lavender Scare: The Cold War Persecution of Gays and Lesbians in the Federal Government.* Chicago: University of Chicago Press, 2004.

Johnson, Giff. "Youth Lead Youth in Marshall Islands." *Japanese Organization for International Cooperation in Family Planning Review,* no. 15 (1988): 35–36.

Johnston, Lynda, and Robyn Longhurst. *Space, Place, and Sex.* Lantham MD: Rowman and Littlefield, 2010.

Jones, Claudia. "An End to the Neglect of the Problems of the Negro Woman!" *Political Affairs,* June 1949.

Joya, Malalai. *A Woman among Warlords: The Extraordinary Story of an Afghan Who Dared to Raise Her Voice.* New York: Scribner, 2009.

Joyce, Davis D. *An Oklahoma I Had Never Seen Before: Alternative Views of Oklahoma History.* Norman: University of Oklahoma Press, 1998.

Kaplan, Amy. *The Anarchy of Empire in the Making of U.S. Culture.* Cambridge: Harvard University Press, 2005.

Katz, Jonathan Ned. *The Invention of Heterosexuality.* Chicago: University of Chicago Press, 1995.

Kauanui, J. Kēhaulani. "Native Hawaiian Decolonization and the Politics of Gender." *American Quarterly* 60, no. 2 (2008): 281–87.

———. "'A Structure, Not an Event': Settler Colonialism and Enduring Indigeneity." *Lateral* 5, no. 1 (2016).

Kelly, Liz. "The Everyday/Everynightness of Rape: Is It Different in War?" In *Gender, War, and Militarism: Feminist Perspectives,* edited by Laura Sjoberg and Sandra Via, 114–23. Santa Barbara CA: Praeger Security International, 2010.

Kessler, Suzanne. *Lessons from the Intersexed.* New Brunswick: Rutgers University Press, 1998.

Keyso, Ruth. *Women of Okinawa: Nine Voices from a Garrison Island.* Ithaca: Cornell University Press, 2000.

Khalidi, Rashid. *Resurrecting Empire: Western Footprints and America's Perilous Path in the Middle East*. Boston: Beacon Press, 2004.

King, Iain, and Whit Mason. *Peace at Any Price: How the World Failed Kosovo*. Ithaca: Cornell University Press, 2006.

Kirch, Patrick. *On the Road of the Winds: An Archaeological History of the Pacific Islands before European Contact*. Berkeley: University of California Press, 2002.

Klip, Andre, and Goran Sluiter, eds. *The International Criminal Tribunal for the Former Yugoslavia, 2001–2002*. Cambridge, UK: Intersentia, 2005.

Kraska, Peter. *Militarizing the American Criminal Justice System: The Changing Roles of the Armed Forces and the Police*. Boston: Northeastern University Press, 2001.

LaDuke, Winona. *The Militarization of Indian Country*. East Lansing: Makwa Enewed, 2012.

Lawrence, Jane. "The Indian Health Service and the Sterilization of Native American Women." *American Indian Quarterly* 24, no. 3 (Summer 2000): 400–419.

Lebovic, James. *The Limits of U.S. Military Capability: Lessons from Vietnam and Iraq*. Baltimore: Johns Hopkins University Press, 2010.

Levitas, Daniel. *The Terrorist Next Door: The Militia Movement and the Radical Right*. New York: St. Martin's Griffin, 2004.

Lewis, Carolyn. *Prescription for Heterosexuality: Sexual Citizenship in the Cold War Era*. Durham: University of North Carolina Press, 2010.

Liebman, Marvin. *Coming Out Conservative: An Autobiography*. San Francisco: Chronicle Books, 1992.

Lieom-Loeak, Anono, and Marie Maddison. "Women's Organizations." In *Life in the Republic of the Marshall Islands*, edited by Anono Lieom-Loeak, Veronica Kiluwe, and Linda Crowl, 82–95. Suva: University of the South Pacific Centre, 2004.

Limber, Susan, and Brian Wilcox. "Application of the UN Convention on the Rights of the Child to the United States." *American Psychologist* 51, no. 12 (1996): 1246–50.

Little, Douglas. *American Orientalism: The United States and the Middle East Since 1945*. Durham: University of North Carolina Press, 2008.

Lockman, Zachary. *Contending Visions of the Middle East: The History and Politics of Orientalism*. Cambridge, UK: Cambridge University Press, 2010.

Lorde, Audre. *A Burst of Light*. Ithaca: Firebrand Books, 1988.

——. *Sister Outsider: Essays and Speeches*. Berkeley: Crossing Press, 1984.

Loyd, Jenna, Matt Mitchelson, and Andrew Burridge, eds. *Beyond Walls and Cages: Prisons, Borders, and Global Crisis*. Athens: University of Georgia Press, 2012.

Lugo-Lugo, Carmen, and Mary Bloodsworth-Lugo, eds. *A New Kind of Containment: "The War on Terror," Race, and Sexuality*. Amsterdam, Netherlands: Rodopi, 2009.

Lyons, Paul. *American Pacificism: Oceania in the US Imagination*. New York: Routledge, 2006.

MacKinnon, Catharine. *Sexual Harassment of Working Women: A Case of Sex Discrimination*. New Haven: Yale University Press, 1979.

Madigan, Tim. *The Burning: Massacre, Destruction, and the Tulsa Race Riot of 1921*. New York: St. Martin's Press, 2003.

Martin, Shannon, and Kathleen Hansen. *Newspapers of Record in a Digital Age: From Hot Type to Hot Link*. Westport CT: Greenwood Publishing, 1998.

Martin, William. *With God on Our Side: The Rise of the Religious Right in America*. New York: Broadway Books, 1996.

Masco, Joseph. *The Nuclear Borderlands: The Manhattan Project in Post-Cold War New Mexico*. Princeton: Princeton University Press, 2006.

———. *The Theater of Operations: National Security Affect from the Cold War to the War on Terror*. Durham: Duke University Press, 2014.

Massing, Michael. *Now They Tell Us: The American Press and Iraq*. New York: New York Review of Books, 2004.

Matsuda, Matt. *Pacific Worlds: A History of Seas, Peoples, and Cultures*. Cambridge, UK: Cambridge University Press, 2012.

McAlister, Melani. *Epic Encounters: Culture, Media, and U.S. Interests in the Middle East since 1945*. Berkeley: University of California Press, 2001.

McConnell, Malcolm. *Just Cause: The Real Story of America's High-Tech Invasion of Panama*. New York: St. Martin's Press, 1991.

McIntosh, Ian. "Polynesian Voyaging and Pacific Self-Determination." *Cultural Survival Quarterly* 24, no. 1 (2000).

McIntyre, W. D. "The Partition of the Gilbert and Ellice Islands." *Island Studies Journal* 7, no. 1 (2012): 135–46.

McKelvey, Tara, ed. *One of the Guys: Women as Aggressors and Torturers*. Berkeley: Seal Press, 2007.

Mecca, Tommi. *Smash the Church, Smash the State! The Early Years of Gay Liberation*. San Francisco: City Lights Books, 2009.

Meintjes, Shelia, Anu Pillay, and Meredeth Turshen, eds. *The Aftermath: Women in Post-Conflict Transformation*. London: Zed Books, 2001.

———. "There Is No Aftermath for Women." In *The Aftermath: Women in Post-Conflict Transformation*, edited by Sheila Meintjes, Anu Pillay, and Meredeth Turshen. London: Zed Books, 2001.

Mejía, Olga. "A Crime against Humanity." In *The U.S. Invasion of Panama: The Truth behind Operation "Just Cause,"* edited by Independent Commission of Inquiry on the U.S. Invasion of Panama. Cambridge: South End Press, 1991.

Merlet, Myriam. "Haiti: Women in Conquest of Full and Total Citizenship in an Endless Transition." In *Women's Activism in Latin America and the Caribbean: Engendering Social Justice, Democratizing Citizenship*, edited by Elizabeth Maier and Nathalie Lebon, 127–39. New Brunswick: Rutgers University Press, 2010.

Meyerowitz, Joanne. *How Sex Changed: A History of Transsexuality in the United States*. Cambridge: Harvard University Press, 2002.

Michel, Lou, and Dan Herbeck. *American Terrorist: Timothy McVeigh and the Oklahoma City Bombing*. New York: HarperCollins, 2001.

Mladjenovic, Lepa. "Caring at the Same Time: On Feminist Politics during the NATO Bombing of the Federal Republic of Yugoslavia and the Ethnic Cleansing of Albanians in Kosovo, 1999." In *The Aftermath: Women in Post-Conflict Transformation*, edited by Sheila Meintjes, Anu Pillay, and Meredeth Turshen. London: Zed Books, 2001.

Mohanty, Chandra, and Biddy Martin. "What's Home Got to Do with It?" In *Feminism without Borders*, by Chandra Mohanty, 85–105. Durham: Duke University Press, 2004.

Mohanty, Chandra, Minnie Bruce Pratt, and Robin Riley, eds. *Feminism and War: Confronting U.S. Imperialism*. London: Zed Books, 2008.

Morgensen, Scott. "Settler Homonationalism: Theorizing Settler Colonialism within Queer Modernities." *GLQ: A Journal of Lesbian and Gay Studies* 16, no. 1–2 (2010): 105–31.

———. *Spaces between Us: Queer Settler Colonialism and Indigenous Decolonization*. Minneapolis: University of Minnesota Press, 2011.

Morrison, Marjorie. *The Inside Battle: Our Military Mental Health Crisis*. New York: Military Psychology Press, 2012.

Ms. Dribo and Ms. Lorennij's Fifth-Grade Class at Ebeye Public Elementary School. *Life in the Marshall Islands: Then and Now*. Ebeye: The Unbound Bookmaker, 2014.

Mulligan, Connie. "Early Environments, Stress, and the Epigenetics of Human Health." *Annual Review of Anthropology* 45 (2016): 233–49.

Murray, Nancy. "Profiled: Arabs, Muslims, and the Post-9/11 Hunt for the 'Enemy Within.'" In *Civil Rights in Peril: The Targeting of Arabs and Muslims*, edited by Elaine Hagopain, 27–68. Chicago: Haymarket Books, 2004.

Musicant, Ivan. *The Banana Wars: A History of United States Military Intervention in Latin America from the Spanish-American War to the Invasion of Panama*. New York: Macmillan, 1990.

Na'puti, Tiara. "Speaking the Language of Peace: Chamoru Resistance and Rhetoric in Guåhan's Self-Determination Movement." *Anthropologica* 56, no. 2 (2014): 301–13.

National Research Council's Committee on Radiological Safety in the Marshall Islands Board on Radiation Effects Research. *Radiological Assessments for the Resettlement of Rongelap in the Republic of the Marshall Islands*. Washington DC: National Academy Press, 1994.

Nelson, T. S. *For Love of Country: Confronting Rape and Sexual Harassment in the U.S. Military*. New York: Haworth Maltreatment and Trauma Press, 2002.

Newcomb, Steven. *Pagans in the Promised Land: Decoding the Doctrine of Christian Discovery*. Golden CO: Fulcrum Publishing, 2008.

Nokov, Julie, Barbara Sutton, and Sandra Morgen, eds. *Security Disarmed: Critical Perspectives of Gender, Race, and Militarization*. New Brunswick: Rutgers University Press, 2008.

Nusair, Isis. "Gendered, Racialized, and Sexualized Torture at Abu Ghraib." In *Feminism and War*, edited by Chandra Talpade Mohanty, Minnie Bruce Pratt, and Robin Riley. London: Zed Books, 2008.

Nyong'o, Tavia. *The Amalgamation Waltz: Race, Performance, and the Ruses of Memory*. Minneapolis: University of Minnesota Press, 2009.

O'Brien, Patty. *The Pacific Muse: Exotic Femininity and the Colonial Pacific*. Seattle: University of Washington Press, 2006.

Ogilvy-Stuart, A. L., and S. M. Shalet. "Effect of Radiation on the Human Reproductive System." *Environmental Health Perspective* 101, Suppl. 2 (July 1993): 109–16.

Office of the Under Secretary of Defense for Acquisition, Technology, and Logistics. *Fiscal Year 2016 Operational Energy Annual Report*.

Parenti, Christian. *Lockdown America: Police and Prisons in the Age of Crisis*. London: Verso, 1999.

Parsons, Keith, and Robert Zaballa. *Bombing the Marshall Islands: A Cold War Tragedy*. Cambridge, UK: Cambridge University Press, 2017.

Peacock, Margaret. *Innocent Weapons: The Soviet and American Politics of Childhood during the Cold War*. Chapel Hill: University of North Carolina Press, 2014.

The People of Rongelap. "Is Rongelap Atoll Safe?" Statement at "Resettlement of Rongelap Atoll, Republic of the Marshall Islands," hearing before the Committee on Energy and Natural Resources, United States Senate, 102nd Congress, September 19, 1991.

Perdue, Theda, and Michael Green. *The Cherokee Nation and the Trail of Tears*. New York: Penguin Books, 2008.

Personal Responsibility and Work Opportunity Reconciliation Act of 1996, H.R.3734, 104th Congress, 1996.

Pettman, Jan Jindy. *Worlding Women: A Feminist International Politics*. New York: Routledge, 1996.

Pfeil, Fred. *White Guys: Studies in Postmodern Domination and Difference.* London: Verso, 1995.

Poblete-Cross, JoAnna. "Bridging Indigenous and Immigrant Struggles: A Case Study of American Samoa." *American Quarterly* 63, no. 3 (2010): 501–22.

Policy Concerning Homosexuality in the Armed Forces, Title 10, U.S. Code, Section 654.

"The Politics of Reproductive Violence: An Interview with Shana Griffin by Clyde Woods." *American Quarterly* 61, no. 3 (September 2009): 583–91.

Power, Lisa. *No Bath but Plenty of Bubbles: An Oral History of the Gay Liberation Front, 1970–73.* London: Cassell, 1996.

Price, Kimala. "What Is Reproductive Justice?" *Meridians: Feminism, Race, Transnationalism* 10, no. 2 (2010): 42–65.

Proctor, William. *The Gospel According to the New York Times: How the World's Most Powerful News Organization Shapes Your Mind and Values.* New York: Broadman and Holman, 2000.

Puar, Jasbir. *Terrorist Assemblages: Homonationalism in Queer Times.* Durham: Duke University Press, 2007.

Puechguirbal, Nadine. "Gender and Peacekeeping: A Few Challenges." *Peace and Conflict Monitor*, April 23, 2008.

Rajiva, Lila. *The Language of Empire: Abu Ghraib and the American Media.* New York: Monthly Review Press, 2005.

Ray, Ronald. *Gays: In or Out?* New York: Maxwell Macmillan, 1993.

Reavis, Dick. *The Ashes of Waco: An Investigation.* Syracuse: Syracuse University Press, 1998.

Reddy, Chandan. *Freedom with Violence: Race, Sexuality, and the US State.* Durham: Duke University Press, 2011.

Redmont, Jane. *Generous Lives: American Catholic Women Today.* Chicago: Triumph Books, 1992.

Regan, Patrick. *Organizing Societies for War: The Process and Consequences of Societal Militarization.* Westport CT: Praeger, 1994.

Renda, Mary. *Taking Haiti: Military Occupation and the Culture of U.S. Imperialism, 1915–1940.* Durham: University of North Carolina Press, 2000.

"Resettlement of Rongelap Atoll, Republic of the Marshall Islands." Hearing Before the Committee on Energy and Natural Resources, United States Senate, 102nd Congress, September 19, 1991.

Rich, Adrienne. "Compulsory Heterosexuality and Lesbian Existence." *Signs* 5, no. 4 (Summer 1980): 631–60.

Richie, Beth. *Arrested Justice: Black Women, Violence, and America's Prison Nation.* New York: New York University Press, 2012.

Rigby, Barry. "The Origins of American Expansion in Hawaii and Samoa, 1865–1900." *International History Review* 10, no. 2 (May 1988): 221–37.

Roberts, Dorothy. "Feminism, Race, and Adoption Policy." In *The Color of Violence*, edited by INCITE! Women of Color Against Violence. Cambridge: South End, 2006.

———. *Killing the Black Body: Race, Reproduction, and the Meaning of Liberty*. New York: Vintage Books, 1997.

Robinson, William, and Terry Hamilton. "Radiation Doses for Marshall Islands Atolls Affected by U.S. Nuclear Testing: All Exposure Pathways, Remedial Measures, and Environmental Loss of 137Cs." *Health Physics*, no. 98 (2010): 1–11.

Rozema, Vicki. *Voices from the Trail of Tears*. Winston-Salem: John F. Blair, 2003.

Ryan, David, and John Dumbrell, eds. *Vietnam in Iraq: Tactics, Lessons, Legacies, and Ghosts*. New York: Routledge, 2007.

Said, Edward. *Covering Islam*. New York: Vintage Books, 1997.

———. *Culture and Imperialism*. New York: Vintage Books, 1994.

———. *Orientalism*. New York: Vintage Books, 1979.

———. *Representations of the Intellectual*. New York: Vintage Books, 1994.

Salaita, Steven. *The Holy Land in Transit: Colonialism and the Quest for Canaan*. Syracuse: Syracuse University Press, 2006.

Salt, Jeremy. *The Unmaking of the Middle East: A History of Western Disorder in Arab Lands*. Berkeley: University of California Press, 2009.

Sapphire. *American Dreams*. New York: Vintage Books, 1996.

Sasson, Jean. *The Rape of Kuwait: The True Story of Iraqi Atrocities against a Civilian Population*. New York: Knightsbridge, 1991.

Schmidt, Tyler. *Desegregating Desire: Race and Sexuality in Cold War American Literature*. Oxford: University of Mississippi Press, 2013.

Schudson, Michael. *Discovering the News: A Social History of American Newspapers*. New York: Basic Books, 1981.

Schwarz, Daniel. *Endtimes? Crisis and Turmoil at the New York Times, 1999–2009*. Albany: SUNY Press, 2012.

Scott, Ridley, dir. *G.I. Jane*. Largo Entertainment, 1997.

Secretariat of the Pacific Regional Environmental Program. *Report of the SPC/UNEP/ASPEI Intergovernmental Meeting on Climate Change and Sea Level Rise in the South Pacific, Majuro, Marshall Islands, 17–20 July 1989*. Nouméa, New Caledonia: South Pacific Regional Environmental Program, 1989.

Sedgwick, Eve. *Epistemology of the Closet*. Berkeley: University of California Press, 1990.

Seidman, Steven, Chet Meeks, and Francie Traschen. "Beyond the Closet? The Changing Social Meaning of Homosexuality in the United States." *Sexualities* 2, no. 1 (February 1999).

Selfa, Lance. *The Democrats: A Critical History*. Chicago: Haymarket Books, 2008.

Servicemembers Legal Defense Network. *Conduct Unbecoming: The Eight Annual Report on "Don't Ask, Don't Tell, Don't Pursue, Don't Harass."* Self-published, 2002.

———. *Freedom to Serve: The Definitive Guide to LGBT Military Service.* Self-published, July 27, 2011.

Shaheen, Jack. *Reel Bad Arabs: How Hollywood Vilifies a People.* Ithaca: Olive Branch Press, 2009.

Sharma, Nandita. "White Nationalism, Illegality and Imperialism: Border Controls as Ideology." In *(En)gendering the War on Terror: War Stories and Camouflaged Politics,* edited by Krista Hunt and Kim Rygiel. London: Ashgate, 2006.

Shawyer, Lois. *And the Flag Was Still There: Straight People, Gay People, and Sexuality in the U.S. Military.* New York: Harrington Park Press, 1995.

Shigematsu, Setsu, with Anuradha Kristina Bhagwati and Eli PaintedCrow. "Women-of-Color Veterans on War, Militarism, and Feminism." In *Feminism and War,* edited by Chandra Talpade Mohanty, Minnie Bruce Pratt, and Robin Riley. London: Zed Books, 2008.

Shilts, Randy. *Conduct Unbecoming: Gays and Lesbians in the U.S. Military, Vietnam to the Persian Gulf.* New York: St. Martin's Press, 1993.

Sideris, Tina. "Rape in War and Peace: Social Context, Gender, Power and Identity." In *The Aftermath: Women in Post-Conflict Transformation,* edited by Sheila Meintjes, Anu Pillay, and Meredeth Turshen. London: Zed Books, 2001.

Signorile, Michelangelo. *Queer in America: Sex, The Media, and The Closets of Power.* Madison: University of Wisconsin Press, 1993.

Simons, Geoff. *The Vietnam Syndrome: Impact on U.S. Foreign Policy.* New York: St. Martin's, 1998.

Sjoberg, Laura. *Gendering Global Conflict: Towards a Feminist Theory of War.* New York: Columbia University Press, 2013.

Smith, Andrea. "Queer Theory and Native Studies: The Heteronormativity of Settler Colonialism." GLQ 16, no. 1–2 (2010): 41–68.

Smith-Norris, Martha. *Domination and Resistance: The United States and the Marshall Islands during the Cold War.* Honolulu: University of Hawaii Press, 2016.

Snorton, C. Riley. *Nobody Is Supposed to Know: Black Sexuality on the Down Low.* Minneapolis: University of Minnesota Press, 2014.

Somerville, Siobhan. *Queering the Color Line: Race and the Invention of Homo-sexuality in American Culture.* Durham: Duke University Press, 2000.

Staff of the *Los Angeles Times. Understanding the Riots: Los Angeles before and after the Rodney King Case.* Los Angeles: Los Angeles Times Syndicate, 1996.

Stanley, Eric, and Nat Smith, eds. *Captive Genders: Trans Embodiment and the Prison-Industrial Complex*. Oakland: AK Press, 2011.

Steffan, Joseph. *Honor Bound: A Gay Naval Midshipman Fights to Serve His Country*. New York: Avon Books, 1992.

St. John, Harold, and Kuaika Jendrusch. "Plants Introduced to Hawaiʻi by the Ancestors of the Hawaiian People." In *Polynesian Seafaring Heritage*, edited by Cecilia Kapua and Nancy Mower, 122–23. Honolulu: Kamehameha Schools, 1980.

Stockton, Kathryn Bond. *The Queer Child, or Growing Sideways in the Twentieth Century*. Durham: Duke University Press, 2009.

Stoler, Anne. *Carnal Knowledge and Imperial Power: Race and the Intimate in Colonial Rule*. Berkeley: University of California Press, 2002.

Stone, Robert, dir. *Radio Bikini*. Robert Stone Productions, 1988.

Stratton, Jon. *Coming Out Jewish*. New York: Routledge, 2000.

Stryker, Susan. *Transgender History*. Berkeley: Seal Press, 2008.

Sublime. *Sublime*. MCA Records, 1996.

Sullivan, Andrew. *Virtually Normal: An Argument about Homosexuality*. New York: Alfred Knopf Press, 1995.

Sycamore, Mattilda Bernstein. Introduction to *Don't Ask to Fight Their Wars*, edited by Ryan Conrad. San Francisco: Against Equality Press, 2011.

Tamez, Margo. "The Texas-Mexico Border Wall and Nde Memory: Confronting Genocide and State Criminality, Beyond the Guise of 'Impunity.'" In *Beyond Walls and Cages: Prisons, Borders, and Global Crisis*, edited by Jenna Loyd, Matt Mitchelson, and Andrew Burridge. Athens: University of Georgia Press, 2012.

Teaiwa, Teresia. "Bikinis and Other S/pacific N/oceans." In *Militarized Currents: Towards a Decolonized Future in Asia and the Pacific*, edited by Setsu Shigematsu and Keith Camacho, 15–32. Minneapolis: University of Minnesota Press, 2010.

Teller-Elsberg, Jonathan Nancy Folbre, James Heintz, and the Center for Popular Economics. *Field Guide to the U.S. Economy*. New York: The New Press, 2006.

Ticktin, Miriam. "The Gendered Human of Humanitarianism: Medicalizing and Politicizing Sexual Violence." *Gender and History* 23, no. 2 (2011): 250–65.

Trask, Haunani-Kay. "The Color of Violence." In *The Color of Violence*, edited by INCITE! Women of Color Against Violence. Cambridge: South End, 2006.

Trent, Barbara, dir. *The Panama Deception*. Empowerment Project, 1992.

Tripp, Charles. *A History of Iraq*. Cambridge, UK: Cambridge University Press, 2000.

Tuck, Eve, and K. Wayne Yang. "Decolonization Is Not a Metaphor." *Decolonization: Indigeneity* 1, no. 1 (2012): 1–40.

United Nations Children's Fund. *State of the World's Children 2015 Country Statistical Tables.*

United Nations Food and Agriculture Organization. *Marshall Islands and FAO Partnering to Improve Food Security and Income Earning Opportunities.* 2015.

United Nations High Commission on Refugees. UNHCR *Guidelines on Formal Determination of the Best Interests of the Child.* May 2006.

"U.S., Soviets to Cut Chemical Weapons." In CQ *Almanac 1990,* 46th ed., 709–11. Washington DC: Congressional Quarterly, 1991.

U.S. Department of Defense. *Population Representation in the Military Services: Fiscal Year 2010.*

U.S. Department of Defense Inspector General. *Tailhook 91—Part 2, Events of the 35th Annual Tailhook Convention.* February 1993.

U.S. Department of Health and Human Services. *Indicators of Welfare Dependence, Annual Report to Congress, 2008.*

U.S. Department of Justice. *Report to the Deputy Attorney General on the Events at Waco, Texas, February 28 to April 19, 1993.* October 8, 1993.

U.S. Department of State. *Trafficking in Persons Report.* June 2016.

U.S. Department of the Census. *Poverty Status of People, by Age, Race, and Hispanic Origin, 1959–2011.*

U.S. House of Representatives. *Military Involvement in the Government Operations at Waco Activities of Federal Law Enforcement Agencies toward the Branch Davidians.* Report, House of Representatives, 104th Congress, 2nd Session, No. 395, August 2, 1996.

Veran, Cristina. "Oceania Rising." *Cultural Survival Quarterly* 37, no. 2 (2013): 12–13.

Vigil, Ariana. "Heterosexualization and the State: The Poetry of Gloria Anzaldua." *Chicana/Latina Studies* 1, no. 16 (2016): 86–109.

———. *War Echoes: Gender and Militarization in US Latina/o Cultural Production.* New Brunswick: Rutgers University Press, 2014.

Vizenor, Gerald. *Manifest Manners: Narratives on Postindian Survivance.* Lincoln: University of Nebraska Press, 1999.

Von Hippel, Karen. *Democracy by Force: US Military Intervention in the Post-Cold War World.* Cambridge, UK: Cambridge University Press, 1999.

Wallensteen, Peter, Johan Galtung, and Carlos Portales. *Global Militarization.* Westport CT: Westview Press, 1985.

Walsh, Julianne. "Adoption and Agency: American Adoptions of Marshallese Children." Presentation at Out of Oceania: Diaspora, Community, and Identity conference, University of Hawaii at Manoa, October 22, 1999.

Walter, Jess. *Every Knee Shall Bow: The Truth and Tragedy of Ruby Ridge and the Randy Weaver Family.* New York: ReganBooks, 1995.

———. *Ruby Ridge: The Truth and Tragedy of the Randy Weaver Family.* New York: HarperPerennial, 2012.

Walton, Douglas. *Appeal to Pity: Argumentum ad Misecordium*. Albany: SUNY Press, 1997.

Weeks, Jeffrey. *Against Nature: Essays on History, Sexuality, and Identity*. London: Rivers Oram Press, 1991.

Welch, Michael. *Detained: Immigration Laws and the Expanding I.N.S. Jail Complex*. Philadelphia: Temple University Press, 2002.

———. *Scapegoats of September 11th: Hate Crimes and State Crimes in the War on Terror*. New Brunswick: Rutgers University Press, 2006.

Wells-Petry, Melissa. *Exclusion: Homosexuals and the Right to Serve*. New York: Regnery Gateway, 1993.

Westad, Odd. *The Global Cold War*. Cambridge, UK: Cambridge University Press, 2005.

Williams, Deanna Perez, and Ann Hampton. "Barriers to Health Services Perceived by Marshallese Immigrants." *Journal of Immigrant Health* 7, no. 4 (October 2005): 317–26.

Wolfe, Patrick. "Settler Colonialism and the Elimination of the Native." *Journal of Genocide Research* 8, no. 4 (December 2006): 387–409.

Wolinsky, Marc, and Kenneth Sherrill, eds. *Gays and the Military: Joseph Steffan Versus the United States*. Princeton: Princeton University Press, 1993.

Yamazaki, James. *Children of the Atom Bomb: An American Physician's Memoir of Nagasaki, Hiroshima, and the Marshall Islands*. Durham: Duke University Press, 1995.

Yates, Lawrence. *The U.S. Military Intervention in Panama: Origins, Planning, and Crisis Management*. Washington DC: Center of Military History, 2008.

Yee, Jessica, ed. *Feminism for Real: Deconstructing the Academic-Industrial Complex of Feminism*. Ottawa: Canadian Centre for Policy Alternatives, 2011.

Zangana, Haifa. *City of Widows*. New York: Seven Stories Press, 2007.

Zeeland, Steven, *Barrack Buddies and Soldier Lovers: Dialogues with Gay Young Men in the U.S. Military*. New York: Harrington Park Press, 1993.

Zimmerman, Jean. *Tailspin: Women at War in the Wake of Tailhook*. New York: Doubleday, 1995.

Zirojević, Olga. "Kosovo in the Collective Memory." In *The Road to War in Serbia: Trauma and Catharsis*, edited by Nebojša Popov, 189–211. Budapest: Central European University Press, 2000.

INDEX

Johnson, Shoshana, 180n27
Jones, Claudia, 7
Joya, Malalai, 128
Just Cause (McConnell), 29
Justus Township siege, 69

Kanaka Maoli, 107, 124. *See also*
    Hawai'i
Kaplan, Caren, 26
Karimata, Nobuko, 42
Kassebaum, Nancy, 45, 56–57
Katz, Jonathan Ned, 54
Kauanui, J. Kēhaulani, 22
Keju-Johnson, Darlene, 103, 120
Kelso, Frank, II, 36–37
Kili Island, 119
King, Rodney, 61. *See also* Los Ange-
    les Uprising
Kiribati, 123
Kissinger, Henry, 111
Kokajoor im Koonmaanlok Kora.
    See Women United Together
    Marshall Islands (WUTMI)
Kony, Joseph, 130–31
Korea, 137
Koresh, David, 66–68
Kosovo, 48–50
Kramer, Larry, 80, 81, 84, 166n18
Kristof, Nicholas, 41
Kulick, Don, 4
Kuromiya, Kiyoshi, 85
Kuwait, U.S. invasion of, 31–34, 53,
    57–58
Kwajalein Atoll, 109, 112, 116, 119

Labaton, Stephen, 67
LA Riots. *See* Los Angeles Uprising
Las Vegas music festival shooting, 133
Latino communities, 132
Ledet, Kendrick, 41, 42, 43

lesbian community. *See* LGBTQ
    communities
Lesbians and Gays against Inter-
    vention, 85
LGBTQ communities: academic
    theories and studies on, 81;
    antiwar activism from, 138–39;
    and Don't Ask, Don't Tell pol-
    icy, 2–3, 93–101, 134, 182n36;
    and "gay witch hunts," 89–91;
    HIV/AIDS activism in, 86–87,
    97, 98, 165n8; and militant
    queerness, as term, 80; poli-
    tics of (1980s), 81, 82–88; and
    same-sex marriage rights, 76,
    97–98, 99, 132, 170n61; termi-
    nology and, 80, 86, 164n2; and
    transgender service member
    rights, 82, 88, 100, 135. *See also*
    homosexuality
Libya, 130, 132
Life in the Marshall Islands, 114
"The Long War," 140–41. *See also*
    War on Terror
Lorde, Audre: on demilitarization,
    22; on feminist solidarity, 49, 80,
    81; on power of the erotic, 3–4;
    on self-expression, 24; on U.S.
    military interventions, 84, 141
Lormil, Rose Margui, 39
Los Angeles Times, 17, 32
Los Angeles Uprising, 61–65, 77
Lynch, Jessica, 129, 131, 180n27
Lyons, Paul, 106, 107

Macke, Richard, 43
MacKinnon, Catharine, 8
Mahmudiyah killings, 129
Maldonado, Diana, 90
Mali, 132
Malta Summit (1989), 10

Navajos, 132
Netherlands, 89
Newcomb, Steven, 23
New Guinea colony, 108
New Republic, 88
Newsday, 68
news media archive, 17–18
Newsweek, 18, 62
New York City Pride Parade, 86–87
New York Times: on David Koresh,
    66–67; on Don't Ask, Don't Tell,
    93; on feminism, 2; on Iraq vio-
    lence, 56, 58, 127; on Okinawan
    occupation, 41; as research
    archive, 17; on sexual violence
    incidents, 31, 34, 39, 40, 46; on
    Timothy McVeigh, 73
Niger, 132
9/11 attacks. *See* September 11,
    2001, attacks
Noriega, Manuel, 25
Nuclear Claims Tribunal, 116
nuclear weapons testing: on Bikini
    Atoll, 107, 109; British, 123; and
    Hanford site and Columbia River
    tribes, 109; on Mescalero Apache
    lands, 109; reproductive health
    and, 15, 103, 110–14. *See also*
    Marshall Islands
Nunn, Sam, 93, 169n50

Oak Creek Sikh *gurdwara* massacre,
    132, 133
Oath Keepers, 133
Obama, Barack, 99
Obergefell v. Hodges, 97
Okinawa, U.S. occupation of, 41–44
Okinawa Women Act against Mili-
    tary Violence, 42, 137
Oklahoma, mass-casualty incidents
    in, 70–71

Oklahoma City bombing, 70, 71–
    74, 77
Operation Desert Storm, 53. *See
    also* Gulf War
Operation Greenhouse, 121
Operation Just Cause, 25, 29–31
Organization of Women's Freedom
    in Iraq (OWFI), 138
OutServe, 98–99
OutWeek, 97
Overland Park Jewish Community
    Center massacre, 132, 133

Pacific Proving Grounds, 103. *See
    also* Marshall Islands
Pacific War, 108
PaintedCrow, Eli, 132
Pakistan, 41, 132
Palin, Sarah, 136
Panama, 25, 29–31
Panama (Buckley), 29
Panamanian Project, 30
Parris Island scandal, 89–91
Partial Nuclear Test Ban Treaty
    (1963), 112
peace initiatives, 135–37
Peacock, Margaret, 59
Peinam, Matafele, 121
Personal Responsibility and Work
    Opportunity Reconciliation Act
    (1996), 76–77, 118
Philippines, 106, 108, 132, 137
Piestewa, Lori, 131–32, 180n27
plants, 113, 123
police brutality, 54, 61–65
Portales, Carlos, 9
post–Cold War era, overview, 11–
    13, 19
poverty and class, 63, 76–77
Pratt, Nicola, 59–60
prison abolition movement, 139–40

Wake Island, 108

Wake Up Queers or We're All Through, 87, 166n18

Wald, Matthew, 44

Wallensteen, Peter, 9

Wall Street Journal, 17, 32, 71

Walters, Barbara, 74

Warner, John, 96

War on Terror, 3, 12–13, 28, 126–35, 140

Washington Navy Yard shooting, 133

Washington Post, 17, 31, 58

Webb, James, 36

white nationalism, 132–33

Wilentz, Amy, 38

Williams, Peter, 97

Winchell, Barry, 99

women: Marshallese activist organizations for, 120–21; peace and antiwar movement of, 135–38; and reproductive health and nuclear weapons testing, 15, 103, 110–14; and reproductive justice, 104; sex trafficking of, 118, 121; sexual exploitation of, 107–8; treatment of Afghan and Iraqi, 2, 127–30. *See also* sexual violence; women in the military

"women and children" phrase, 57

Women Cross DMZ, 137

women in the military: Combat Exclusion Policy on, 44; *G.I. Jane* on, 26, 50; inclusion arguments and realities of, 50–52; rise of, 27, 37

Women's International League for Peace and Freedom, 16

Women United Together Marshall Islands (WUTMI), 120–21

Woodward, James, 91

World War II, 108

Yakima Nation, 109

Yamazaki, James, 112

Yang, K. Wayne, 122

Yates, Lawrence, 29

Yemen, 132

Youth to Youth in Health (YTYIH), 120–21

Yugoslav Wars, 47, 130, 138. *See also* Kosovo

Zangana, Haifa, 34, 51, 59

Zimmerman, Jean, 37

In the Expanding Frontiers series

To order or obtain more information on these or other University of Nebraska Press titles, visit nebraskapress.unl.edu.